Income Distribution

Martin Schnitzer

The Praeger Special Studies program—utilizing the most modern and efficient book production techniques and a selective worldwide distribution network—makes available to the academic, government, and business communities significant, timely research in U.S. and international economic, social, and political development.

Income Distribution
A Comparative Study of the United States, Sweden, West Germany, East Germany, the United Kingdom, and Japan

PRAEGER SPECIAL STUDIES IN INTERNATIONAL ECONOMICS AND DEVELOPMENT

Praeger Publishers   New York   Washington   London

339. 2
S 361

Library of Congress Cataloging in Publication Data

Schnitzer, Martin.
    Income distribution.

    (Praeger special studies in international economics and development)
    Includes bibliographical references.
    1. Income distribution—United States. 2. Income distribution—Europe—Case studies. 3. Income distribution—Japan. I. Title.
HC79.I5S36   339.2   73-26

PRAEGER PUBLISHERS
111 Fourth Avenue, New York, N.Y. 10003, U.S.A.
5, Cromwell Place, London SW7 2JL, England

Published in the United States of America in 1974
by Praeger Publishers, Inc.

Printed in the United States of America

The purpose of this book is to present data on income distribution for six rather diverse countries: the United States, Sweden, West Germany, East Germany, the United Kingdom, and Japan. The subject of income distribution is a key problem in any society, and the failure of society to solve this problem in a satisfactory manner can lead to social upheaval. The modern welfare state reflects a trend that began with the inception of capitalism toward modifying the distribution of income. New institutional and social arrangements have developed that have as their goal a more even distribution of both income and wealth.

The methodology used in this book is as follows: The data on income distribution were obtained from tax returns in the case of Sweden, Japan, the United Kingdom, and West Germany; available studies on income and wealth distribution in Sweden and West Germany, which were translated into English; and statistical yearbooks and first-hand statistical reports for all countries. Comparisons between countries were generally avoided for the reason that truly comparable data are difficult to devise. A weakness in using tax returns to compare differences in income distribution between countries is that no two countries use exactly the same standards in terms of income included, exemptions, deductions, and so forth. In Japan there is considerable income that is not covered in the tax returns; in Sweden virtually all income is included. The statistical data for some countries, in particular the United Kingdom and West Germany, are also more comprehensive than they are for other countries.

The author is indebted to the following persons who assisted him in obtaining the necessary data for the book: Dr. James Meade of Cambridge University, Dr. Jack Revell of the University College of North Wales, and Dr. A. B. Atkinson of the University of Essex; Professor Pebbe Selander of the University of Uppsala and Mr. Ingvar Ohlsson of the Swedish National Bureau of Statistics; Dr. Peter Mitzscherling and Mr. Gerhard Goseke of the Deutsches Institut für Wirtschaftsforschung for data on East Germany; and to Crista Pirie and Kersten Siff, who helped with the translations.

CONTENTS

LIST OF TABLES

LIST OF FIGURES

Income Distribution

1

A PERSPECTIVE OF
INCOME DISTRIBUTION

The purpose of this book is to compare the distribution of income in six countries: the United States, Sweden, West Germany, East Germany, the United Kingdom, and Japan. In a vital sense the distribution of income has been a key issue that has pervaded Western society since the beginning of capitalism. In fact, the development of the modern welfare state reflects a continuing trend in modifying the distribution of income to achieve more equality. Moreover, Marxism is nothing more than a radical challenge to the alleged failure of capitalism to achieve distributive justice. Vast disparities in the distribution of both income and wealth have created environments that have been ripe for social disorders. Certainly the distribution of income was an important issue in the most recent national election in the United States, an issue that by no means was resolved by the election of President Nixon.

It is necessary to establish a frame of reference with respect to the meaning of income distribution. There are actually two meanings—functional income distribution and personal income distribution. Functional income distribution refers to claims on national output that arise out of the ownership of economic resources. These claims are incorporated in the concept of national income, which represents income earned by the owners of economic resources—land, labor, and capital. This income takes the form of wages and salaries, rent, interest, and profit. Personal income, on the other hand, involves the distribution of income among different income classes. It includes that part of national income actually received by persons or households, and income transfers from government and business. It is measured on a before-tax basis, except for individual contributions to social insurance. In comparing income distribution among persons and households, the concept of personal income is more appropriate than functional income, although the former depends upon a prior distribution of the latter. National income is the logical starting point for an

1

analysis of income distribution, but personal income becomes more important when the objective is to analyze the extent to which governments attempt to alter the functional distribution of income.

It is important to note that governments can exert an influence on both the functional distribution of income and the personal distribution of income. Through fiscal and monetary policies, governments can affect the total demand for goods and services. The functional distribution of income depends to some extent on total demand, for the market prices paid to the owners of economic resources, that is, land, labor, and capital, are connected to the types of goods and services in demand. Moreover, governments can also alter the distribution of functional income among groups. For example, they can favor the distribution of labor income as opposed to property income by promoting the organization of unions. With respect to personal income, governments can intervene to alter its distribution through the use of income taxes and transfer payments. The incomes of some persons are increased through transfer payments, while the incomes of others are reduced by taxation. In addition, shifts in the distribution of personal income can be effected through government purchases of goods and services. Educational expenditures and medical care are bound to have a redistributive effect on income.

While the national income is produced by the combination of productive resources and is received by the owners of these resources, in the final analysis it is consumed by individuals and families. The factor that is of most importance in connection with their standard of living and general economic welfare is the amount of income received from all sources. A fact in the distribution of personal income, which holds true for not only the United States but for other countries as well, is the existence of great inequality. Many millions of persons may receive less than average incomes, while a relatively small number of persons have extremely large incomes. The highest incomes received by persons or families may be literally thousands of times greater than the incomes received by other persons or families at the lower end of the income scale. Moreover, inequality in the distribution of wealth is always greater than that in the distribution of income.

In subsequent chapters primary emphasis will be placed on the use by governments of tax and transfer payment policies to redistribute income in accordance with defined social goals. An effort will be made to analyze both pre-tax and post-tax income distribution in each of the six countries studied. Another purpose is to find out the actual extent to which social welfare expenditures and progressive income taxes redistribute income. Inequality in income distribution will be compared by using such measures as the range between the highest and lowest incomes before taxes, and the range or ratio between the average income for the highest and lowest quintiles, or the upper and lower one-fifth of income earners. An attempt will be made to arrive at some sort of judgment as to what constitutes a just distribution of income. However, there are indeed a large variety of institutional factors at work in any prevailing system of income distribution. This fact means that any attempt to pass value judgments based on a single set of factors, such as inequality of talents among people, may hold little promise.

As a frame of reference, it is necessary to distinguish between real income and money income. Real income is the purchasing power of money income, which depends upon the relationship between money income and the general price level. Symbolically, real income can be defined as the money income divided by the general price level, or 1 (real income) = i (money income) ÷ p (price level). Money income simply refers to the monetary value of income from wages and other sources. So income distribution can be looked at in two ways—real income and money income. The easier way to look at income distribution is from the standpoint of money income, for real income often depends upon subjective valuations that are difficult to measure. So, unless specified to the contrary, subsequent discussions of income distribution will be concerned only with money income. This approach, however, may well overstate differences in economic well-being among social groups. Psychic income, which involves satisfaction derived from employment or from a clean environment, is also not taken into consideration.

Before examining the processes of income distribution in the six countries used in this study, it is desirable to look at the institutional arrangements prevalent in both capitalist and socialist countries that have an effect on the processes. Income distribution in a market economy depends upon a different set of factors than income distribution in a socialist economy. For one thing, the pricing process operating in the market for economic resources—land, labor, and capital—is of paramount importance in determining income distribution in a market economy. The process of redistributing income is effected by the government through taxes and transfer payments. In a socialist country the process of income distribution is in the hands of the state and is tied to economic planning. The use of prices to regulate the distribution of income is considered wasteful and thus undesirable. Distribution can be effected by regulating wages, social services, and taxes.

The remainder of the chapter is divided into three parts. The first part involves an analysis of the factors influencing the distribution of income in a capitalistic market economy. There has been considerable modification of income distribution through state intervention. The second part presents the factors that affect income distribution

3

in a socialist country, such as East Germany. The Marxist theory of income distribution is provided as a frame of reference. The final part discusses the question of equity in the distribution of income.

INCOME DISTRIBUTION IN
A CAPITALIST MARKET ECONOMY

Income distribution in a market economy is based on institutional arrangements, such as the pricing process, that are associated with this type of system. High prices are set on scarce agents of production and low prices on plentiful agents. In terms of rewards to labor, those persons whose skills are scarce relative to demand enjoy a high level of income, while those persons whose skills are not scarce do not. In a market economy people are supposedly rewarded on the basis of their contribution to marketable output, which, in turn, reflects consumer preferences and incomes. The implication is that persons whose productivity in value terms is low will earn little, regardless of whether the low productivity is attributable to lack of effort, lack of skill, or low demand for the skill.

Income in a market economy emanates from two sources: income from wages and salaries, or self-employment, and property income. Property may be regarded as a stock of claims on the value of wealth, whether it be natural resources or man-made capital and consumer durable goods. The structure of property claims in a capitalist economy is generally a complex one; individual claims on wealth owned by corporations, for example, may be represented by common or preferred stock, by corporate bonds, and by notes and mortgages. Ultimately, property rights can be traced to the objects of wealth underlying them, or to claims on income to which the wealth gives rise. In national income accounting, labor income consists of wages, salaries, and entrepreneurial income, while property income takes the form of rent, interest, and profit. Thus there is a fundamental dichotomy between labor and nonlabor income.

The Marginal Productivity Concept

The most basic theory underlying income distribution in a market economy involves the marginal productivity concept. This concept can be applied to the distribution of both labor and property incomes. Accordingly, the income received by an owner of a productive resource tends to be determined by supply and demand, under competitive conditions, so that it equals the marginal contribution that the resource is able to make to the exchange value of goods and services. With

4

respect to labor income, it will pay employers best to take on that number of workers that makes their marginal revenue product equal to their wage. In this way the demand for labor is determined. The same reasoning is also applied to the distribution of property income. Resource owners tend to be remunerated according to the marginal revenue products of the resources they own.

The marginal productivity concept is based on the law of diminishing returns, which holds that an increased amount of a resource applied to a fixed quantity of other resources will yield a diminished marginal product. Thus if employers were to take on a number of workers so large that their marginal revenue product was not worth the wage that had to be paid, they would soon find that number excessive. The number of workers that any employer would prefer to take on is that number that maximizes his profit, and that number is given by the equality of wages to the marginal revenue product of the last worker employed. Below this point an employer would be reducing his revenues more than his receipts, and so diminish his profit. Above this point profit is not being maximized.

However, the marginal productivity theory of income distribution is subject to much criticism. First of all, the assumptions upon which it is based are open to question. For one thing, it is assumed that a truly competitive economy exists and that all units of an economic resource are basically alike, so that they may be interchanged in production and may contribute to the production of a number of goods and services with different exchange values. Thus, the use of an economic resource would be carried to the point where the productivity of the last unit of the resource in its most important use would be equal to that of the same unit in any other use.

Given that the above assumptions are wrong, there is no close correlation between the income received by resource owners and the value of the marginal revenue products of the resources they provide. So in a complicated modern economy, it is inconceivable that marginal productivity analysis is sufficient in itself to explain the distribution of income. This does not, however, deny the validity of the concept. It can be said that decisions made by individuals or groups, such as trade unions, governments, or large-scale enterprises, within the framework of demand and supply, determine income distribution. Generally, the demand for an economic resource is derived from the goals of production, either maximum profit or the volume of production, as determined by institutional considerations. The supply of an economic resource is based upon numerous and varying economic and sociological factors that represent a composite of quality and quantity variables, such as education.

Capitalism and the Welfare State

Despite Marxist predictions of inevitable collapse, capitalism has shown a surprising ability not only to survive but also to expand and to adapt to the democratic conditions of modern industrialized society, which, it must not be forgotten, it has strongly helped to create. One manifestation of this adaptation has been the development of what can be called "welfare statism." Actually, a precursor of the "welfare state" was the social welfare program developed in Germany in 1883, when Bismarck's opposition to socialism and his jealousy of the trade union movement led him to sponsor health insurance and old-age insurance. Bismarck, a political pragmatist of the first order, realized that social legislation was necessary in order to remove the causes upon which socialism was developing. Another precursor of the welfare state was the social welfare program of the Liberal government in the United Kingdom. Developed in 1908, the program included social insurance for health and unemployment, old-age pensions, and assistance to low-income workers through the statutory fixing of minimum wages.

The fundamental premise of the welfare state as it has developed in the capitalistic countries is that governments must intervene to achieve certain economic and social objectives. Altering the distribution of income has been one of those objectives. Under a purely capitalistic market economy, it was held that market forces would compensate people on the basis of their contributions to total output. However, this idea has been modified because it was easy to recognize the fact that large incomes accrued to some persons, not on the basis of their contributions to national input, but through inherited wealth or other accidents of birth, or through the exercise of other special privileges. Moreover, capricious economic and social changes often worked hardships on the most productive of individuals. The Social Darwinist concept of "survival of the fittest" made little sense when a depression caused millions of efficient and productive persons to be out of work.

In general, the development of the welfare state stems from a dissatisfaction with the distribution of income. One result of market capitalism, as mentioned previously, has been an extreme inequality in the distribution of income. This inequality can be attributed primarily to the receipt of income from claims on property, such as interest, rent, and dividends. Thus, efforts have been made to effect a more equitable distribution of income. The methods that governments have used most widely to alter the distribution of income have been graduated income and inheritance taxation and transfer payments. Policies directed toward the maintenance of full employment also have an effect upon the distribution of income. Certainly a hallmark of the welfare state has been the priority attached to achieving a high level of employment.

TAX POLICIES AND
THE DISTRIBUTION OF INCOME

The progressive income tax affects the distribution of income in two ways. First, the tax directly reduces the disposable income of individuals. It can be said that the progressive income tax accomplishes a redistribution of income in the direction of greater equality because the proportionate share of the upper-income groups in the total income is reduced and the proportionate share of the lower-income groups is raised. The progressiveness of the income tax structure brings about this result because the effective rate of taxation—the ratio of total taxes paid to incomes received—increases with the size of the income. This means, in other words, that the proportionate share of the total tax burden is greater for the upper-income groups, hence there will be a redistribution in the direction of greater equality.

Second, there is an indirect effect on incentives. However, it is difficult to measure the negative influence of progressive income taxation on the will to work. It may be presumed that highly progressive taxation has a restraining influence on the creation of income. Not only would high marginal tax rates cause people to think twice before adding to their work output, but they may well have an injurious effect on savings and on the supply of venture capital. Moreover, the effect of high income tax rates may well discourage entry into high-risk activities. Compensation differentials are also lowered, and unless other reasons exist for individuals to acquire skills and education, a reallocation of talent may be the end result. The restraining effect of progressive taxation is probably not constant but is undoubtedly dependent on other factors, such as the general level of economic activity. But it may be expected to intensify in proportion to the rise in the standard of living. The incentive to wage earners to increase their efforts probably becomes less as the still unsatisfied consumer demand declines in importance. For most families, the purchase of a second car can hardly be as important as the first.

There is another effect of progressive income taxation that has some relation to incentives. High taxes tempt people to evade paying them, so that those who are unwilling or unable to evade paying some of their income tax must carry a proportionately greater share of the burden. Injustice may also arise for those whose income, for any reason, varies greatly from one year to the next. Moreover, the existence of special tax concessions, or "loopholes," can well distort the base of the income tax by lightening the tax burdens of special taxpayer groups.

Income redistribution through progressive taxation is affected by a number of factors. One such factor is the ownership of property. In some countries income from property of any kind is taxed more heavily than income from employment. For example, in Sweden there is no exemption from either the national or local income tax on interest from government securities. On the other hand, in the United States interest from state and local bonds is exempt from the federal income tax. Legislative and other provisions have been provided to evade payment of at least a part of the tax. Capital gains from the ownership of property are subject to specially favorable treatment. The effect of so-called "loopholes" in the income tax laws of the United States has been to make the actual rates less than the nominal rates. In addition, the incidence of the income tax may be quite unequal for persons at the same income level for the reason that the amount of the tax can vary widely depending upon the source of the income. Thus widespread inequity has been introduced into the tax system.

Other factors that have an effect on income redistribution through income taxes include marital status, special allowances for such things as home ownership, and the rate of economic growth of a country. The income tax systems prevalent in the capitalistic countries favor married persons over singles. Income is redistributed in favor of those families with dependents and against those who are without children or who are single. In the United States personal exemptions and minimum standard deductions provide allowances that in essence increase as income increases. But the allowances work in reverse in that they benefit least those families that need them the most, and benefit most those families that need them the least.

What is the effect of progressive income taxation upon the redistribution of income? One way to answer this question is to compare the present distribution of the tax burden with what it would be if taxation were proportional, that is, if a certain fixed percentage of all incomes were paid in taxes. It is likely that once the comparison is made, a progressive system of income taxation will result in a rather small shift of the tax burden to the higher income groups. The most important consideration in judging how far the progressive income tax system tends to redistribute incomes is to know who benefits from the relief afforded by this form of taxation, and the extent of this benefit per taxpayer.

The progressivity of the income tax also depends upon how other taxes are levied. In particular, indirect taxes, such as sales and excise taxes, introduce the element of regressivity into any tax system. Regressivity occurs when the tax rate decreases as the tax base increases; the rate of tax and the base are inversely related. Some forms of tax that are nominally proportional in rate, for example, sales tax, may, however, be classified as regressive if these taxes are related to income as the base. So it can be said that indirect taxes help to moderate the progressivity of the income tax. On a relative basis, the amount paid in indirect taxes by upper-income groups is less than the amount paid by lower-income groups. As a matter of fact, the absolute burden of indirect taxes upon lower-income groups is rather substantial in such countries as Sweden and West Germany.

It is also necessary to comment on social security taxes, for certainly a social security system brings about a redistribution of income. There will be a redistribution of income in favor of a given group if the benefits received are in excess of the social security taxes paid; if the opposite is true there will be a redistribution of income at the expense of the group in question and in favor of other groups. However, social security taxes proper usually are not adequate to cover all outlays of funds in the social security system. A part of the latter's cost must be covered by general government revenues. For example, in West Germany the federal government, through transfers from the budget, finances a part of old-age and survivor's pensions, family allowances, and part of maternity benefits. It is possible in this case that the amount of income redistribution brought about by the social security system is negligible. This statement hinges on the incidence of the taxes that provide the revenue for the West German federal budget.

A final set of taxes that would have an effect on income redistribution are the so-called "wealth" taxes. Estate and inheritance taxes fall into this category. The taxation of transfers of wealth provides one means through which a government can insure some greater equality of opportunity without, at the same time, causing major disincentive effects. Certainly a cardinal objective of the welfare state has been a reduction in the concentration of wealth in the hands of a few families. It is felt that a concentration of wealth results in a concentration of economic power that is often perpetuated from generation to generation. However, it may be argued that since estate and inheritance taxes impinge directly on property, they constitute a particularly heavy burden on savings. Since savings are the source of capital formation, the downward redistribution effects of the taxes will be nullified through unemployment.

Key to the analysis of income redistribution is the incidence of taxation. The term "incidence" refers to the final resting place of a tax after further shifting becomes impossible. Generally speaking, the more direct the tax, the more difficult it is to shift it to someone else; the more indirect the tax, the greater the possibility of transferring its burden from the point of impact to the point of incidence. This is explained by the fact that a direct tax usually is applied to a tax base close to the individual, such as income or wealth, Direct taxes, in most instances, are further removed from subsequent market transactions after the taxes are imposed than are bases of indirect taxes. Thus, direct taxes, such as the personal income tax, are not especially conducive to the further market transactions that are necessary for the shifting of a tax. On the other hand, indirect taxes, such as retail sales and excise taxes, are more closely associated with market transactions, and hence are more conducive to tax shifting than direct taxes.

In a market economy tax shifting occurs through the mechanism of supply and demand. This means that shifting will usually occur through a change in the market price of an economic good or productive resource. Taxes may be shifted either forward or backward. The former occurs when the price of a good is increased as a result of a tax allowing a part or all of the tax to be transferred onto someone else. On the other hand, if the result of the tax is a decrease in the price of a factor of production, and if this permits transference of all or a part of the tax burden, the tax has been shifted backward. Forward shifting ordinarily results in the rise in the price of an economic good in the product market, and backward shifting results from the reduction in the price of a productive resource in a factor market. In the first instance the burden of the tax has been shifted onto the consumer, while in the latter case the burden has been passed backward to the factor of production.

There are a number of factors that affect the extent to which a tax can be shifted. Probably the most important are the elasticities of the taxes that provide the revenue for the West German federal budget. elastic the demand for a product, the more nearly price will rise by the full amount of the tax and the more complete the shifting. The more inelastic the conditions of supply, the less the market price will rise and the less the extent of shifting. A second factor is the degree of monopoly in a particular market. In general, the greater the control of prices in a market, the easier it is for a firm to shift taxes. Finally, the more broad-based the tax is, the easier it is to shift it. With a broad-based tax, consumers have no alternative to spend in areas where there is no tax, and sellers are in a position to raise prices in order to shift the tax. In particular the value-added tax, used by many countries, including Sweden and West Germany, is an example of a broad-based tax that is levied on consumption.

It is possible that a system of social welfare expenditures might function in such a way as to bring about a redistribution of income from upper-income to lower-income groups. This is rarely the case in actuality, however. This particular pattern of income redistribution would come about if practically all of the beneficiaries of social welfare expenditures were found in the lower income brackets and the system were financed wholly by a progressive income tax. This, of course, is not the case, for most existing systems adhere to a greater or lesser degree to the principle that the beneficiaries should at least contribute in part to the cost of the system. This is particularly true with respect to social security, but less true for more general government expenditures of a welfare nature.

Redistribution of Income by Means of
Government Expenditures

In contrast to progressive income taxation, government expenditures offer a greater possibility of affecting the redistribution of income in a country. Government expenditures can be broken down into two categories. The first category involves direct government expenditures on goods and services that directly benefit various segments of society. Tax revenues are repaid in the form of benefits such as free education, police protection, and free institutional and hospital care. Being financed by taxation, even those who do not benefit by these services contribute to their cost, which results in an indirect redistribution of income. This is the case even when the services are of a general nature, as different income groups pay widely differing amounts for them. These expenditures can be regarded as nonmonetary transfers. The recipients of these services benefit through obtaining them at a price below their real cost as measured by the government expenditures for the resources necessary to provide the services. However, these services absorb resources and must be distinguished from expenditures that result solely in a transfer of income from one group to another group.

The second type of government expenditure is the transfer payment. A transfer payment is distinguished from other government expenditures in that no equivalent value in either product or productive services is received in exchange. Transfer payments are of two basic types. First, there are those transfers that benefit certain sectors of society. Family allowances benefit families with children, housing allowances generally benefit low-income families, and old-age pensions benefit those who have retired from work, Second, there are grants to certain economic sectors, such as agricultural subsidies, that result in lower prices for certain goods and services. Presumably, the resulting increase in a country's real social income through broader consumption of agricultural products at lower prices is far greater than the reduction of social income through the taxes needed to pay the subsidy. The theoretical possibility of such a net gain has been established, but is difficult to measure.

The extent to which governments redistribute income can be measured in part by a comparison of transfer payments to national income, which is the factor cost of producing gross national product, or, more specifically, the aggregate earnings of labor and property that arise from the production of goods and services by a nation's economy. It is a concept of fundamental importance, for it represents to an economy as a whole the major source of money income or spending power for the purchase of the bulk of the national output. So the relationship of transfer payments to national income indicates the extent to which the percentage of earned income has been redistributed by government action. However, the relationship does not indicate the extent to which there is a horizontal or vertical redistribution of income. In many situations transfer payments merely redistribute income within the same income groups.

It is necessary to emphasize the point that income redistribution that results from transfer payments cannot be separated from the incidence of taxation. In particular, it is important to compare the monetary benefits of family allowances, old-age pensions, and other social welfare transfers to the incidence of the taxes employed to finance these benefits. Typically, social security taxes are inadequate to finance all transfers, so the total costs are in part covered by general tax revenues. This is the actual situation in France, Sweden, West Germany, and other countries. This creates the problem of examining not only the incidence of social security taxes, but the parallel incidence of the taxes used to finance the deficit. Moreover, it is difficult to separate direct from indirect taxes, for any allocation of tax revenue from different tax sources to social security expenditures will be arbitrary, as there is no way to determine for most government budgets the exact use of revenue from a particular source.

Various types of public expenditures may be initiated that have as their primary objective the equalization of opportunities for earning incomes. One example involves expenditures for education. Individual opportunities for earning of income in the marketplace tend to be equalized as educational services are financed publicly and made available to all members of the group. However, the equalizing of opportunities through education is not the same thing as producing equality in the distribution of income. In fact, it may well be that there are other factors that are more important than education in affecting income distribution. A recent study made in the United States contends that education actually plays a minor role in determining income distribution.[1] Heredity, environment, and just plain luck are rated as being more important. The study concludes that even if every person received an equally good education, American society in terms of income distribution would hardly be more equal than it is now.

Government Stabilization Policies

There are no clear boundaries between stabilization policies and other types of government activities. In general, it can be said that stabilization policies involve the use of a government's fiscal and monetary powers to influence employment, output, and growth in productive capacity, as well as the level of prices. Certain parameter changes are made in the operation of these policies, including changes in the level of money and credit and changes in tax rates and government expenditures. In addition, there are manpower policies that attempt to create jobs for specific individuals, groups, and locations, and control policies that can involve the control of capital movements. Stabilization policies exert a major impact on an economy in terms of the level of expenditures and the level of taxation. They exert their influence directly by affecting demand and, therefore, employment and income.

The central objective of stabilization policies has been the maintenance of a high level of employment. A very large part of government activity in the modern welfare state has been directed toward achieving, or at least approximating, this goal. It can be said that stabilization policies have accomplished a complete turnabout in employment from the depression before World War II. In no country has this turnabout been more apparent than in Sweden. For example, the average rate of unemployment in the period from 1923 to 1930 was 11 percent; in the period from 1930 to 1933 the rate was 19 percent; and in the period from 1933 to 1937 the average rate was 16 percent.[2] However, after the war Sweden made use of a national income budget as a means of providing the general framework for the coordination of economic activity, both public and private. Economic policy coordination between public and private groups was extensive and thorough, the fiscal and monetary policies were utilized to maintain high levels of aggregate demand. As a result, unemployment has usually averaged less than 2 percent annually since the war, and the supply of labor in some areas has been so short that workers have been imported from other countries.

It can be said that modern capitalism probably owes its existence to Keynesian economics. Keynesian doctrine has been incorporated as a matter of course in the apparatus of the welfare state and constitutes an important part of the theoretical background against which all stabilization policies are formulated. So governments are able to intervene in the economic process, maintain stability, and preserve some of the basic institutions of capitalism. Crises and depressions, with their concomitant effects upon the distribution of income, have been eliminated. But this is not to say that Keynesian economic policies have provided a satisfactory solution to the conflict between the goals of achieving full employment and avoiding inflation. In recent years inflation rather than unemployment has been the major problem in such countries as Sweden and West Germany. The efforts of governments to curb inflation have increased their tolerance of unemployment. In the United States, for example, the long-accepted goal of 4 percent unemployment as a goal of stabilization policy appears to have been replaced by acceptance of a higher unemployment rate of 5 percent or better coupled with more stable prices.

INCOME DISTRIBUTION UNDER SOCIALISM

Income distribution under socialism can be examined in two ways. First, there is the Marxist theory of income distribution, which is based upon an adaptation of Ricardian ideas, particularly with respect to a labor theory of value. Marx's theory of income distribution was a part of his overall theory of the development and decline of capitalism. In actual practice, however, there is a departure from his theory in the socialist countries today. Although this departure is explained away in part by the assertion that socialism is just a stage on the way to communism, the fact remains that income distribution in such countries as the Soviet Union and East Germany is tied to pragmatic economic objectives.

The Marxist Theory of Income Distribution

At any given time—according to Marx—the way in which men make a living is conditioned by the nature of the existing productive forces. These productive forces are three in number: natural resources, capital equipment, and human resources. Since men must make use of these productive forces in the process of making a living, some sort of relationship between men and the productive forces is necessary. Specifically, a property relationship is involved. Men may own certain productive forces individually, as in a capitalist economy; or they may own them collectively, as in a socialist society. In addition to the relationships between men and the productive forces, there are relationships between men and men, for, except under very primitive or isolated conditions, men find it desirable to cooperate, to engage in social production. The relationships between men and productive forces and between men and men Marx calls the relations of production, and the sum total of these relations of production constitutes the economic structure of society.

The Marxist theory of income distribution is based on the labor theory of value, which, in essence, asserts that the value of a commodity is determined by the labor time necessary for its production. Marx stated that the one thing common to all commodities is labor. Because labor power is the source of all economic or exchange value, exploitation exists whenever a worker fails to receive the whole value of his output. Although all value is created by the workers, it is expropriated by employers in the form of surplus value, which can be defined as the difference between the value created by the workers and the value of their labor power. The employers, or capitalists, are owners of the nonhuman agents of production—capital equipment and land. It is through their ownership of the physical means of production that the capitalists exploit the working class and extract surplus value from it.

Income in the Marxist schema is divided into two categories—surplus value, which is the source of all profit, and labor income. Capitalists try to wring as much surplus value out of their workers as possible to maintain or improve their relative share in the income total. The ratio of surplus value to labor income, or profit to wages, is really the foundation of the Marxist theory of income distribution. A rise in the ratio of surplus value to labor income represents an increase in the rate of exploitation. A decline in the ratio represents the reverse. Given the relationship between surplus value and labor income, the capitalists attempt to increase their share of the income total. They have the advantage over labor because a normal condition of a capitalist society is a continuous excess of labor supply over demand. This excess causes the market wage to fall toward a real wage equal to the minimum subsistence standard of living.

The traditional Marxist approach denies the role of demand in the determination of value. The idea of marginal utility is rejected because it is in conflict with the assumption that value is objectively determined by the labor content, not by subjective valuation of the amount used. So value in the Marxist rubric can be expressed in the formula $c + v + s$, where c represents raw materials and capital consumption, v represents variable outlays on wages, and s represents surplus value in the form of rent, interest, and profit. The c component, raw materials and capital, although clearly not labor, is explained away by Marx, who regarded it as stored-up labor from past periods. Thus the remainder, $v + s$, represents net output, which consists of the two basic income shares, wages and profit.

The distribution of income eventually precipitates the downfall of capitalism. This would occur after a series of business crises. Under capitalism there are certain inevitable forces at work to bring about its eventual collapse. There is a continuing struggle among the capitalists to increase their share of the total income. To do this, they try to wring as much surplus value out of their workers as possible. Hours become longer, and women and children are employed. As long as there is a surplus of labor, the workers will receive no more than the value of their labor power. The intensity of competition among the capitalists also leads to capital accumulation, which leads to a decline in the relative share of wages in total income. But the end result is self-defeating for the reason that with falling wages, aggregate demand also falls, and the workers are not in a position to consume the products that the capitalists are turning out.

After the collapse of capitalism, two phases of communism are to occur. The first phase, which Marx called the "lower phase" or "socialism," is a transitional phase in which, among other things,

15

income distribution is based upon ability rather than need. For the period of "socialist transition," the principle of distribution based on performance is necessary to create a society of abundance. So the term "socialist" is applied to the countries controlled by the Communist Party, including the nine Eastern European countries. These countries describe themselves as socialist—the Union of Soviet Socialist Republics. The higher phase, or "communism," is to be marked by an age of plenty, distribution according to needs, and the absence of money. Individuals are supposed to derive satisfaction from being a part of such a social order—from contributing to it and sharing its ambience. All vestiges of capitalism are to disappear and the state is to wither away. However, when this higher phase is scheduled to begin is anybody's guess. In the Soviet Union some reference has been made to the second phase as starting around 1980.

Income Determination Under Socialism

Income distribution under socialism refers to the allocation of national income by distributive shares, primarily in the form of wages and salaries. Since property is owned by the state, there is no income in the form of rent paid to landowners. Interest does figure in the national income to some extent, as a part of income received by individual producers may be considered as interest on the relatively small amounts of capital they own. Interest is also used as a device to encourage personal savings, which are regarded as necessary to put a brake on excess consumer demand, and interest rate differentials exist in favor of long-term savings deposits. Profits, which are distributed in the form of dividends or retained by corporate shareholders in a capitalist system, occupy a different role under socialism. They are used as a criterion of enterprise performance and, up to a point, of the efficiency of production.

The basic Marxist principle, "from each according to his ability, to each according to his needs," does not govern the distribution of income in any socialist country. Whether it will in the future, when pure communism is supposed to be established, remains to be seen. Instead, the principle has been amended to "to each according to his ability." Thus piecework pay, wage differentials, and bonuses to outstanding workers have always been a part of the reward structure of socialist countries. This reliance on material incentives was justified by Lenin himself when he stated that socialism could be established "with the help of enthusiasm born of the great revolution, on personal profit, on self-interest, on economic calculation." The Leninist principle has been accepted ever since as being applicable to the transition stage that can be called the lower phase of communism, or socialism.

Income distribution is determined by the state within the framework of the economic plan. The total amount of wages to be paid, and the production counterpart to support the wage funds, depends on the division of the national income between accumulation and consumption, and further of consumption between the social consumption fund and the wage fund. The total wage fund is partitioned into wage funds for all economic fields. In its economic planning the government is able to determine the total wages for the economy by multiplying the planned number of workers by the rates of wages it has set. Wages are changed as seems necessary to effectuate government policy and achieve particular production ends. For example, in order to attract more workers to a given industry, the wages it pays may be raised while other wages remain static or are allowed to decline. Direct pressure on the part of workers would in general have little effect on wage determination.

The degree of state control over the wage fund at the microeconomic, or firm, level is smaller. Some latitude is allowed to enterprise managers in determining the size and the use of the fund. Typically, the wage fund consists of several components, including basic wages. This component can be subdivided into two categories, time rates and piece rates. Both are based on work output indicators. In addition, bonuses may also be paid from the wage fund. The wage fund also provides for extra wages that are based on the difficulty of work, including payments for night, holiday, and Sunday work, and wages for state holidays, vacations, and participation in public duties. As it stands, a typical worker receives a payment according to his work grade from the wage fund plus a bonus based on a performance standard.

Another source of income is provided from the material incentives fund. This fund is tied to enterprise profit. The significance and success of the profit criterion lies mainly in the fact that a direct link has been established between profit and incentive payment so that it is in the interest of enterprise personnel—and at the same time of society—to strive to maximize enterprise profit. The proportion of enterprise profits channeled into this fund varies in different socialist countries. For example, in East Germany up to 20 percent of net profits can be placed in the fund. In East Germany, Poland, and Romania the size of the fund is based on complicated formulas in which a distinction is made between planned and above-plan profits, and further between profits made by exceeding production targets and those achieved by reductions in prime costs.

Government Expenditures

Wages are only one side of the coin, however. When various government expenditures for free and subsidized consumer services,

17

such as medical benefits and family allowances, are taken into consideration, total income for most workers is increased. For example, it is estimated that transfer payments and subsidized services amount to around 35 percent of average monthly earnings for wage and salaried workers in the Soviet Union.[3] However, the extent to which incomes are redistributed through the medium of transfer payments must be examined carefully. First, it is necessary to point out that most transfer payments are made to people regardless of their income category. Second, many transfers take place laterally within income groups. Single persons are usually taxed more heavily than married persons. The family allowance favors couples with children.

It is also necessary to mention the provision of free education, which provides the opportunity for qualified persons to prepare themselves to participate in the distribution of income. Unquestionably, free education has been used to break down class barriers and to provide upward mobility for many persons. However, this upward mobility has been promoted by rapid industrialization in the socialist countries. Studies now indicate that mobility and success in the selection of occupations are related to the position of a person's family.[4] In other words, it is less likely that a factory worker's child, regardless of talent, will enter a university and receive the training necessary to become a professional worker than is the case for the children of scientists, technicians, and Party officials. It is far less likely for a worker's child to move up the occupational ladder to become a scientist or manager than it is for a scientist's or manager's child to move down the ladder and become a worker.

Taxes

What effects do taxes have on the redistribution of income in the socialist countries? To answer this question, the features of socialist tax systems must be examined. The most important feature is the predominance of indirect taxation over direct taxation. This is surprising in view of the fact that Marxist doctrine would hold that the use of such taxes discriminates against the working classes because they are regressive and inequitable. There are reasons for this reliance on indirect taxation, however. First, indirect taxes are easier to administer and harder to avoid than direct taxes. They are collected from thousands of enterprises rather than millions of persons. Second, it is felt that indirect taxes have less effect on work incentives than income taxes. Third, the role of the government, as reflected by the size of the state budget, is more important in the socialist countries, so taxation by necessity must be higher. Direct taxes would not provide the revenues that are necessary to support budgetary expenditures.

18

The two most important taxes in the socialist countries are the turnover tax and deductions from enterprises' profits. The turnover tax represents the difference between the producer's and the retail price, excluding the wholesale and retail margins for trading enterprises. It is in actuality a broad-based sales tax on consumption goods, since it applies, on a gross basis, to all transactions through which a tangible economic good passes. Thus it exercises an influence on the redistribution of income. This is true because of its regressivity to income as a base. It should be remembered that the turnover tax is often a "cascade" tax, the amount getting larger as the number of transactions increase. Products that are usable both in original form and as components of other products may be taxed more than once. Products such as grain and flour may be taxed at successive stages in the production process. Therefore, the final market price of many consumer goods could contain a number of turnover taxes.

Deductions from profits represent another important type of levy. Profit, as defined in socialist terms, can represent the difference between the total income of an enterprise from the sale of its products and its production costs. Profit can also represent the difference between the government-determined price for a given commodity and the cost to an enterprise of producing it. When profits are made by an enterprise, they are utilized in two ways—one part is remitted to the state and the other part is retained by the enterprise. In some socialist countries, as in Hungary, deductions from profits are made only after gross profits are divided into different funds, including the wage fund and the material incentives fund. The part that is returned to the state can be viewed as a transfer of revenue rather than a direct tax. However, since it is a part of total profits over and above costs of production, it is incorporated in the final selling price. In this respect, deductions from profits can be considered to have the same effect as the turnover tax, since each can be shifted forward to consumers.

Income taxes are also used in the socialist countries. As a revenue source to the state, they are of no particular importance. The taxes are levied on persons, cooperatives, and enterprises. The rates are progressive depending on the source and size of income. Discriminatory rates are used so as to inhibit the accumulation of excessive profits by nonstate enterprises and to prevent private enrichment. For each socialist country, there are typically several sets of rates that are based on the source of income. For example, in East Germany the degree of tax progression on professional persons not directly employed by the state is markedly higher than the progression on incomes earned by wage and salary earners. The degree of progression is even higher for private craftsmen and entrepreneurs. Personal income taxes are also levied on farmers selling privately

19

grown produce directly to consumers. However, irrespective of the socialist country involved, it can be said the rate of tax progression, particularly on wage incomes, is far lower than the rates prevailing in the Western capitalist countries.

Socialist systems of social security conform to a particular pattern. First, taxes to finance social security are paid into a special state social insurance budget. Disbursement of the social insurance funds is the responsibility of socialist trade unions. Second, although there are some variations from country to country, the general pattern is for workers, enterprises, and governments to contribute to the cost of social insurance. The rates of social insurance taxes are rather high in comparison to the capitalist countries. For example, in Hungary the tax to finance old-age pensions, health care, and maternity benefits is 10 percent of earnings for the worker and 10 percent of payrolls for the enterprise. The family allowance is financed by a special tax on the wages of childless workers. Finally, it is important to note that a major part of social insurance expenditures is financed out of the general tax revenues of the state budget. In East Germany, Hungary, and the Soviet Union the amount is in excess of 40 percent of total expenditures. The apportionment of state expenditures, however, varies for the different types of social welfare services. The cost of the family allowance is borne entirely by the state out of general tax revenues.

Income Differentials Under Socialism

The claim of a "classless society," which is commonplace in socialist countries, obviously does not apply to income classes but to exploitative classes. The reasons for income differentials are quite apparent. Income policy has clear-cut aims within the broader scope of economic growth strategy. Workers are expected to deploy themselves where wanted and to advance their skills. Income differentiation is based on pragmatic consideration of worker self-interest. Moreover, with the economic reforms of the 1960s, the socialist countries have moved further away from the utopian ideal of a perfectly egalitarian society by introducing incentives and bonuses, which in themselves tend to differentiate among workers. Despite all of the rhetoric about the workers' state, all surveys indicate that the salaries of average workers are far below those of intellectuals, scientists, technicians, and other professional workers. In some Soviet factories, for example, some executives earn 10 or 20 times as much as workers.[5]

There is another sort of gap between rhetoric and reality in the socialist countries; it separates claims of egalitarianism from the facts of special privileges for a small elite. These privileges involve, among other things, special shops in which party officials, scientists, technicians, and other members of the elite can buy products not available to the average worker. Plant managers and government officials are entitled to such emoluments as a chauffeur-driven car for their constant use, as well as personal secretaries and assistants. The elite group is able to live in villas, arrange repairs on their homes, and have their groceries delivered by state enterprises free of charge. There is a whole compendium of special privileges denied to the average worker: greater freedom, better medical care, and the opportunity to travel abroad. The last privilege entitles a person to receive a hard currency allowance, which would entitle him to buy Western cars and clothing unavailable at home immediately, without the usual wait of up to five years or more required for a person using local currency. Moreover, children of the elite often enjoy educational advantages no worker's child could hope for.

It is rather obvious then that a truly egalitarian society does not exist in such socialist countries as East Germany, Hungary, Poland, and the Soviet Union. It is a myth that the workingman is first among equals. In fact, the worker with hammer or the horny-handed peasant with hoe, long glorified in socialist folklore, is being replaced by a more sophisticated type who in his way of life differs hardly at all from clerks or professional people. The socialist countries, in particular Hungary and East Germany, are concerned with greater efficiency through economic reform, which seems essential if they are to achieve the long-term prosperity necessary for stability. But egalitarianism would tend to contradict the objective of efficiency, for with the latter comes income differentiation, so that responsibility and initiative can be rewarded.

Income inequality in the socialist countries, then, can be attributed to the desire for growth and the value system. Growth involves industrialization, which in itself exercises a pull toward an unequal distribution of income. With respect to values, the stated goal of socialism is to base income distribution on need rather than production achievement. This goal presumes the creation of a society of abundance, which is supposed to be created during the transition period from socialism to full communism. Whether that transition comes about remains to be seen. Despite the fact that the worker is the eulogized paradigm of virtue, there is no question but what the power to make decisions is concentrated in the hands of the Communist Party. It is to be doubted that those who are in a position to benefit the most from the maintenance of the status quo would voluntarily surrender positions, power, and emoluments to create the ultimate egalitarian society where everyone is an equal part of the social and economic order.

EQUITY AND INCOME DISTRIBUTION

It is difficult to reach an agreement on what is an optimum distribution of income. Individuals and groups view an economic system from their own positions in society. Unanimity of opinion is therefore impossible, and it is highly doubtful if an agreed upon concept of optimum distribution can be achieved. If such is the case, the actual effect of taxes and government expenditures on the distribution of income will not be determined on the basis of a particular theory of optimum distribution, but rather as a result of a struggle between the dominant political forces at a particular moment in time. The results will be strongly modified, of course, by political decisions made in the past. This does not mean that theories will play no role whatever, for each group must have a rationalization of its position.

We would not be on secure grounds in asserting that perfect equality in the distribution of income and wealth would be necessary to the existence of an economic optimum. There is no way to make objective comparisons of satisfactions or utilities as between persons. There is also no way to measure aggregate satisfactions for the whole population of an economy because of differences among individuals with regard to their capacities to experience satisfactions. Certainly the assumption that all persons have equal capacities for satisfaction is incapable of scientific proof. Thus apart from any questions of the distribution of money income, it is necessary to know more about the psychological basis of human wants before a given condition can be considered an economic optimum. To what extent is it possible for income to measure the magnitude of basic human needs or wants? Utility analysis is rather unsatisfactory from the point of view of psychology.

The question of what constitutes an equitable distribution of income is difficult to answer. It is hard to justify on purely ethical grounds the position that those persons who contribute most to output should receive the most income, which would happen in a market economy. Problems arise because individuals and families differ with respect to age distribution, health problems, and in many other ways, and therefore have different needs in an objective sense. Unfortunately, there are no accepted ethical standards for determining the degree to which contributions to output should be rewarded, nor are there any acceptable economic standards for determining how much effort any individual is making. The end result is that the Western market-oriented countries have accepted the idea that income distribution is much too important to be left solely to market-determined forces. There is acceptance of the idea that income ought to be redistributed in favor of those with lower incomes at the expense of those with higher incomes.

There is an apparent conflict, particularly in the United States, between the goals of an egalitarian society and the existence of marked income inequality. Studies indicate that since the end of World War II, the United States had made almost no progress toward closing the considerable income gaps between the nation's highest- and lowest-paid workers.[6] To the contrary, the share of wage and salary income going to people who are already well paid is gradually increasing, while the share paid to low-ranking workers is falling. But this is inconsistent with government policies that imposed a progressive income tax in 1913 and that introduced expensive programs designed to alleviate poverty. It also appears inconsistent with policies designed to provide education for all, for education is supposed to be the great equalizer of all men. Apparently, there may be factors that are more important than education, or the lack of it, in explaining differences in incomes among persons and groups.

Is income inequality necessary for economic growth? This is a difficult question to answer. It is generally argued that growth is tied to performance. The theme is that the whole incentive structure is based on having income differences. Industrial growth and income distribution are correlated in that in order to have the former, it is necessary to have increased financial resources, which are obtained only through higher profits. But in any economy based primarily upon the ownership of private property, measures designed to increase profits may well have an effect on the distribution of income and wealth that is in conflict with the goal of equality in the distribution of income.

On the other hand, it may well be possible to have economic growth with a more even distribution of income. It is contended that Japan, which has the most rapid rate of economic growth of all industrial countries, has the most equal distribution of pre-tax income. This distribution refers to average income by quintiles, with the ratio of the highest to the lowest average being less than 5 to 1.[7] On an a priori basis, however, one is tempted to attribute the high rate of economic growth to various characteristics of the Japanese culture rather than to a relatively equal distribution of income. Actually, the Japanese growth rate is an integral extension of a century of development, the roots of which can be traced to the emergence of a mercantile class during the latter part of the Tokugawa Shogunate. Growth continued during the Meiji period up to the present, and the basic reasons for it have survived—a pervasive spirit of enterprise that combines the profit motive with economic nationalism.

From an economic standpoint, few persons would argue for complete income equality. The result in terms of resource allocation, loss of productivity, and lack of incentives would probably be disastrous to any modern society. Even in China, despite the egalitarian tone set by the Cultural Revolution, there remain significant differences in income. For example, it is reported that at the Kwangkhow Machine Tool plant, monthly incomes range from $16 for new workers to $60 for the plant director.[8] There is a greater disparity of incomes between industrial and agricultural workers, with cash incomes for the latter running as low as one-sixth of factory wages. The stated goal of the Chinese system is to make pay scales for all types of workers more nearly equal. Whether or not this will be accomplished remains to be seen. However, there appears to be a considerable degree of equality in the consumption of material goods. So it is entirely possible that in terms of the distribution of real income, the Chinese have achieved one of the most egalitarian of all current societies.

There are no well-accepted standards for determining when the process of income distribution has gone far enough, or even when it has gone too far. For example, take the case of Brazil. In 1970 the upper tenth of all income earners received 48 percent of total income, compared to 40 percent in 1960.[9] On the other hand, the share of the lowest 40 percent declined from 11.6 percent to 10 percent. In 1970 the richest 5 percent received 39 percent of national income, while the poorest 60 percent received 21 percent. Obviously there is an unhealthy imbalance in the distribution of income, exacerbated in part by the existence of a large component of unskilled labor. Given the fact that Brazil is an underdeveloped country, it can be said that a greater degree of income inequality exists than is the case in advanced industrial countries. It can be said that economic growth and technological developments should lead to greater equality in the distribution of income over time. Evidence tends to support this statement, at least with respect to Great Britain, where the top 1 percent of income earners received 12.5 percent of total income in 1938, compared to 7.9 percent in 1963.[10]

Some industrial countries display more income inequality than others. Comparisons are made difficult by differences in statistical observation and classification, and also on account of all the dimensions inherent in the concept of income distribution. Typically, the data used would have to involve the distribution of income before taxes. It would appear that Sweden has a relatively egalitarian society in comparison to most industrial countries. For example, in 1963 the highest 10 percent of income earners in Sweden received 28 percent of total income, compared to 41 percent for the top 10 percent in West Germany and 37 percent for the top 10 percent in France.[11] In the same year the highest 1 percent of income earners in Sweden received 6 percent of total income, compared to 10 percent for the top 1 percent in France and 12 percent for the top 1 percent in West Germany. However, these percentages do not take into consideration the effects of progressive income taxation and public expenditures. Statistics on income distribution, which allow for these factors, would show a still more equal distribution of income in Sweden than in the other countries.

Measurements of Income Inequality

There are various measures of income inequality, including the Lorenz curve and the Pareto and Gini coefficients. Of these measures, the Lorenz curve is most commonly used. The starting point for the Lorenz curve involves the use of an arithmetic scale that begins with an assumption of income equality as a starting point. Equality in the distribution of income is found when every income-receiving unit receives its proportional share of the total income. If incomes were absolutely uniformly distributed, the lowest 20 percent of income earners would receive exactly 20 percent of the total income; the lowest 80 percent would get exactly 80 percent of total income; and the highest 20 percent would get only 20 percent of the income. In using a Lorenz curve, the curve of absolute equality would actually be a straight line extending upwards from left to right showing that 20 percent of income earners on the horizontal axis receive 20 percent of the income shown on the vertical axis, 40 percent of income earners receive 40 percent of the income, and so on. Any departure from this line is a departure from complete income equality. The measure of the degree of inequality in income distribution is the concavity of the Lorenz curve relative to the straight line indicating complete equality.

An illustration of the Lorenz curve is presented in Figure 1. The straight line OAF is the line of perfect equality. The line OBF represents a departure from equality. There are certain weaknesses in the use of the Lorenz curve as a measure of income distribution. First, one cannot tell by inspection of the curves just how unequal the distribution of income is. By making use of percentages, the Lorenz curve conceals the number of income units in the different income brackets. It is also true that the slope of a curve at various points gives no more information than the curve itself. On the other hand, the Lorenz curve is excellent as a device for the visual presentation of inequalities in the distribution of income. It also can measure the effects of changes in the levels of taxing and government spending on the distribution of income.

The Lorenz curve is also applicable to the distribution of wealth. The curve for the distribution of wealth would generally deviate much more from the diagonal line and show a greater inequality of distribution. It is possible for two countries to show similar Lorenz curves for income distribution but entirely different curves for wealth distribution. The Lorenz curve for wealth reflects the fact that older and more stratified industrial societies display more wealth inequality than newer societies.

25

FIGURE 1

A Lorenz Curve

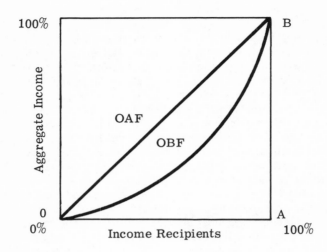

Through the use of a measure of concavity, it is possible to avoid reliance solely on visual comparisons of Lorenz curves in order to draw inferences with respect to income distributions of various types. This measure is called the Gini concentration coefficient. In a Lorenz diagram the Gini concentration coefficient is the ratio of the area between the diagonal and the Lorenz curve to the total area below the diagonal. For a perfectly equal distribution the Gini coefficient is zero. The greater the inequality, the larger the concentration coefficient, and conversely, the greater the equality, the smaller the concentration coefficient. The Gini concentration coefficient, then, is tied to the concavity of the Lorenz curve—the greater the concavity, the greater the coefficient. The coefficient, however, is basically an average, and does not tell anything about the extent to which inequality of distribution may be marked in various segments of the income distribution.

The Gini concentration coefficient, or index, is found by dividing the area between the diagonal line on the Lorenz curve that represents complete income equality and a line of inequality by the total area below the diagonal of equal distribution. With reference to Figure 1, it should be remembered that the Lorenz curve is based on a ranked cumulative distribution in both directions, that is, of income and number of recipients. Inequality is shown by the distance between the straight line and the curve connecting points O and B in the diagram. The Gini concentration coefficient is obtained by dividing the area between this line and curve by the triangular area OAB. For example, assume that the area under the diagonal of equal distribution, OAB, is equal to 5,000, and assume that the area between the diagonal and the curve OCB is equal to 2,500. The Gini coefficient is 0.50. The coefficient then can range from 0 to 1. The closer the coefficient is to zero, the more equal the income distribution; the closer the coefficient is to 1, the more unequal the distribution.

SUMMARY

To understand the subject of income distribution in a market economy, it is first necessary to differentiate between the concepts of functional income distribution and personal income distribution. The functional distribution of income refers to distribution according to the resource classes represented by land, labor, and capital. In national income accounting, compensation of employees represents income received by the owners of labor resources, while profits, interest, and rental income represent income received by the owners of land and capital. Some income, such as income to proprietors, can include income from both sources. The personal distribution of income, as the concept implies, relates to individual persons and their incomes. What matters with this concept is how much someone earns, not whether it comes from wages or property income. There is an obvious link between personal and functional income distribution in that if the amount of production factors each person has to offer is given, then factor prices determine how incomes will be divided among individuals. Of the two concepts, personal income distribution is of more concern with respect to the subsequent discussion of income distribution.

Opinions differ as to what is the most fair or the most desirable distribution of personal income. Unfortunately, however, there is no set answer. It is easy to think up desiderata with respect to what constitutes equity in the distribution of income, but often they are highly subjective and are of little relevance in diverse industrial societies. The norms and the interests of various people differ. But in general it can be said that the most important aspect of the development of the welfare state in Western society has been a drive for more equality in the distribution of income. There is less willingness to tolerate wide disparities in the distribution of both income and wealth.

27

NOTES

1. Further reference is made to the study by Christopher Jencks in Chapter 2.

2. Martin Schnitzer, "Unemployment Programs in Sweden," Joint Economic Committee of the U.S. Congress, 88th Congress, 1st Session (Washington: U.S. Government Printing Office, 1964), p. 11.

3. Bureau of Labor Statistics, "Labor Developments in the U.S.S.R.," BLS Report No. 311 (Washington: U.S. Department of Labor, 1966), p. 39.

4. One such study is by Peter Ludz, The German Democratic Republic from the Sixties to the Seventies (Cambridge: Harvard University Center for International Affairs, November, 1970).

5. John Dornberg, The New Tsars: Russia Under Stalin's Heirs (Garden City: Doubleday & Co., Inc., 1972), p. 281.

6. These studies are referred to in Chapter 2.

7. Lester Thurow and Robert Lucas, "The American Distribution of Income: A Structural Problem," Joint Economic Committee, 92d Congress, 2d Session (Washington: U.S. Government Printing Office, 1972), p. 4.

8. Fortune, October 1972, p. 144.

9. The Washington Post, November 10, 1972, p. 54.

10. R. J. Nicholson, "The Distribution of Personal Income," Lloyds Bank Review, January 1967, p. 12.

11. Olle Lindgren and Erik Lundberg, "Sweden's Economy in an International Perspective," Skandinaviska Banken Quarterly Review 1 (1971): 1-5.

2

INCOME DISTRIBUTION
IN THE UNITED STATES

There have been a number of studies on the subject of income distribution in the United States. Therefore, the purpose of this chapter is really not to provide anything new, but rather to present and synthesize what has already been done. The chapter will serve as a frame of reference for chapters that are to follow. It is assumed, however, that the reader is more familiar with the tax system of the United States than with systems of the other countries considered in the book. The U.S. tax system, in particular the personal income tax, has been subjected to much criticism. Indeed, a number of tax avoidance loopholes exist—many of which are effectively available only to upper-income taxpayers—contributing to considerable erosion of the federal personal income tax base. As an end result, the effective progressivity of the federal personal income tax deviates considerably from the nominal progressivity that would be suggested by the marginal tax rate brackets, which range from 14 to 70 percent.

The United States presents a paradox with respect to the distribution of income. Average figures of income wealth show the United States at the top in comparison with other countries. The United States has the highest per capita income of all countries. Yet the distribution of its income is quite unequal. Although the average income of the United States would indicate a prosperous nation, the fact is that the living standards of a part of the population are quite low. There is conflict with the idea of narrowing the income spectrum that has been an American ideal for more than half a century. The nation has imposed a progressive income tax since 1913, enforced a graduated estate tax since 1916, and passed expensive programs designed to alleviate poverty since the New Deal. Overall these policies appear to have had little effect on reducing the extent of income inequality in the United States.

Why, then, do extremely large differentials in income exist in the United States? In part the basis for unequal incomes is found in income derived from the sales of labor services. The labor supply is divided into noncompeting groups in such a way that many persons can perform the functions required by occupations in the lower groups, while comparatively few persons can fill the requirements of the occupations in the higher groups. Rather large differences in the marginal productivity of labor units therefore exist among the labor groups. Although wages do not adjust themselves with perfect accuracy to these intergroup differences in marginal productivity, great differences in wages or payment for labor services are found among workers in different groups. Thus even if there were no other sources of income for various individuals, a considerable degree of inequality in income distribution would result from this factor alone.

Much more important, however, is the fact that in the United States, as well as in other capitalist economies, individuals can own land and capital and can turn these objects of wealth over to various enterprises on the basis of the income to be derived from their use in production. In return these individuals receive income for the use of their land and capital as well as for the use of their labor services. This fact might make for equality rather than inequality in income distribution if those individuals who had small labor incomes had large incomes from land and capital, while those individuals who had large labor incomes received small property incomes. However, the actual situation is the other way around. The ownership of land and capital may well help an individual to acquire a large labor income. Conversely, the receipt of a large labor income makes possible the acquisition of land and capital. Inequality in the distribution of income becomes even greater when the institution of inheritance is allowed to operate. Individuals who amass great fortunes are allowed to transfer them to their heirs, who may continue to receive income from wealth.

Fundamentally, then, inequality in the distribution of income in the United States can be traced to a set of institutional arrangements, such as private property, that prevail. The pricing process, referred to in Chapter 1, is certainly one of these arrangements. As has already been mentioned, the high and low prices for productive resources not only result from the operation of the pricing system, but provide a necessary mechanism for the rational allocation of the resources and for the attainment of equilibrium on the basis of market forces. But high prices for the relatively scarce resources mean large incomes for their owners, while low prices for the relatively plentiful resources provide low incomes for their owners, and inequality in the distribution of income results.

Income inequality can be reduced through taxation and government expenditures. Once individuals have received their high and low incomes on the basis of the pricing process, progressive income taxation can lower the differential. The influence of inheritance in increasing and perpetuating inequality can also be reduced by progressive inheritance taxation. Government expenditures on education are supposed to break down the purely environmental barriers to movement between labor groups, and also permit each person to obtain the highest and most remunerative employment for which his abilities qualify him. The government can also use a part of public revenues to subsidize the production of various goods for the use of the poor.

INCOME DISTRIBUTION IN THE UNITED STATES

The purpose of this chapter is simply to present data concerning the distribution of income in the United States. Current studies indicate that at best there has been little or no shift in the distribution of income over the last twenty-five years. There are many facets to the whole subject of income distribution. First, there is the issue of equity that was a part of the McGovern plan to redistribute income. The original failure to develop a plausible plan destroyed credence in his subsequent efforts to present a viable program. Second, there is the relationship of education to income distribution. Has mass education had an effect in reducing income inequality? A current and controversial study purports to show that education has done little to reduce income inequality in the United States.[1] In fact, other factors, such as luck, environment, or heredity, may be equally or more important in determining one's position on the income ladder. Finally, there is the effect of tax policies on income distribution. Many experts take the position that effective tax rates on high income earners have been declining over time, because of a combination of loopholes and rate reductions. Conversely, rates on lower income earners have increased through the use of regressive sales taxes.

Functional Distribution of Income

The total national income of the United States amounted to $934.9 billion in 1972.[2] Salary and wage payments amounted to $626.4 billion, or about 64 percent of the national income total. Various supplements to wages and salaries, including employer contributions for social insurance, came to $78.7 billion. The income of unincorporated enterprises, less inventory valuation adjustments, amounted to $55.6 billion. Income of farm proprietors, including changes in inventories, was $19.6 billion. Rental income was $25.6 billion, corporate profits, less inventory valuation adjustments, $87.7 billion, and income from net interest, $41.3 billion.

Although these broad figures have some use in comparing different countries, they do not reveal many things that it is desirable to know. For example, it is not known how the large item for wages and salaries was divided as between the wages of ordinary types of workers and salaries going to business managers. Were all of the workers fairly well paid, or did most of them receive very low incomes while a few received extremely large ones? Did some of the large salaries and bonuses paid to corporate executives contain, as they often do, an element of profits? Did profits contain elements of income that should have been imputed to certain other productive factors? Finally, statistics for the national income as a whole and for the broad shares of income going to the owners of productive factors tell nothing as to the incomes that the citizens of the economy received as individuals and as families.

Personal Income Distribution

The national income is consumed in the final analysis by individuals and families. The factor that becomes important in connection with their standard of living is the amount of income received from all sources, rather than the rate at which income is paid for each unit of land, labor, or capital. In 1972 personal income from all sources amounted to $935.8 billion. Included in this total were government transfer payments to individuals and families of $99.1 billion, and business transfer payments of $4.9 billion.[3] Transfer payments, both government and business, have tripled since 1960. Other sources of personal income included wages and salaries of $626.4 billion, dividends of $26.4 billion, net interest paid by government and consumers of $31.6 billion, rental income of $25.6 billion, and various types of proprietary income of $76.4 billion. But these statistics do not present a breakdown of income received by individuals and families at various levels of income and the extent of income inequality that exists in the United States. Moreover, the statistics do not reflect the fact that inequality in the distribution of wealth is always greater than that in the distribution of income.

All of the numerous studies of personal income distribution indicate the existence of considerable income inequality. In 1929 the 8 percent of all families that had incomes of $5,000 or more received some 42 percent of the incomes of all families, and the highest 20 percent received 59 percent of personal income.[4] On the other hand, the bottom one-fifth of all families received only 4 percent of total income. The upper one-half of the families received 81 percent of the total income of all families, while the lower half received only 19 percent. Personal income in 1929 amounted to $85.9 billion.[5] Out of this total, and contributing to the concentration of income in the upper one-fifth of all families, dividends and interest amounted to $8.3 billion, or about one-tenth of personal income. On the other hand, transfer payments, which normally redound to the advantage of the lower-income groups, amounted to $900 million, or a little more than 1 percent of personal income. In 1972, however, transfer payments accounted for more than 10 percent of personal income, while dividends and interest accounted for around 6 percent.[6]

Some shifts in the distribution of income occurred during the Depression. In 1935-36, the highest 20 percent of families received 51 percent of personal income, while the lowest 20 percent received 5 percent of personal income.[7] Families that had incomes of $5,000 or more, or less than 3 percent of the total, received about 21 percent of the incomes of all families. Contributing at least in part to the shift in income distribution was a decline in interest and dividend payments to less than half of the 1929 total. In 1935-36, the upper half of all families received 78 percent of total income, while the lower half of the families received 22 percent of total income.

Income Distribution in 1971

Recent decades have witnessed no real movement toward greater equality in the distribution of income in the United States. In fact, a study by Peter Henle of the Library of Congress indicates that the share of wage and salary income going to the top fifth of male wage earners increased from 38 percent to 40.5 percent between 1958 and 1970.[8] At the same time, the bottom fifth's share of wages and salaries decreased from 5 percent to 4.5 percent. Another study by Lucas and Thurow indicates that there has been no shift in the share of income going to the highest and lowest fifth of all families in the period from 1947 to 1969.[9] The three-fifths in the middle brackets received about the same share of income throughout the period. There have been, however, some shifts in both absolute and relative measures of dispersion in income distribution. For example, over the twenty-two-year period the average income of the highest one-fifth of all families fell from 8.6 to 7.3 times that of the lowest one-fifth of all families.[10]

Table 2.1 presents the distribution of income for families and individuals in 1971. A family unit, as used in the table, is defined as a group of two or more persons related by blood, marriage, or adoption who reside together in the same dwelling. In 1971 more than half of all families had two or more income earners. Income

TABLE 2.1

Number of Families and Unrelated Individuals
(by total money income in 1971)

Total Money Income	Families	Unrelated Individuals
Under $1,000	784,000	1,749,000
$1,000 to $1,999	1,339,000	3,365,000
$2,000 to $2,999	2,242,000	2,457,000
$3,000 to $3,999	2,574,000	1,657,000
$4,000 to $4,999	2,888,000	1,324,000
$5,000 to $5,999	3,027,000	1,062,000
$6,000 to $6,999	2,955,000	945,000
$7,000 to $7,999	3,327,000	850,000
$8,000 to $9,999	6,560,000	1,168,000
$10,000 to $11,999	6,686,000	702,000
$12,000 to $14,999	7,674,000	526,000
$15,000 to $24,999	10,399,000	386,000
$25,000 and over	2,841,000	120,000
Median income	$10,285	$3,316
Total	53,296,000	16,311,000

Note: Families and unrelated individuals as of March 1972.

Source: U.S. Bureau of the Census, "Current Population Reports, Consumer Income 1971" (Washington, D.C., December 1972), p. 1.

in the table includes income from a number of sources. One such source is income from wages and salaries, bonuses, tips, and commissions, before deductions for taxes. Capital gains, however, are excluded from income. Since capital gains are received primarily by higher-income groups, their income tends to be understated. Another source of income is derived from both farm and nonfarm self-employment. Dividends, interest on savings or bonds, rent royalties, and income from estates are a third source of income. Other income sources include various types of transfers, including social security pensions and benefits, other pensions, unemployment compensation, veterans' benefits, and compensation for employment accidents.

The median and mean (average) are absolute values that are used to measure central tendency in any distribution. As indicated in the table, the median family income in 1971 was $10,285, and the median income for unrelated individuals was $3,316. When incomes of both groups are combined, the median income was $8,563, reflecting the fact that families receive around 84 percent of personal income. The median income for white families was $10,670 and for black families $6,640; the median income for males was $6,910 and for females $2,410.[11] However, these figures reflect the fact that a much larger proportion of males work full-time than females. When full-time yearly income is compared, the median income for males was $9,630 and for females $5,700. In 1971 the median income for nonfarm families was $10,430, compared to a median income of $7,190 for farm families. Median family income also varied by regions, ranging from a low of $8,890 in the South to a high of $11,020 in the Northeast. Finally, the median income of families with both husband and wife employed was $12,850 in 1971, compared to a median income of $9,740 for families where the wife was not employed.

The mean, or average income, for all families in 1971 was $11,853 and for all unrelated individuals $4,774.[12] Again there were regional, sex, and color variations in averages. On a regional basis, mean income varied from a high of $12,280 in the Northeast to a low of $10,431 in the South. Male heads of families averaged $11,366, while female heads averaged $5,585. Families with two or more income earners averaged around 50 percent more than families with single income earners. White family income averaged $11,997, while black family income averaged $7,695. There were also variations in average incomes based on the amount of education, with the average income ranging from $20,212 for family heads with five or more years of college to $7,170 for a family head with less than eight years of elementary education. Then, too, age, as might well be anticipated, was also responsible for differences in averages with workers in the middle-age brackets (35 to 54) possessing the highest average.

Table 2.2 presents the degree of inequality in the distribution of family income in the United States for the year 1971. Both complete equality and complete inequality of income distribution are shown relative to the actual distribution of income during that year. The deviation from complete equality and complete inequality is apparent. The table may be then translated into a Lorenz curve that graphically compares the actual distribution of income to complete equality or inequality of distribution (Figure 2). The diagonal line A represents complete equality where each family unit earns an identical income. The right-angled curve B represents complete inequality where one family earns the entire income of the society. The actual 1971 distribution of family income in the United States is represented by

TABLE 2.2

A Comparison of Family Income Distribution
in the United States in 1971 to Complete Equality
and Inequality in the Distribution of Family Income

Percentage of Family Units Cumulated from Poorest to Richest	Complete Equality	Complete Inequality	1971 Distribution
0	0	0	0
20	20	0	5.5
40	40	0	17.4
60	60	0	34.8
80	80	0	58.5
100	100	100	100.0

Source: U.S. Bureau of the Census, "Current Population Reports, Consumer Income 1971" (Washington, D.C., December 1972), p. 38.

curve C, which lies between the two curves representing complete equality and complete inequality of income distribution. Curve C may be moved inward toward curve A or outward toward curve B through government tax and expenditure policies.

One measure of income inequality involves a comparison of mean family incomes for different income classes. This measure is presented in Table 2.3. The mean for the income class $50,000 and over is $66,988, which is more than 50 times larger than the mean income of $1,261 recorded for the income class $1,000 to $1,499 and almost six times larger than the mean income of $11,583 for all families. Moreover, this mean income of $66,988 does not reflect that capital gains are excluded from its computation, with the end result that the amount actually may be understated considerably. Also presented in the table is the number of earners per family. As would be expected, there is a positive correlation between the number of earners and the size of average family income, with the exception at the highest income level.

Family income can also be broken down by quintiles to show the variation in mean incomes for the lowest and highest quintiles. In 1971 the average income of the lowest one-fifth of all families was approximately $3,200, and the average income of the highest one-fifth of all families was approximately $24,100—a ratio of about 8 to 1

FIGURE 2

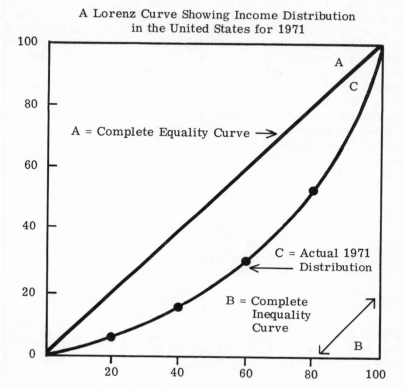

A Lorenz Curve Showing Income Distribution
in the United States for 1971

between the lowest and highest quintile means.[13] The absolute difference in average incomes of the lowest and highest fifths of families
apparently has widened considerably since 1947. In that year the
difference between the lowest and highest averages was $10,565; in
1971 the difference in averages was $20,900 (in 1971 dollars). In
1971 the average income of the highest 5 percent of all families was
approximately $33,180, and the average income of the lowest 5 percent
of all families was approximately $1,600—a ratio of about 21 to 1 in
favor of the highest 5 percent of all families.

Family income is derived from two basic sources—earnings
and income other than earnings. Earnings are broken down into three
categories—wages and salaries, nonfarm self-employment income,
and farm self-employment income. Income from sources other than
earnings can be broken down into public and private pensions,

dividends and other income from the ownership of property, public
assistance payments, and unemployment and workmen's compensation
and other income transfers. The manner in which each source of
income is distributed has an impact on the pattern of income distribution. For example, approximately 5 percent of all families receive
about 40 percent of dividend, interest, rent, and royalty incomes,
while the lowest two-thirds of all families receive less than 20 percent
of income of this type. About 40 percent of self-employment income
is also received by about 5 percent of all families.

Table 2.4 presents sources of income by income classes. For
the sake of space, various types of transfer payments are combined
into one column, and the same holds true for farm and nonfarm self-
employment income. These combinations in no way affect the inter-
pretation of the table. Some classes are aggregated to save space.

TABLE 2.3

Average Family Income and Number of Wage Earners
for Income Classes in 1971

Income Class	Mean Family Income	Earners per Family
Under $1,000	$ -161	0.83
1,000 to $ 1,999	1,261	0.71
2,000 to 2,999	2,238	0.67
3,000 to 3,999	3,223	0.88
4,000 to 4,999	4,502	1.07
5,000 to 5,999	5,466	1.27
6,000 to 6,999	6,456	1.37
7,000 to 7,999	7,461	1.46
8,000 to 8,999	8,446	1.57
9,000 to 9,999	9,448	1.63
10,000 to 11,999	10,887	1.74
12,000 to 14,999	13,325	1.94
15,000 to 24,999	18,514	2.24
25,000 to 49,999	31,179	2.40
50,000 and over	66,988	1.94

Source: U.S. Bureau of the Census, "Current Population Reports,
Consumer Income, 1971" (Washington, D.C., December 1972), p. 23.

38

TABLE 2.4

Family Income Classified by Source, 1971
(millions of dollars)

Income Classes	Wages and Salaries	Self-Employment	Transfers	Property Income
Under $1,000	183	—	138	22
1,000 to 2,000	605	90	1,351	46
2,000 to 4,000	5,045	702	8,301	468
4,000 to 6,000	16,600	2,079	9,620	1,223
6,000 to 8,000	31,759	3,216	7,473	1,462
8,000 to 10,000	48,078	3,732	5,563	1,391
10,000 to 12,000	62,051	5,387	4,543	1,589
12,000 to 15,000	89,442	4,601	4,705	2,347
15,000 to 25,000	165,996	13,669	7,322	5,533
25,000 and over	68,480	21,132	2,835	8,658
	488,239	54,977	51,851	22,739

Source: Bureau of the Census, "Current Population Reports, Consumer Income 1971" (Washington, D.C., December 1972), p. 25.

Income Distribution, 1947-71

There has been a stability in the distribution of income over the twenty-four-year period, 1947-1971, which is remarkable in view of the great changes that have taken place in the American economy. For one thing, it would be logical to expect mass education, particularly at the college level, to broaden employment opportunities and to break down class barriers. But it would appear that mass education has done little to reduce income inequality. This is a point that can be reserved for later observations. It would also appear that the social welfare programs of the Great Society have also had no impact on changing the distribution of income. However, the various poverty and job training programs may be too immediate in terms of time to discern any noticeable effect. An increase in government transfer payments from $10 billion in 1947 to $92 billion in 1971 also appears to have had little effect in changing income distribution patterns during the period.

The stability in the distribution of income is evident in Table 2.5, which presents the percentage share of aggregate before-tax income received by each one-fifth (quintile) of families as well as the top 5 percent of all families for the years 1947, 1950, 1960, 1965, and 1971. In 1947 the bottom one-fifth of all families received 5 percent of aggregate income; in 1971 the bottom one-fifth received 5.5 percent of income. It may also be observed that the percent of total money income received by the highest quintile declined from 43 percent to 41.6 percent between 1947 and 1971, while the percentage received by each of the other quintiles showed a modest increase during the period. Moreover, the share of the top 5 percent of all families showed a decrease from 17.2 percent to 14.5 percent during the period. For the period from 1965 to 1971, negligible changes were registered for all quintiles. In 1947 the highest 40 percent of families received 66.1 percent of aggregate income, compared to 33.9 percent for the lowest 60 percent; in 1971 the percentage relationship had shown virtually no change—65.3 percent to 34.7 percent.

Income of unrelated individuals, which is not included in Table 2.5, showed more significant shifts toward equality during the period. The income share of the highest fifth of unrelated individuals decreased from 59.1 percent in 1947 to 50.4 percent in 1971, while the income of the lowest one-fifth increased from 1.9 percent of total income in 1947 to 3.4 percent in 1971.[14] The income share of the top 5 percent of all unrelated individuals decreased from 33.3 percent in 1947 to 20.6 percent in 1971. Gains were made by the middle three quintiles during the period. In 1947 the share of income going to the second

TABLE 2.5

Percentage Distribution of U.S. Family Income
by Quintiles, 1947-71

Income Rank	1971	1965	1960	1950	1947
Lowest fifth	5.5	5.3	4.9	4.5	5.0
Second fifth	11.9	12.1	12.0	12.0	11.8
Third fifth	17.4	17.7	17.6	17.4	17.0
Fourth fifth	23.7	23.7	23.6	23.5	23.1
Highest fifth	41.6	41.3	42.0	42.6	43.0
Total	100.0	100.0	100.0	100.0	100.0
Top 5 percent	14.5*	15.5	16.8	17.0	17.2

*Estimate

Source: U.S. Bureau of the Census, "Current Population Reports, Consumer Income 1971" (Washington, D.C., December 1972), p. 38.

quintile was 5.8 percent; in 1971 the share had increased to 8.1 percent. The share of income going to the third and fourth quintiles was 11.9 percent and 21.4 percent in 1947; in 1971 the shares had increased to 13.9 percent and 24.2 percent, respectively.

In absolute terms (not shown in the table), the median family income of all families in the United States during 1971 was $10,285, compared to $3,031 in 1947.[15] When translated in terms of constant dollars for 1971, median income in 1947 was $5,480, so the actual gain was a compounded rate of around 3 percent over the twenty-four-year period. Shifts have also occurred in the relationship of the median incomes of whites and blacks and other races. In 1947 the median income of the minority groups was 51 percent of the median income for whites; in 1971 the relative relationship was 63 percent. Most of the gain in the median income of blacks and other races occurred during the period from 1965 to 1971, with an increase from $3,994 in 1965 to $6,714 in 1971.

However, all income classes have apparently made gains over the period from 1947 to 1971. In particular, there was a marked increase in the number of families with incomes of $10,000 or more.[16] The number of families in this category increased from 5.7 million in 1947 to 27.6 million in 1971 (over half of all families in 1971). Using constant 1971 dollars as the base, twice as many families had incomes under $4,000 in 1947 as had incomes above $10,000, whereas in 1971 four times as many families had incomes above $10,000 as had incomes below $4,000. In 1971 one out of every four families and unrelated individuals had incomes of $15,000 and over, and 51.7 percent had incomes in excess of $10,000, compared to 15.4 percent in 1947. At the other end of the income spectrum, the percentage of families and individuals making less than $5,000 declined from 44 percent in 1947 to 18.5 percent in 1971. Even after allowing for changes in the consumer price index, the end result is that all income earners, family or otherwise, have made gains during the period.

Trends in Income Distribution, 1958-70

Peter Henle of the Library of Congress analyzed Census data covering wages and salaries and earnings of male workers during the period from 1958 to 1970. He has found that there has been a slow but persistent trend toward inequality in the distribution of earnings and also in the distribution of wages and salaries. His study is limited to money income received as wages, salaries, or earnings from self-employment. Using the Gini index to measure inequality in the distribution of earnings, Henle obtained the following results:[17]

1. The Gini index of the earnings for full-time male workers decreased from .317 in 1958 to .315 in 1970. (The closer the Gini index is to zero, the more equal the income distribution.)

2. The Gini index for total earnings of males increased from .399 in 1958 to .428 in 1970.

3. The Gini index for wages and salaries of full-time male workers increased from .254 in 1958 to .281 in 1970.

4. The Gini index for wages and salaries for all male workers increased from .328 in 1958 to .356 in 1970.

A comparison of data by occupation and industry also confirmed a pattern of increased income inequality. The distribution of earnings for male workers in all occupations showed a trend toward more inequality during the twelve-year period. Certain occupations, however, showed a trend toward more equality, in particular, managers and officials. Increased inequality was found for the occupational groups—farm and nonfarm laborers, clerical, craftsmen, operatives, and services. When male workers were divided by industry groups, there were variations in income inequality. The industry in 1970 with the most unequal distribution of income was agriculture. The Gini index for agriculture was .416. At the opposite end of the scale from agriculture, public administration, with a Gini index of .230, had the most equal distribution of income. Industries associated with manufacturing and transportation showed a more equal distribution of income than the trade and service industries.

According to Henle, the reason for the increase in income inequality lies in the structure of the U.S. job market.[18] The number of high-paying jobs, such as engineer, computer programmer, and upper-level civil servant, has increased and salaries in these categories have risen markedly. There are shifts in the composition of employment among occupations and industries that widen the income gap between lower-paying jobs in agriculture and higher-paying jobs in service and professional areas. Moreover, the number of very low-paying jobs—janitor, dishwasher, and hospital orderly—has not declined. There has also been an influx into the job market of young people, who, despite generally higher educational levels, act as a drag on the lower end of the market. In addition, there has been an increase in women and part-time workers, who often command relatively low pay. The end result is that employers have found so many people to be hired for relatively little money that they have not gone all out to upgrade jobs and salaries.

DISTRIBUTION OF WEALTH IN THE UNITED STATES

The distribution of wealth in the United States is much more unequal than the distribution of income. Inequality of wealth is a contributing factor to inequality in incomes, for property income is received by a minority of persons. Although wealth in itself is not a bad thing, there is certainly a conflict between the way in which it is concentrated in the hands of a few and the American belief in equality of opportunity. With wealth goes economic power and prestige. The wealthy can afford to send their children to the best schools and provide them with the right contacts in employment. Inheritances also compound inequality through generations. Those who are wealthy can finance their own or others' campaigns for political office and thus successfully obtain political power. In no country is this more pronounced than the United States. The wealthy can hire expensive and successful lawyers to widen the scope of legitimate tax avoidance for themselves and also to resolve in their favor any legal conflicts between themselves and the less wealthy.

Table 2.6 presents the results of a study of wealth distribution made by the Federal Reserve Board in 1962. As is indicated in the table, the wealthiest 1 percent of all families owned 26.8 percent of all private assets, while the poorest 25 percent of all families had no net assets. In the same year, however, the poorest 25 percent of families received approximately 10 percent of total income. The richest 20 percent of all families owned around 77 percent of all assets, while receiving 42 percent of total income. The correlation of wealth with income is readily apparent in the table.

Another study, made by Robert Lampman, shows that there has been some decline over time in the share of personal sector wealth held by wealth-holders.19 In 1922 the top 1 percent of all adults owned 31.6 percent of the equity wealth in the United States, and the top 0.5 percent owned 29.8 percent. In 1929 the percentages had increased to 36.3 and 32.4 respectively. During the Depression the percentages declined to a point below the 1922-1929 level. A low point was reached in 1949 when the top 1 percent of all wealth-holders owned 20.8 percent of all equity wealth, and the top 0.5 percent held 19.3 percent. However, inequality increased during the 1950s. In 1956 the top 1 percent of wealth-holders controlled 26.0 percent of wealth, and the top 0.5 percent held 25 percent. The degree of inequality was still considerably less in 1956 than in either 1922 or 1929.

THE IMPACT OF TAXATION ON INCOME AND WEALTH DISTRIBUTION

Both direct and indirect taxes have an impact on the redistribution of income and wealth. The most important direct tax in the United States is the personal income tax levied by the federal government. The rates of the tax are progressive and thus should have a

TABLE 2.6

Family Distribution of Net Worth in 1962

Net Worth Class (thousands)	Cumulative Distribution of Families	Cumulative Distribution of Net Worth
Negative	8.1	-0.2
$0 to 1	25.4	0
1 to 5	42.7	2.1
5 to 10	56.9	6.6
10 to 25	81.3	23.8
25 to 50	92.5	40.9
50 to 100	97.6	55.9
100 to 200	98.6	61.3
200 to 500	99.5	74.2
500 and over	100.0	100.0

Source: Federal Reserve Bulletin, "Survey of Financial Characteristics" (Washington, D.C., March 1964), p. 291.

redistributive effect in that a larger part of the income of a rich person is taxed than is the income of a poor person. In actuality, however, the effectiveness of progressivity in reducing income inequality has been rather limited. Indirect taxes, such as sales taxes, tend to be regressive because they are levied on consumption. Social insurance contributions also may be considered regressive, as they apply only to labor income and are stopped once a cut-off point ($10,800 in 1973) is reached. Overall then in the United States there is a mix of taxes that tend to exert some sort of counterbalancing effect in terms of their impact upon income redistribution and to a lesser extent upon wealth distribution.

It is necessary to look at the most important taxes that affect income earners to arrive at some conclusion pertaining to their effect on incomes. First is the personal income tax levied by the federal government. What is its effect upon income redistribution? Second are other taxes, in particular sales and excise taxes, that also have to be taken into consideration. Finally, it is possible to obtain an idea of the overall incidence of taxation upon all income groups.

The Effect of Income Taxation on Income Distribution

An article that appeared on the front pages of all of the nation's major newspapers in March 1973 underlined a very significant issue in the state of the American economy.[20] The article stated that 276 persons with income in excess of $100,000 in 1971 had paid no federal income tax for that year. This number was down somewhat from a year earlier, when some 394 individuals had incomes of more than $100,000 and paid no federal income tax. Moreover, of the 276 nontaxpayers in the over-$100,000 class in 1971, 72 had incomes in excess of $200,000. What all of this means is that the American commitment to the "ability to pay" principle of income taxation has been substantially vitiated through the increased effectiveness of loopholes in the highest tax brackets, where most income is produced by investment rather than salary. These loopholes serve to reduce the effective rate of the federal personal income tax to the point where the average rate of tax paid by the top 1 percent of taxpayers in 1967 was only 26 percent, even though the nominal, or marginal, tax rate on incomes ranged up to 70 percent. The end result of the loopholes is to erode the base of the personal income tax.

However, the 276 persons who paid no taxes in 1971 are really the tip of the iceberg, for there are thousands of other persons who pay small amounts in taxes on their incomes. But even separate and apart from tax loopholes that permit avoidance of income taxation, personal income is reduced considerably by a series of escape provisions before taxable income is reached. For example, transfer payments are not included in the total taxable income of individuals. Around 10 percent of personal income also escapes tax liability by being either filed on nontaxable returns or not being reported. Personal deductions, both itemized and standard, also reduce the base of the personal income tax. Furthermore, personal exemptions constitute another category of erosion between personal income and taxable income. There are other exclusions, such as imputed income and income in kind, that are not included in taxable income. As an end result, a series of exclusions reduce personal income to a taxable income total that is less than half its original amount. Federal income tax revenues, as a result of the exclusions, amounted to 10 percent of personal income in 1971 and 19.8 percent of taxable income.[21] Comparable percentages for Sweden for the same year were 33 percent and 51 percent respectively.[22]

The main issue, however, concerns the reduction in the effective progressivity of the personal income tax, with the concomitant effect on income inequality. Certainly it can be said that a paramount reason for the apparent increase in income inequality in recent years is that special tax-law provisions work in such a way that income is reduced before it is even subject to the tax. But it is to be emphasized that some of the tax preferential treatment benefits a wide range of average taxpayers, not just the rich. For example, homeowners can deduct the interest cost on a mortgage from their income, as well as the cost of property taxes, while not being required to pay taxes on the imputed income derived from ownership of a house.

The effective rate of taxation has been reduced through preferential tax treatment. Thus the progressivity of the income tax, as reflected in the minimum and maximum marginal rates of 14 percent and 70 percent, is actually far less for many taxpayers. Table 2.7 presents the effective income tax rates paid by various income classes in 1972. The effective rate in the table is an average rate for each income class. There is very little change in the average effective rate in the income classes from $15,000 to $50,000. The average effective rate of 34.2 percent for incomes of $1 million and over is much less than the marginal tax rate of 70 percent that would be applied to additional dollars of income earned in this tax bracket.

There are two issues involved with respect to the loophole provisions of the personal income tax—equity and loss of revenue to the U.S. Treasury. The subject of equity is directly related to

TABLE 2.7

Effective Income Tax Rates by Income Classes for 1972

Income Classes	Effective Rate
$ 0 and under 3,000	0.5 percent
3,000 and under 5,000	1.7
5,000 and under 10,000	5.1
10,000 and under 15,000	8.6
15,000 and under 20,000	10.5
20,000 and under 25,000	11.8
25,000 and under 50,000	13.9
50,000 and under 100,000	22.2
100,000 and under 500,000	31.0
500,000 and under 1,000,000	32.8
1,000,000 and over	34.2
All classes	11.0

Source: Charles L. Schultze and others, Setting National Priorities: The 1973 Budget (Washington: The Brookings Institution, 1973), p. 434.

46

inequality in the distribution of income. In particular, attention is being given to a group of taxpayers, namely those in the upper-income brackets, who in general are the main beneficiaries of tax loopholes. For example, preferential treatment of capital gains creates in essence a tax welfare system for those persons who need benefits the least. Philip Stern in his book The Rape of the Taxpayer cites average capital gains of $640,667 yearly to persons making $1 million or more, while persons in the income bracket $10,000 to $15,000 average $24 yearly.[23] Moreover, nine out of every ten taxpayers are unable to take advantage of capital gains provisions. When all tax loopholes are taken into consideration, there is on the average a saving of $720,490 yearly to a person who makes over $1 million, which, as Stern points out, is tantamount to an average increase in weekly take-home pay of $13,855.[24] The tax loopholes reduce the effective rate from 63 percent to 32 percent. But at the other end of the income spectrum, tax loopholes are virtually meaningless.

The loss in revenue to the U.S. Treasury as a result of tax loopholes is large. Estimates of the loss range from $36 billion to $77 billion annually.[25] The Treasury Department estimated that tax loopholes resulted in a loss of $36 billion in 1971.[26] In a separate study, Pechman and Okner estimated a loss of $77 billion in 1972 to the Treasury as a result of tax preferences.[27] Included in their estimate are tax benefits, such as income splitting for married couples, that are not normally considered in the category of loopholes. But whatever the estimate, the significance is clear. The progressivity of the personal income tax is reduced, and the loss to the Treasury deprives the federal government of revenue that could be devoted to domestic needs. As Stern points out in his book, $2 billion of tax welfare benefits is distributed among the 3,000 richest American families. This amount is equal to the total amount spent by the federal government to provide food stamps in 1971.

To be objective, however, it is necessary to point out that preferential treatment of various groups of taxpayers, with the subsequent loss of revenue to the U.S. Treasury, is not an unmixed evil. It is certainly possible to suggest that the federal government would not spend the additional $36 billion or $77 billion derived from loophole closures wisely. The common notion that money buys solutions to all social problems is under attack. There is a certain group of prominent social scientists who keep telling the public and the politicians that no amount of extra money spent on schools will make much difference in how children perform.[28] It is also apparent that much of the money spent on the many poverty programs went to those persons who were nonpoor—bureaucrats, politicians, sociologists, and professors.[29] Moreover, once programs are put into effect and vested interests in them develop, they are maintained at the expense of the taxpayer long after they have outlived their usefulness.[30]

In most cases, tax loopholes are designed to accomplish an economic or social objective. Two prime examples of such loopholes and their objectives are presented below. It is necessary to compare the advantages gained by the economy as a whole to the disadvantages reflected in the loss of revenue and equity in the income tax system. It can be argued, for example, that favorable treatment of capital gains stimulates the flow of risk capital, and that depletion allowances encourage exploration for oil. The end result is that society gains. Moreover, almost any personal income tax system must include some quite arbitrary definitions as to what constitutes income for tax purposes. Important definitional and measurement problems arise in connection with those receipts that do not constitute ordinary income, but that yet retain certain characteristics of personal income. Income in kind and capital gains are examples of such problems.

Capital Gains

A controversy exists over the treatment of capital gains in a preferential manner from the treatment of ordinary income. In particular, capital gains realized on the sale or exchange of capital assets held for more than six months receive preferential tax treatment. The tax liability on these gains is determined by including in adjusted gross income only 50 percent of the excess of the net long-term (more than six months) gain over net short-term (less than six months) capital losses. The tax is then computed at regular rates on the adjusted gross income of the taxpayer. As a result of this procedure, the capital gain is taxed at only one-half the marginal rate applied to ordinary income. On the other hand, capital gains realized on the sale or exchange of capital assets held for less than six months are fully taxable as ordinary income.

There are, however, certain arguments advanced to support the favorable treatment of capital gains. The most important argument is that the lower rate of taxation produces a favorable economic effect. Individuals in the upper-income brackets—who constitute an important source of investment capital—favor investments that combine probabilities of capital accretion with low current income yield and some degree of risk. Favorable treatment of gains thereby offsets some of the depressant effect that the progressive federal income tax would otherwise have on various forms of investments through reducing the capacity and willingness of wealthy individuals to take risks. In this connection, it is also argued that capital gains serve as rewards to individuals who are willing to take risks. It also may be argued that preferential treatment of gains prevents an investor from being "locked in" to an investment that has risen in value. Hesitation to sell an asset because of a capital gain may result in a distortion of business and investment decision-making.

The arguments in favor of capital gains taxation, however, are in direct conflict with the concept of equity inherent in the progressive income tax. Favorable treatment of gains redounds primarily to the advantage of taxpayers in the higher-income brackets, thus reducing the effective rate of progressivity of the personal income tax. There is also the loss of revenue to the U.S. Treasury, revenue that could be used in solving many of the domestic social problems. There is also the argument that capital gains often represent an unearned increment of income, attributable to a rise in property value or in corporate bonds, for which the owner is in no way responsible. By all principles of tax justice, it can be argued that unearned income should be taxed as much as earned income. It may also be argued that favorable treatment of capital gains can create a negative effect on capital markets by encouraging the retention of profits within companies.

Exemption of State and Local Government Bond Interest

Another very controversial tax loophole involves the exemption of state and local bond interest from federal income taxation. The basic point in the controversy lies in the fact that the rich purchase these bonds because the interest is tax exempt. As a vehicle of investment, state and local bonds are really not within the reach of the average taxpayer, for even if he could buy a bond or two, the tax saving would be meaningless. But to a wealthy investor who is in the 50 percent marginal rate bracket, a 6 percent yield on a municipal bond translates itself into a 13 percent yield on a taxable security. This results in risk capital being diverted to the private sector because of the tax subsidy, with a distortion of resource allocation between the public and private sectors. This can occur, for example, when a locality or state uses tax-exempt bonds to finance industrial facilities that are used to attract industries from other geographical areas.

However, there are also arguments in favor of exempting interest from state and local bonds from federal income taxation. For one thing, it is contended that both state and local governments would have to borrow at much higher interest rates were it not for the tax exemption provision. The higher interest rates would mean additional costs to both state and local governments. The credit rating of many localities is low in comparison to higher levels of government and to large corporations, so the only advantage in borrowing is through the tax-exempt municipal bond. Then, too, it is argued that removal of the exemption feature represents an impingement on the part of the federal government on state sovereignty.

49

It would appear on balance that capital gains should be treated as regular income and taxed as such. It does not necessarily follow that investment will be adversely affected, and it is also apparent that many gains result from pure speculation on the stock market or in property. As for the exemption of interest on state and local bonds, it should be eliminated and a subsidy or grant arrangement introduced in its place. For example, the federal government could pay state and local governments some fixed proportion of their annual interest payments if they issued taxable bonds. In both cases, equity is the key factor. Only the wealthy really are in a position to gain through the use of each device. It is likely that income tax rates could be reduced for all classes of taxpayers provided that various loopholes that erode the base of the income tax are closed.

The Effects of Other Taxes on Income and Wealth Distribution

In terms of the general retail sales tax and most excise taxes, the fact that the rates tend to be proportional as applied to the tax base renders these taxes regressive. Since the marginal and average propensities to consume tend to be lower at higher income levels, the purchase of items subject to sales taxes is ordinarily a smaller proportion of the higher incomes. Moreover, the regressivity is accentuated when services are exempt from the tax base of a general retail sales tax, since these tend to be consumed more, in a relative sense, by higher-income taxpayers. The effective progressivity of the personal income tax may be viewed as being neutralized to some extent by the regressive distribution effect of general sales and excise taxes. It should be recognized, however, that the exemption of food and drug purchases from the general sales tax base in certain states, and also the occasional use of tax credits, reduce the effective regressivity of the tax.

Social security contributions can also be considered regressive in terms of their effect on income redistribution. This occurs because payroll taxes apply to only a limited amount of a person's wage or salary. In 1973, for example, the social security tax amounted to 5.8 percent of wage or salary incomes up to $10,800 a year, with a maximum of $632. The tax is regressive because it hits low-income groups the hardest. On a family making $5,000 a year, the tax would amount to 5.8 percent, but on a family making $20,000 a year, the tax would come to around 3 percent. To many families, social security contributions can amount to as much or more than the federal personal income tax. Even a family of four with an income of $12,000 will pay more than half as much to the Social Security Administration in 1973 as to the Internal Revenue Service. Families with both parents working are hit for two full-sized deductions, even though their eventual benefits at retirement will be the same as if only one spouse worked.

Furthermore, it is argued that the employer's share of social security contributions may be shifted either forward, in the form of higher prices to consumers, or backward, in the form of lower wages to employees. To shift the contribution forward presupposes the assumption that it is simply a part of labor costs, which, like other costs of production, will be passed on to the consumer via price increases. The extent to which the contribution can be passed on depends on a complex set of variables, including the elasticities of supply and demand and the degree of monopoly in a particular market. The tax may also be shifted backward to the employee through a reduction in money wages. In a competitive market situation, the wage, including the employer's contribution to social security, will be equal to the marginal product of labor. Thus an increase in the employer's tax for social security, ceteris paribus, would be shifted backward by a reduction in money wages.

There are other taxes that would have some impact on income and wealth distribution. One such tax is the property tax. In general, the property tax is considered to be regressive. Income does not measure one's ability to pay property taxes. In particular, owner-occupied residences do not provide a direct relationship to taxpaying ability. Instead, the ability to pay taxes is derived ultimately from either current income or from the long-term accumulation of wealth. Renters and older persons on fixed incomes also can find that the property tax is regressive. However, it is possible that the positive effect of public services provided from property tax revenues can offset to some degree the regressive effect of the tax.

The incidence of the major taxes on individuals and families appears to be proportional through a wide range of incomes, with some progressivity achieved at the higher levels. One study made by Lester Thurow on the impact of taxes on the American economy indicates that there is little change in tax incidence for families up to the income level of $15,000.[31] As this study incorporates data for 1965, only 6.5 percent of all families had incomes above this level. At the lowest income levels, social security contributions, property taxes, and general consumption taxes constituted a much greater percentage of total income than the personal income tax. For example, for the income class $4,000 to $5,000, social insurance, consumption, and property taxes accounted for 16.4 percent of income, compared to 6.9 percent for the personal income tax. For the income class $10,000 to $15,000, social insurance, consumption, and property taxes took 13.2 percent of family income, compared to 10.7 percent for the personal income tax.

It is more difficult to determine the effect of taxes upon the distribution of wealth. Most taxes are levied on income or consumption and have little effect upon the holding of existing wealth. Sales taxes in particular would have no impact on either the accumulation of wealth or on existing wealth. The personal income tax would have some impact upon wealth accumulation, but not upon existing wealth. When the income tax is capitalized, it will have a greater impact on the incomes of the rich than of the poor since, given the progressivity of the tax, the rich have to pay higher taxes than the poor. The effect of estate and gift taxes, which are considered taxes upon wealth, appears to be minor. They have failed to achieve one of their primary initial objectives, namely, the prevention or constraint of the continuing accumulation through successive generations of very large family concentrations of wealth. Also, given the incomplete coverage of wealth taxes, many types of wealth are left untaxed. This would include life insurance policies, annuities, retirement plans, trusts, and unrealized capital gains. Finally, the impact of the estate and gift taxes as measured in monetary terms is small. Measured as a percentage of net worth, they were levied at an average rate of 0.2 percent in 1965.[32]

The effect of all taxes upon the distribution of wealth as measured by net worth is presented in Table 2.8. The effective tax rates on net worth range from 4.5 percent for those with negative net worth to 31.1 percent for those with net worths between $20,000 and $49,999. Actually, the effective rate is less for the very wealthy-- those with a net worth of $500,000 and over. There is little effective progression between wealth classes. Moreover, since a great majority (81 percent) of persons have a net worth of less than $25,000, it is apparent that taxes do not have much impact upon the distribution of wealth.

THE IMPACT OF GOVERNMENT EXPENDITURES ON INCOME DISTRIBUTION

It should be evident that the government sector affects the distribution of income, for it collects taxes and dispenses various services and benefits. Taxes have the effect of altering the flow of income from the private sector to the public sector of the American economy. But taxes re-enter the income stream in the form of expenditures on goods and services and transfer payments. Taxes are not collected from nor services transferred to income recipients in the same proportion. Some persons are bound to pay out more in taxes than they receive back in direct government benefits, while others are bound to receive more in benefits than they pay out in taxes. The end result

TABLE 2.8

A Comparison of the Effect of Taxes on Net Worth

Size of Net Worth	With Taxes	Effective Tax Rate
Negative	$ -538	4.5%
$ 0 - $ 999	302	11.2
1,000 - 4,999	2,809	16.7
5,000 - 9,999	7,305	20.1
10,000 - 24,999	16,281	21.6
25,000 - 49,999	35,309	21.3
50,000 - 99,999	67,042	23.8
100,000 - 199,999	129,958	28.6
200,000 - 499,999	293,655	31.1
500,000 and over	1,176,281	27.2
Total	22,588	25.0

Source: Lester C. Thurow, The Impact of Taxes on the American Economy (New York: Praeger Publishers, 1972), p. 77.

is a redistribution of income that leaves some persons better off and others worse off than before income distribution was modified through public action.

Government expenditures can be divided into two categories— direct expenditures on goods and services and income transfers that involve no equivalent value in product or productive services in exchange. The impact of the first type of expenditure upon income redistribution is difficult to measure, for many government services are collective in nature in that they are enjoyed by everyone. These services are indivisible among recipients, and cannot, as a practical matter, be provided by the market mechanism. National defense is a case in point, for expenditures for this purpose clearly yield benefits to the citizens of a country, but it is equally obvious that this is a kind of benefit that cannot be consumed or enjoyed on an individual basis. The productive character of public activities results from the fact that expenditures by government units create values that benefit society.

An idea of the redistributive effect of transfer payments can be gained by examining census data on family income by sources in 1971. Public assistance and welfare payments accrue primarily to families with an aggregate income of $6,000 or less. To families with incomes of $1,000 or less, public assistance and welfare payments

53

accounted for approximately 18 percent of total income, while all
transfers, including social security benefits and unemployment compensation, accounted for 40 percent of total income.[33] The distributive pattern of all social welfare payments, exclusive of public
assistance and welfare payments, shows that a sizable share accrues
to families in the upper-income brackets. For example, families with
incomes of $15,000 or more received almost one-third of the total
of unemployment and workmen's compensation, government pensions,
and veterans' payments, and also almost one-third of private pensions. It would appear that low-income groups in general are not
particularly helped by the existing system of social welfare.

Table 2.9 presents the distribution of social welfare payments
by income classes for 1971. Private pensions, annuities, and alimony
are excluded from the table, as they do not represent any part of the
tax transfer payment mechanism. As might be expected, they show

TABLE 2.9

The Distribution of Social Welfare Payments by
Income Classes, 1971
(millions of dollars)

Income Classes	Social Security and Related Transfers	Public Assistance
0 and under 1,000	61	60
1,000 and under 2,000	758	494
2,000 and under 3,000	2,190	1,203
3,000 and under 4,000	3,236	1,071
4,000 and under 5,000	3,579	921
5,000 and under 6,000	3,260	544
6,000 and under 7,000	2,816	363
7,000 and under 8,000	2,549	257
8,000 and under 9,000	2,256	209
9,000 and under 10,000	1,825	124
10,000 and under 12,000	3,459	184
12,000 and under 15,000	3,491	118
15,000 and under 25,000	5,585	115
25,000 and over	1,590	33

Source: Bureau of the Census, "Current Population Reports,
Consumer Income 1971" (Washington, D.C., December 1972), p. 25.

a proportional relationship, increasing as family incomes increase. Income transfers from the government sector are then divided into two categories—income from the various social insurance programs, such as unemployment compensation and veterans' benefits, and income from public assistance and welfare transfers.

The public sector may also influence income distribution through the use of subsidies. A subsidy may be differentiated from a transfer payment in that it is designed to create incentives to alter specific market behavior, while welfare payments are designed to raise the income level of certain groups. A subsidy requires a specific economic performance from the recipients in the particular market to which the subsidy is tied. Subsidies can take a number of forms. A subsidy can be derived from the expenditure side of a government budget in the form of an outright payment to a private economic unit. Partial expenditure subsidies occur when government provides a productive resource or an economic good to a private economic unit at a price beneath the cost of providing the resource or good.

EDUCATION AND INCOME INEQUALITY

Thomas Jefferson said, "We hold these truths to be self-evident: that all men are created equal . . ."34 This statement, when taken out of context, appears patently ridiculous. After all, everyone knows from his personal experience that people are different and unequal. Neither Congress nor the Supreme Court can repeal the human condition that some people can run faster and jump farther than others. But Jefferson went on to make the statement, "There is a natural aristocracy among men. The grounds of this are virtue and talents. . . . There is also an artificial aristocracy, founded on wealth and birth, without either virtue or talents. . . . The natural aristocracy I consider as the most precious gift of nature."35 But how can we all be equal if some of us are naturally going to wind up better than the rest of us? That is the issue underlying the whole concept of income distribution in the United States.

Education in the United States is held to be the great equalizer of all men. Certainly no one idea has captured the attention and belief of American society so completely as that mass education can solve all problems and make everyone equal. During the 1960s an idea emerged that assigned to the federal government the responsibility for providing equality of opportunity. This meant government programs by the score designed to remove the barriers of privileged birth—legal action to break down racial discrimination and social programs to remedy the handicaps of the poor. Equality of opportunity has ascended to the highest place in the American pantheon of cherished ideals. Given that equality of opportunity might someday be reached, the result will be the same income inequality, a replica of the same disparities of income that already exist. Since people are different and unequal, equality of opportunity means they will wind up different and unequal. In theory, it can't turn out any other way.

Now education has come under attack. In a provocative study called Inequality, Christopher Jencks and his associates conclude that even if schools could be reformed to assure that every person received an equally good education, adult society would hardly be more equal than it is now.36 They argue that economic success is not primarily due to the kind of schooling a person has but "to luck or to subtle, unmeasured differences in personality and on-the-job competence." / At first glance, this argument would be rendered ineffective by citing Bureau of the Census tables that show a direct relationship between educational attainment and income levels. However, as Jencks points out, comparisons can be misleading. For example, when individuals have similar family backgrounds and similar test scores, but very dissimilar educational attainments, income differences are reduced by about 40 percent.37 So there are factors other than education that are responsible for income disparities between, say, a person who is a high school dropout and a person who has finished college. Jencks estimates a correlation between educational attainment and income of 0.353—a generally low coefficient.38

The notion that education is the instrument of equality, the balance-wheel in the social machinery, has been questioned by others than Jencks. The Coleman Report, published in 1966, analyzed studies involving more than 600,000 children.39 Coleman concluded that there were far fewer differences in physical facilities, curriculums, and teachers than anyone had suspected. Moreover, he found that the greatest variation in the achievement of students occurred not between schools but within the same school. His conclusion: "Family background differences account for much more variation in achievement than do differences in schools." In 1969 Arthur Jensen published an essay arguing that genes were largely responsible for the average fifteen-point I.Q. difference between American blacks and whites.40 What this means basically is that if a person's ability is really determined by heredity, there is not much education or family environment can do to achieve economic equality. Only those who are genetically well endowed will rise to the top.

Other doubts have risen as well. There is debate about the purpose of a college education, which has come to be looked on rather narrowly as an insurance for a career with some status and good pay. It would appear that there is underemployment—if not unemployment— of many college graduates today. The Bureau of Labor Statistics has estimated that only 20 percent of the jobs in the 1970s will require education beyond high school.[41] It is also projected that over the next decade an average of 2.5 persons will be competing for every job that requires a college education. Yet more than one-half of America's high school graduates opt each year for a college education. All of this should not denigrate the true purpose of education, which is to improve men's minds and make society better. But one can see why the plethora of college graduates produced might have little impact on income distribution.

SUMMARY

The purpose of this chapter has been to review some of the current findings on the subject of income distribution in the United States. The results may be summarized as follows: When income distribution is viewed as a long-run phenomenon—if the period from 1929 to 1971 can be considered long-run—income inequality has been reduced. In 1929 the top 20 percent of all families and individuals received more than one-half of total income. The Depression altered the distribution of income to some extent. However, a leveling-off point was reached by 1947. In a shorter time period, from 1947 to 1971, the top and bottom fifths of families and individuals have received about the same percentage of income. However, during this period all income groups showed gains, but the absolute difference in the average incomes of the lowest and highest one-fifth of all families has widened.

The personal income tax has had little impact on altering the distribution of income. The effective rate of progression has been reduced through a series of loopholes that have been written into the tax laws over time. In general these loopholes have worked to the advantage of upper-income families. Capital gains realized from the sale of assets are subject to a lower tax rate than ordinary income, and interest income from state and local bonds is completely exempt from federal income taxation. These and other loopholes were designed to encourage certain activities that have been deemed beneficial to the national economy. The end result, however, has been to deprive the U.S. Treasury of additional revenue, which might or might not be wisely spent. Perhaps a more serious condemnation of the loopholes is that they violate the ability-to-pay principle that is the rationale for the use of the personal income tax. The ordinary taxpayer has to carry the burden of the tax.

NOTES

1. Christopher Jencks, Inequality: A Reassessment of the Effect of Family and Schooling in America (New York: Basic Books, Inc., 1972).

2. Council of Economic Advisers, Economic Report of the President (Washington, 1973), p. 210.

3. Ibid., p. 210.

4. M. Leven, H. G. Moulton, and C. Warburton, America's Capacity to Consume (Washington: The Brookings Institution, 1934), Chapter 5.

5. Economic Report of the President, p. 212.

6. Ibid., p. 212.

7. U.S. National Resources Committee, Consumer Incomes in the United States, Their Distribution in 1935-36. (Washington, 1938).

8. Peter Henle, "Exploring the Distribution of National Income," Monthly Labor Review, December 1972, pp. 16-21.

9. Thurow and Lucas, op. cit., p. 7.

10. U.S. Bureau of the Census, "Current Population Reports, Consumer Income 1971," Current Population Reports, Series P. 60, No. 85 (Washington, December, 1972), p. 38.

11. Ibid., p. 3.

12. Ibid., p. 4.

13. Computations based on Table A, page 1, and Table 4, page 25, in "Consumer Income 1971."

14. Ibid., p. 38.

15. Ibid., p. 5.

16. Ibid., p. 38.

17. Henle, op. cit., p. 17.

18. Ibid., pp. 24-25.

19. Robert Lampman, Changes in the Share of Wealth Held by Top Wealth-Holders (New York: National Bureau of Economic Research, 1960), pp. 2-22.

20. The Washington Post, March 11, p. 1.

21. Computations based on data provided by the U.S. Treasury.

22. Swedish data based on the monthly journal Sunt Förnuft (March 1973), published by Skattebetalarnas Förening, Stockholm.

23. Philip Stern, The Rape of the Taxpayer (New York: Random House, 1973), p. 94.

24. Ibid., p. 6.

25. Ibid., p. 10.

26. Treasury Staff Study, prepared for the Joint Economic Committee, that appears in The Economics of Federal Subsidy Programs, 92nd Congress, 1st Session, 1972, p. 31.

27. Joseph A. Pechman and Benjamin A. Okner, "Individual Income Tax Erosion by Income Classes," in The Economics of Federal Subsidy Programs, Joint Economic Committee, 92nd Congress, 2nd Session, 1972.

28. In particular, Christopher Jencks and James Coleman.

29. Daniel P. Moynihan, The Politics of A Guaranteed Income (New York: Random House, 1973) p. 70.

30. Ibid., p. 307.

31. Lester Thurow, The Impact of Taxes on the American Economy (New York: Praeger Publishers, 1972), p. 75.

32. Ibid., p. 76.

33. U.S. Bureau of the Census, op. cit., p. 25.

34. Preamble to the Declaration of Independence.

35. Ibid.

36. Jencks, op. cit., Chapter 5.

37. Ibid., p. 144.

38. Ibid., p. 162.

39. James S. Coleman, Equality of Educational Opportunity (Washington: U.S. Government Printing Office, 1966).

40. Arthur R. Jensen, "How Much Can We Boost IQ and Scholastic Achievement?" Harvard Educational Review 39 (1969): 1-123.

41. Reported in Time, April 14, 1973.

CHAPTER

3

INCOME DISTRIBUTION
IN SWEDEN

Sweden is the smallest country used in this study, but in some respects it may be the most important. It is a highly developed industrial country that may well have the highest overall standard of living in the world. In terms of per capita money income, it ranks second only to the United States in the world; in terms of a more equitable distribution of real income, it ranks second to no country. In measuring how well a country provides for the economic and social well-being of all its citizens, Sweden would rank very high. It displays a willingness and ability to act in order to correct problems that arise in society. The approaches that it has used to create employment, eliminate poverty, and create aesthetic beauty in its cities are very resourceful and have been emulated by other countries. This is not to say, however, that Sweden is free from internal economic and social problems.

Although Sweden unquestionably deserves a high rating on the attainment of important economic and social goals, it is necessary to point out circumstances that have provided a framework favorable to the development of the country. First of all, it avoided participation in the two major wars of this century—wars that dissipated the resources and talents of other European countries. The Swedish foreign policy of nonalignment, which it followed during both wars, was prompted to a major degree by a series of conflicts in which it participated in the eighteenth and nineteenth centuries—conflicts that gained little in terms of territory and prestige but that lost much in terms of lives and property. Second, Sweden is a very homogeneous country; unlike the United States and the Soviet Union, which have extremely heterogeneous populations, there are no minority or racial problems. Third, the population of Sweden is small relative to the land area and resource base.

The economic system of Sweden has been called the "middle way" by Marquis Childs.[1] This term, when it was first used in the 1930s, referred to a sort of middle-ground approach between the unfettered economic individualism of American capitalism and the collectivism of Russian communism. The goal of Swedish policy during the 1930s was to modify the excesses of capitalism while avoiding the outright socialization of the agents of production. The Swedish system has also been called "functional socialism,"[2] which means that certain equity goals of socialism, such as a more equitable distribution of income, have been realized without recourse to formal nationalization of the agents of production. Instead, there has been a selective socialization of some of the more important functions within a totality of private ownership. However, the term "mixed economic system" seems to be as appropriate as any in describing the Swedish economy. In this system some functions of ownership are socialized, while others are not.

Social welfare measures in Sweden are comprehensive. One of the basic characteristics of the economy is the provision of a number of welfare measures to insure the average person against the vicissitudes of life. There is security from the cradle to the grave that does indeed provide protection for everyone. This security is expensive and is paid for by the taxpayers out of taxes that amount to more than 40 percent of the gross national product. But, given the objectives of the welfare state, which are to provide a more equal distribution of income and social services, the high cost is hardly surprising. Although the policy of creating a more egalitarian society is not without its costs, it can be said that disparities in economic and social power between upper- and lower-income groups based on income and wealth ownership have been narrowed considerably.

A stated objective of Prime Minister Olof Palme is to move Sweden toward even greater equality in the distribution of income.[3] To achieve this objective, broad-based economic and social policies are to be utilized. For one thing, income of lower-income groups is to be raised through state participation in labor market policy. Policies to maintain full employment are to receive highest priority. There is to be an expansion of adult education to equalize employment opportunities for older persons. Welfare benefits, particularly in the area of dental care, are to be broadened. However, there has been no mention in Sweden, at least on the part of the Palme government, of what constitutes a precise and exact end for the efforts to equalize incomes. So the question of how equal can you get is left hanging in the air. It would appear, however, that no Swedish politician is arguing for complete income equality.

THE SWEDISH ECONOMY

Before looking at income distribution and redistribution in Sweden, it is necessary to present some of the basic facets of the economy. In some respects the economy is quite different from the economies of the United States or West Germany. One thing that comes to mind is the strong union organization in Sweden. Nearly everyone belongs to a union—doctors, lawyers, teachers, white- and blue-collar workers, and government employees. Management is also strongly organized. So the organizational structure for centralized collective bargaining is thoroughly developed in Sweden.

The structure of the Swedish economy is somewhat similar to the economies of other mixed capitalistic countries. There is a basic reliance on free enterprise and the market system. Most of the gross national product is contributed by the private sector of the economy, and the institutions of capitalism—freedom of enterprise, private ownership of property, and consumer sovereignty—prevail in Sweden subject to modifications. Nevertheless, government control is substantial as a result of fiscal, monetary, and regulatory measures of the kinds familiar in other highly developed industrial countries, and the Swedish government has large interests in various sectors of the economy.[4] For a variety of reasons, the government, national and local, has entered into certain business activities that it shares to a greater or lesser degree with private enterprises. In Sweden there is also a cooperative movement. Although cooperatives account for only a small fraction of total industrial production, they are especially important in the food industry, accounting for about one-fourth of the nation's food trade.

One measure of the contributions of the private and public sectors to the Swedish economy can be obtained by comparing the amounts of private and public consumption and investment to gross national product. Because of the special interest that centers around government expenditures, these have, in the practice of national income accounting, been treated as a separate category. Government expenditures can be subdivided into the categories of consumption and expenditures. In Table 3.1 the contributions of the private and public sectors to the Swedish gross national product for 1971 are presented. Private consumption and investment accounted for about 65 percent of gross national product. The foreign trade sector of the economy is treated as a separate entity.

More important than the absolute relation of private consumption and investment to gross national product for 1971 is the fact that the private sector has declined in importance to the public sector over the last 25 years. For example, in 1946 private consumption amounted to 68 percent of the gross national product and 87 percent of total consumption; however, in 1971 private consumption amounted to 54 percent of gross national product and 70 percent of total consumption.[5] Private investment expenditures have also shown a decline relative to public investment expenditures over the same period. In 1946 public investment represented less than one-fourth of total investment; by 1971 public investment increased to almost one-half of total investment. In 1946, 17 percent of the gross national product was utilized by the public sector, compared to 34 percent in 1971.[6] Part of this increase in public sector expenditures can be attributed to

TABLE 3.1

The Swedish Gross National Product for 1971

	Millions of Kronor*
Private consumption	97,374
Central government consumption	15,836
Local government consumption	26,635
Private domestic gross investment	20,350
Central government gross investment	8,592
Local government gross investment	9,621
Changes in stock	1,725
Exports of goods and services	44,928
Less: Imports of goods and services	43,107
Gross national product	181,954

*The krona is the Swedish currency unit. In 1971 it was worth approximately $.19.

Source: Statistiska Centralbyran, Statistisk Arsbok For Sverige 1972 (Stockholm, 1972).

problems caused by the rapid urbanization of Swedish society that has taken place over the last twenty years, and part can be attributed to the increased participation of the government in certain sectors of the economy.

Actually, public consumption and investment expenditures do not measure the total contribution of the public sector to the Swedish economy. A considerable part of expenditures in the public sector, particularly by the national government, consists of income transfers to other sectors of the economy. While these outlays do not in themselves make any demands on real resources, the direct transfers from the national government to households and to local governments in particular do result in an immediate demand for goods and services. Transfer payments, such as family allowances, old-age benefits, and unemployment compensation, are excluded from public consumption expenditures for the reason that their recipients are free to use them for private consumption or savings. Public consumption involves goods and services that are supplied by the government. The purchase of educational materials and teachers' salaries would count as public consumption, but educational grants would count as income transfers. The provision of free medical care, however, is considered a part of public consumption expenditures.

National Income

National income in Sweden amounted to 136.6 billion kronor for 1971. On the basis of factor costs involved in the production of the gross national product, wages and salaries were the largest single component, amounting to 99.7 billion kronor. This figure excludes the 14.2 billion kronor in employers' contributions to social security and local and national government contributions to pension funds, which are included in the national income totals. A second component of national income is income of private entrepreneurs, which amounted to 9.2 billion kronor in 1971. Net income from capital, including interest from private insurance funds, amounted to 1.4 billion kronor. Finally, other-factor income, including corporate income, amounted to 12.1 billion kronor. Wages and salaries accounted for approximately four-fifths of factor costs, exclusive of the employers' contributions to social security and public sector contributions to pensions.

Personal Income

Personal income in Sweden amounted to 162.2 billion kronor in 1971. Of this total, transfer payments amounted to 26.1 billion kronor. The remainder of personal income—or household income, to use Swedish terminology—came from wages, salaries, and pension benefits, which amounted to 113.9 billion kronor, other-factor income, including primarily income to self-employed persons and to businesses, which amounted to 20.6 billion kronor, and interest—including interest on the national debt, which was excluded from the national income total—and dividends, which amounted to 1.7 billion kronor. From the total of personal income of 162.2 billion, direct taxes of 43.3 billion kronor and other transfers of 15 billion kronor were made to give a disposable income total of 103.8 billion kronor. When transfer payments are subtracted from direct taxes, household net payment to the public sector amounted to some 17 billion kronor in 1971.

PUBLIC FINANCE

Public finance in Sweden can be divided into three categories—taxes and expenditures of the national government, of the local governments, and contributions and expenditures under social security. Social security occupies an intermediate position between the national government and local government sectors on the one hand, and the household and business sectors on the other. Contributions from households and employers toward social security are routed—in some cases through the national government—to the social security sector. In total, when the three categories of public finance are considered, the impact of both taxes and transfer payments upon income distribution is enormous. Thus, before examining income distribution in Sweden, it is necessary to present the nature of the tax-transfer payment mechanism.

The level of taxation in Sweden compared to gross national product is the highest of any Western industrial country. In 1972 receipts from Swedish taxation plus contributions under the social security system amounted to 44 percent of the gross national product, as contrasted with a corresponding figure of approximately 27 percent for the United States.* No country in the world relies more heavily on the income tax as the prime source of both national and local government revenues. In the field of local revenue, it is important to note that local governments rely almost exclusively on income taxation; there is no other local tax of any consequence. Not only is the local income tax uniform, except as to rate, throughout Sweden, but it is integrated almost completely with the national tax. Income taxation accounts for around 65 percent of total national and local tax revenues.

On the reverse side of the coin, government expenditures, both national and local, are also quite high in relation to gross national product. In particular, government expenditure through transfer payments has had a great impact on income redistribution in Sweden. This transfer of income is accomplished by an extensive system of allowances and subsidies. Direct government expenditures on goods and services are also important. In addition to the standard expenditures on national defense, education, and housing, other expenditures are made through the public enterprises and the government-owned business companies. Social welfare expenditures account for the largest percentage of national government expenditures, while educational and public service expenditures are the largest components of local government expenditures.

National government expenditures are contained in the current and capital budgets and are scheduled to amount to around 60.5 billion kronor for the fiscal year 1973-74.[7] The main part of social welfare expenditures, however, is carried in separate budgets. These expenditures consist primarily of transfer payments, which, of course, are concerned with the redistributive function of government. They do not absorb resources; rather their chief effect is that of redistributing income among individuals and social and economic groups. It is important to note that a large part of social welfare expenditures are financed directly from the current operating budget of the Swedish government. Transfers financed directly out of the current operating budget include the basic old-age pension, family allowances, and housing subsidies. Grants are paid from the operating budget for health insurance and unemployment benefits.

---

*Comparisons were made by using the Swedish and U.S. budgets.

Taxation

The Swedish tax system is relatively easy to describe. The income tax is the most important national and local tax and is levied against both individuals and companies. In 1971 the income tax accounted for 36 billion kronor out of a total tax collection of 60 billion kronor. Another tax, which is of increasing importance as a source of revenue, is the value-added tax. This tax is of recent origin and is patterned after the French value-added tax, which has been adopted by many European countries. Sumptuary taxes, particularly those on alcohol and tobacco, are also of importance. In recent years indirect taxes have increased in importance relative to direct taxes as a source of government revenue. For example, the value-added tax will account for almost one-fourth of total revenue in the 1973-74 national budget, compared to 9.1 percent for the sales tax in the 1960-61 budget.[8]

Table 3.2 presents tax revenues for both national and local governments for the fiscal year 1973-74. Excluded from the table are revenues from public enterprises and other sources of nontax revenues, such as receipts from annual depreciation allowances and the liquidation of assets.

The National Income Tax

Sweden has a national and local income tax. The national income tax is progressive, but all local income taxes are proportional. The rates, however, vary from one locality (commune) to another. The average rate of all local income taxes in 1972 was 24 percent. Local income taxes actually take more income from the bulk of Swedish taxpayers than the national tax, and local income tax revenues account for a larger percentage of total income tax revenues than is true for the national income tax. Local income taxes are levied at the same rate for individuals, partnerships, corporations, and trusts. The national and local government taxes are collected together by one administrative organization, usually by means of withholding from wages and salaries. The county governor's office pays to each local government income taxes collected on its behalf.

Income in Sweden is defined as the total of net income from all sources: wages and salaries, interest, dividends, business activities, rent, and capital gains.[9] Capital gains, unlike in the United States, are treated as regular income, and are subject to both the national and local income taxes. There are variations in the treatment of capital gains. For example, capital gains derived from stocks and bonds are taxed on the full gain if the securities are held for two years or less, and at a decreasing rate if held longer than two years. After a five-year period, 10 percent of the capital gain is taxed as ordinary income. Capital gains on the sale of real estate are also

TABLE 3.2

National and Local Tax Revenues
for the Fiscal Year 1973-74

Taxes	Millions of Kronor
Taxes on income and capital	21,300
Taxes on motor vehicles	3,500
Value-added tax	14,000
Tobacco tax	1,800
Beverage taxes	3,200
Special employers' tax	4,500
Miscellaneous	4,800
Total	53,100
Local	
Income tax	27,000
Total	80,100

Source: Ministry of Finance, The Swedish Budget, 1973-1974 (Stockholm, 1973), p. 87.

taxed as ordinary income. If the property has been held for less than two years, the tax is on the full amount of the gain; after two years the tax is on 75 percent of the gain. Acquisition and improvement costs of up to 3,000 kronor a year can be deducted from the sales price of the property.

Deductions and allowances may be credited against total net income. Deductions may be made from income for necessary costs incurred in obtaining income. In 1971, however, there was a reform of the Swedish tax system. This reform was intended primarily to bring about a more equal distribution of income by easing the burden of taxes on incomes up to the 40,000-45,000 kronor ($8,000-$9,000) income bracket. A major change in the system of personal allowances was made. The personal allowance, which was formerly 4,000 kronor for married couples and 2,250 kronor for single persons, was changed to 4,500 kronor for every person, married or single. The allowance is the same for both national and local income taxes. However, for incomes above 30,000 kronor ($6,000), the personal allowance starts to decrease until a vanishing point is reached at 52,500 kronor (around $10,500). For two persons in the same family with income, both are entitled to the full allowance, provided that their individual incomes are less than 30,000 kronor. In a situation where there is one income earner in a family, a tax credit of 1,800 kronor is permitted. On second incomes of up to the 4,500 kronor allowance, the tax credit declines. The purpose of the tax credit is to aid families in which the wife does not work. But as the wife begins to earn supplemental income, the credit decreases until the allowance is reached; at that point the credit disappears.

Other characteristics of Swedish personal income taxation are as follows:[10]

1. For purposes of the national income tax, all earned income, for example, wages and salaries, is taxed separately by income earner. In other words, a husband and wife have to file separate returns. Joint taxation applies to unearned income, for example, rent, interest, and dividends. No system of joint taxation applies to the local income tax.

2. There are no exemptions for children under either the national or local income tax. Instead, parents receive a family allowance of 1,200 kronor per year for each child under 16. In some cases, a child-care allowance is permitted, particularly when a single person has a child or children under 16 living at home.

3. As far as individuals are concerned, the local income tax is not deductible from income for purposes of the national income tax. In no case is the national income tax deductible for purposes of either the national or local income tax. Neither of the taxes is available as a credit against the other.

The national income tax rates for 1973 range from 10 percent to 54 percent. These rates are only base rates; annually the Swedish Parliament has to determine what percentage of the base rates is to be applied for the year in question. This results in a "mobile tax" that gives the income tax system a degree of flexibility to meet changing revenue or economic needs. By a simple rate statute, Parliament can raise or lower rates without reopening the entire statute or even the rate itself.

The rates of the national income tax are presented in Table 3.3. The tax is computed the same way as the federal personal income tax in the United States. Progression is accomplished by the "bracket" method, whereby each successive higher rate applies only to income in excess of the previous bracket maximum. Until the tax reform of 1971, exemptions tended to reduce somewhat the overall burden of the scheduled rates. The effective rates of total taxable incomes tend to be less than the maximum bracket rates applied to these incomes. For example, the marginal tax rate on taxable incomes between 30,000 and 40,000 kronor is 28 percent, but the effective rate is much less. The total national tax on a net taxable income of 39,000 kronor is 7,020 kronor. The effective rate is 18 percent, compared to a marginal tax rate of 28 percent.

The Local Income Tax

For all practical purposes, however, it is the local income tax that is more important to the bulk of Swedish taxpayers. Local income

TABLE 3.3

National Income Tax Rates for Sweden, 1971

Taxable Income (Kronor)	Amount of Tax (Kronor)
Not more than 15,000	10 percent of taxable income
Exceeds 15,000 but not 20,000	1,500 on 15,000 plus 16 percent of remainder
Exceeds 20,000 but not 30,000	2,300 on 20,000 plus 22 percent of remainder
Exceeds 30,000 but not 52,500	4,500 on 30,000 plus 28 percent of remainder
Exceeds 52,500 but not 70,000	10,800 on 52,500 plus 38 percent of remainder
Exceeds 70,000 but not 100,000	17,450 on 70,000 plus 44 percent of remainder
Exceeds 100,000 but not 150,000	30,650 on 100,000 plus 49 percent of remainder
Exceeds 150,000	55,150 on 150,000 plus 54 percent of remainder

Source: Skandinaviska Enskilda Banken, The Tax System in Sweden (Stockholm, 1972), p. 41.

tax rates, which are proportional, ranged from 19 percent to 28 percent of assessed income for the income year 1972. Computation of taxable income is similar to the computation for the national income tax in that general deductions are deducted from income from all sources to get assessed income.[11] From assessed income, personal allowances are deducted to get taxable income. Given the rates of the national and local income taxes, there are cases in which the total burden of taxes could be quite high. In addition, there is a progressive tax on wealth exceeding 150,000 kronor, whose rates increase to a maximum of 2.5 percent.

The following example of the computation of the national and local income taxes can be used to illustrate some of the fundamentals of income taxation in Sweden. The taxpayer is a married person whose wife has no earned income. (This is not to be taken as a typical or atypical situation.) Assessed income after general deductions is assumed to be 60,000 kronor ($12,000), and the local income tax is assumed to be 24 percent. The local income tax, as mentioned previously, cannot be taken as a deduction from net income. Moreover, there is no personal allowance of 4,500 kronor, for the income of 60,000 kronor is above the point of 52,500 kronor where the allowance vanishes. Since the wife earned no income, the husband is not entitled to use her personal allowance. Instead, the husband is entitled to a tax credit, against the amount of tax due from him, equal to 40 percent of the maximum personal allowance of 4,500 kronor, or 1,800 kronor. This tax credit is available for both local and national tax purposes.

Local Income Tax		National Income Tax	
Assessed income	60,000 kronor	Assessed income	60,000 kronor
Minus allowance	0	Minus allowance	0
Taxable income	60,000	Taxable income	60,000
Income tax of		Income tax	
24 percent	14,400	(Table 3.3)	13,650
Less tax credit	1,800	Less tax credit	1,800
Total Local		Total National	
Tax	12,600	Tax	11,850

In addition to national and local income taxes on personal incomes, there is a basic old-age pension, which is financed by a tax on the employee of 5 percent of income, with a maximum payment of 1,500 kronor a year, and health insurance premiums, which are based on income. Husband and wife are treated separately for pension purposes; no system of joint taxation applies. The three taxes are withheld as a single deduction from an employee's income by the employer. Since the deduction covers both national and local income taxes, and since the rate of the latter tax varies from commune to commune, it is necessary to publish a series of withholding tables. The health insurance premium ranges from 230 kronor a year to a maximum of

533 kronor, and is deductible for both national and local income tax purposes.

The Corporate Income Tax

National and local income taxes are also levied on the incomes of corporations. The national income tax is levied on corporations at a flat rate of 40 percent of net income, and the local income tax is levied at the same rates as for individuals. Since the latter tax is deductible for national income purposes, the combined rates amount to about 54.4 percent of taxable income. Both the national and local income taxes are assessed against corporations in the assessment year on incomes earned in the previous year.[12]

The corporate income tax is levied on net taxable income. To determine net income, a corporation may deduct from its gross receipts all normal operating expenses. It can deduct interest on borrowed capital, certain taxes including the local income tax, pensions, maintenance and repairs, wages and salaries, and rent. In addition, there are special rules governing the taxation of corporate income that are designed to increase the efficiency of Swedish industry as a competitor in world markets. These rules govern depreciation, inventory valuation, and the use of investment reserves for economic stabilization.

The Value-Added Tax

The value-added tax (Mervardeskatt) was introduced in Sweden in January 1969, replacing a general retail sales tax that had been in effect for a number of years. Simply stated, the value-added tax is a tax on what a firm adds in value to the goods it handles. The tax base, in general, is the difference between a firm's total receipts from sales and its payments for materials. The tax base, in other words, is the growth in value attributable to each firm's activities. In essence, it is a tax on wages, profit, and other payments for the factors of production. It is usually imposed at each stage of the production process, not at just the retail stage or the wholesale level.

The Swedish value-added tax is a rather comprehensive levy on general consumption items—goods and services and imports of taxable goods to Sweden.[13] The tax does not apply to export sales, however, and because of a tax-credit mechanism, sales of machinery and capital equipment are, in effect, exempt. With few exceptions, all goods and services are subject to the tax. The tax is levied on heating fuels, growing crops, hunting and fishing rights, consumer and capital goods, stocks and bonds, and lottery tickets. Services are also taxable. For example, cleaning and repair work, catering and leasing, transportation with the exception of passenger service, hotel rooms, and alteration and maintenance work are all subject to the tax.

71

The value-added tax has a single nominal rate of 15 percent for all taxable goods and services. In accordance with a practice common in Europe, the tax is levied on the sales price including the tax itself, making an effective rate of tax, on the price before tax, of 17.65 percent. The effective rate of the value-added tax on the price of an article before it is levied may be determined from the nominal rate by use of the following formula, in which E equals the effective rate and N the nominal rate:

$$E = \frac{N}{1-N}$$

Using Sweden's nominal rate of 15 percent, the result is:

$$E = \frac{15\%}{1-15\%} = 17.65\%$$

One may wonder why an egalitarian society, such as Sweden's, would make use of the value-added tax. First, the value-added tax reflects a continued trend toward greater reliance on indirect taxation in Sweden. This trend began with the imposition of a retail sales tax in 1960. During the period from 1960 to 1970 indirect taxes increased from 7.3 billion kronor to 20.6 billion kronor. The reason for this increase lies in the fact that progressive income taxation in itself is no longer sufficient to pay for Sweden's ever-expanding social welfare programs. As has already been mentioned, the ratio of direct taxes to gross national product is already higher in Sweden than in any other country. Second, the choice of the value-added tax reflects the fact that there is a trend in Europe toward the use of this type of tax. In 1967 the Council of Ministers of the Common Market directed member countries to adopt the value-added tax as the common form of taxation. The European Free Trade Association (EFTA), of which Sweden is a member, also endorsed the use of the tax. So Denmark, Norway, and Sweden adopted it.

The value-added tax, being a tax on consumption, can almost certainly be considered regressive, since consumption as a percentage of income falls as income rises. Thus substituting the value-added tax for part of the personal income tax is to substitute a regressive tax for a progressive tax. In the case of Sweden, however, there was little substitution effect. While advocates of a value-added tax for the United States prefer to substitute its use, at least in part, for the corporate income tax, no such substitution occurred in Sweden. In the adoption of the value-added tax, it was stated government policy that there was to be no transfer of the total tax burden from business to the consumer.

Sumptuary Taxes

Sumptuary taxes are designed to penalize the consumption of certain products that are generally considered to be harmful. The taxation of tobacco and liquor represents a specific example. These taxes have often been rationalized on the grounds that the use of these products is socially undesirable. In Sweden the taxes on both tobacco and liquor are quite high. The tax on tobacco consists of two elements— a flat rate calculated per piece or per package and the value-added tax, which is imposed on the sales price to the consumer. The combined taxes average 88 percent of the sales price of a package of cigarettes. Two taxes are also levied on the sale of liquor—a sales tax, which is added to the price of liquor when sales are made from the wholesaler to the retailer, and the value-added tax, which is imposed on the retail price of the liquor. In general, taxes account for about 85 percent of the retail price of a bottle of whisky and about 55 percent of the purchase price of an ordinary light wine.[14]

Wealth Taxes

Sweden levies a national tax on net wealth, inheritances, and gifts.[15] The wealth tax is a capital tax levied on net assets in excess of 150,000 kronor. Net wealth is defined as the capital value of a taxpayer's assets minus the amount of his debt. With few exceptions, virtually every kind of property—real or movable, tangible or intangible—is subject to the tax; in general, only such items as household goods and certain kinds of personal insurance are exempt. For purposes of the tax, the assets of husbands and wives are lumped together. The capital tax involves double taxation in that income from assets is subject to income taxation. The rate of the net wealth tax ranges from 1 percent on a minimum taxable wealth of 150,000 kronor ($30,000) to 2.5 percent on taxable wealth in excess of 1,000,000 kronor. When income comes entirely from wealth, the impact of the wealth tax can be considerable. For example, an income of 60,000 kronor derived from taxable wealth of 1,000,000 kronor would be subject to a wealth tax of 15,250 kronor and national and local income taxes of approximately 28,000 kronor. However, by law the combined income and wealth taxes may not exceed 80 percent of a taxpayer's taxable income in a given year, provided the income is less than 200,000 kronor.

The Swedish inheritance and gift taxes have special rates based on the consanguinity of the inheritors to the person who is deceased. Three rates are levied upon inheritances. The lowest rate is paid by those inheritors who were closest to the deceased. An exemption of 30,000 kronor is allowed a surviving spouse and an exemption of 15,000 kronor is allowed each child. Inheritances above the exemption level are taxed at rates that start at 5 percent on the first 25,000 kronor ($5,000) and progress to a maximum of 65 percent on inheritances in excess of 5,000,000 kronor. Higher rates with lower exemptions apply to brothers, sisters, cousins, and friends. For example, a friend of a deceased person would pay a 65 percent tax on an inheritance of 50,000 kronor ($10,000). The gift tax is imposed upon donees at the same rates as those of the inheritance tax, and in effect the two taxes constitute one cumulative transfer tax on certain occasions.

Social Security Contributions

Social security contributions and expenditures really can be considered as separate from the main Swedish tax system, as both are handled in a separate budget. Contributions to social security include health insurance payments, which are based on the size of income, and a basic national old-age pension contribution, which is 5 percent of taxable income and reaches a maximum amount of 1,500 kronor. Two income earners in the same family must pay the tax separately. In addition, there is a supplementary pension scheme that pays benefits to retired individuals on the basis of their earnings. Contributions for this scheme come from employers, and no tax is levied on employees. Self-employed persons are subject to the tax, which amounts to 10 percent of earned income, with a maximum contribution of 4,500 kronor.

Membership in a national health insurance program is compulsory for all Swedish income earners. The rates are not set at a national level, but vary from locality to locality. The rates are based on income. In Stockholm, for example, the rate ranges from 230 kronor on a yearly income of 1,800 kronor to 533 kronor on an annual income of 39,000 kronor or more. The amount of the health insurance fee can be used as a general deduction for purposes of both the national and local income taxes. The fee is paid into various insurance funds, which are administered by the national government. In addition to the public insurance program, there is a voluntary health insurance program.

The social security sector thus includes health insurance, compulsory and voluntary; national old-age pensions and supplementary pensions; and industrial injury insurance. Separate from social security is unemployment insurance, which is handled by contributions into unemployment funds administered by unions, and family allowances, which are financed out of general revenues of the national budget. In 1972 revenues of the social security sector amounted to 28.5 billion kronor.[16] Of this total, social security contributions amounted to 16.7 billion kronor, grants from the national and local governments amounted to 8.3 billion kronor, and income from interest accounted for 3.5 billion kronor. When social security contributions of 16.7 billion kronor are added to total tax revenues of 70.3 billion kronor, the total public sector take was 86.9 billion kronor for 1972, or 44.5 percent of gross national product for that year.

Transfer Payments

A part of the public sector's income is returned to the private sector. For example, 37.4 billion kronor in income transfers constituted 39 percent of total public expenditures in 1972.[17] To some extent these income transfers form components in the social security system and are financed with contributions and fees from households, while other income transfers are intended to redistribute income among income brackets. In 1972 total income transfers to households amounted to 28.3 billion kronor. A smaller portion of the public sector's income is returned in the form of subsidies to the business sector and can thus be said to benefit the household sector in the form of lower prices. In 1972 transfers of this type amounted to 6.4 billion kronor. The remaining income transfers of 6.5 billion kronor go to a wide variety of categories, including agriculture and transfers abroad. The public sector, then, returns economic resources in the form of transfers to the private sector, with a varying degree of control over their final use.

Family Allowances

Family allowances are one component of the total of income transfers to households. These allowances are financed entirely from general government revenues; there are no contributions from employers or employees. They are not a part of the Swedish social security system, and are carried as an expense item in the Swedish operating budget. In 1970 the family allowance was paid at the rate of 900 kronor ($175) a year per child under 16. For 1973 the rate had been increased to 1,320 kronor a year. Unlike most countries with family allowances, Sweden does not exclude the first child from receiving the allowance. Like family allowances in France and in some other countries, the family allowance includes more than just payments based on the number of children in a family. There is also a housing allowance for low-income families with children, and various allowances that are payable in special circumstances, such as maternity grants.

Housing allowances, on the other hand, are actually tied to family income, with the purpose of providing assistance to low-income families. The allowance is paid by both the national and local governments, with the latter receiving support in the form of grants from the national government. The total allowance and eligibility levels have been raised each year since 1966. A sliding scale is used based on the size of income and the number of children in a family. For example, a family with three children living in a three-room flat on an annual income of 20,000 kronor ($4,000) would receive national and local government housing allowances in the amount of 6,500 kronor.

Pensions

As family and housing allowances are designed to improve the economic status of the family, pensions are designed to improve the economic position of the aged and disabled. There is a basic, national old-age pension, as well as a supplementary old-age pension, for everyone who reaches 67. However, at his discretion, a Swedish citizen can apply for his old-age pension at the age of 63 or defer it until the age of 70 by accepting a reduction or premium in the pension. Both old-age and supplementary pensions are designed to provide an amount corresponding to 60 percent of the annual earned income averaged during the fifteen best years before retirement. The maximum annual income included in this calculation, as of 1972, is 53,250 kronor (approximately $10,000).[18] There are also basic and supplementary invalidity pensions, which provide the same amounts as the old-age pensions. Both types of pensions provide for children's and housing supplements, as well as for a widow's pension, which amounts to 90 percent of the basic pension and 40 percent of the supplementary pension.

Unemployment Compensation

Unemployment compensation, which is voluntary, covers the majority of persons exposed to the risk of unemployment. Benefits, which range between certain maximum and minimum limits, are paid on a daily basis, and currently can amount to a maximum of 60 kronor ($12) a day for a period of up to 200 days. There is also a dependent's supplement of three kronor a day for the spouse and all children under 16. The compensation is financed by contributions made by all insured persons, which vary according to the unemployment insurance society to which a person belongs, and also by grants from the national government. These grants average two-thirds of the total cost of unemployment compensation.

Sickness and Maternity Benefits

A compulsory health program covers all of the population. There is a guarantee of income for loss of work caused by illness, which amounts to 80 percent of lost income up to an amount of 39,000 kronor a year. Health insurance also covers hospital costs. Certain special services, such as out-patient treatment, are paid for in part by patients. Maternity benefits include a lump-sum cash payment of 1,080 kronor and payments for lost income during a maximum of six months for gainfully employed mothers. In total, disposable income from sickness benefits and other related transfer payments add up to 80 percent of normal disposable income from employment. Sickness benefits are payable as long as the illness causes a reduction in working capacity of not less than 50 percent.

Disability Compensation

Disability benefits are financed entirely by employer contributions, which are based on payroll and range up to a maximum of 1.2 percent. Benefits are of two types, temporary and permanent. Temporary benefits range from 6 to 52 kronor a day, based on income classes and payable for ninety days. There are supplements for children, which range from 1 to 3 kronor a day based on the number of children. Permanent disability benefits amount to eleventwelfths of earnings with a maximum benefit of 12,000 kronor a year. There is also a cluster of ancillary benefits, including a constant-attendant supplement of 1,200 kronor a year and a funeral grant of 600 kronor.

It can be said that most of social welfare expenditures in Sweden are financed by the national and local governments out of general tax revenues. However, the apportionment of these expenditures varies widely for the different types of social welfare service. The cost of the family allowance is borne entirely by the national government out of general tax revenues. Health and hospital services are financed entirely by the national and local governments. Sickness insurance, on the other hand, is financed almost entirely by employer and employee contributions. Unemployment measures are financed primarily by the national government.

INCOME DISTRIBUTION IN SWEDEN

Given the fact that the public sector occupies an important position in the Swedish economy through taxation and expenditures, it is now possible to continue toward the presentation of income distribution. The statistics on income distribution available at present comprise tax assessment data. The concept of income underlying the data is known for assessment purposes as combined net income, a concept obtained by adding together the income received from different sources and deducting all expenses in acquiring the incomes. The use of tax assessment data has several defects. For example, it is not possible to determine whether the income comes from full-time or part-time work, and how many people are supported on the income. Income data also give no information pertaining to the distribution of living standards and welfare among individuals. The use of tax assessment data also involves leaving out a number of persons whose incomes for one reason or another are too low for assessment.

Trends in Income Distribution in Sweden

One major Swedish study has measured the distribution of income for the period from 1951 to 1968.[19] The income statistics were based on the inclusion of everyone in the population 20 years or older. Two measures were used to describe the concentration of income over this period. One measure is called the coefficient of concentration. This measure of dispersion relates the absolute sum of all income differences to the mean income. The lower the value of this measure, the more uniform the distribution of income. A second measure used involved the distribution of income into deciles (tenths). This approach was extended to give the total shares of income received by the top 5 percent and 1 percent of income earners.

Table 3.4 presents the percentage of income received by the top 10 percent and 1 percent of all income earners in Sweden for the period from 1951 to 1968, plus estimates for the year 1969. The distribution shows that the top 10 percent share of total income declined from 34.2 percent in 1951 to 31.4 percent in 1969, and the share of the top 1 percent decreased from 8.5 percent to 6.9 percent. The 1 percent with the highest incomes in 1968 were those with more than 70,000 kronor in income (approximately $14,000), while the top 10 percent were those with more than 31,000 kronor. Also presented in the table is the coefficient of concentration. All measures show a gradual shift over time toward more equality in the distribution of income. One factor to mention is the decline of capital income from 2.9 percent of total income in 1951 to 2.3 percent in 1966. However, capital incomes and the yield from other forms of wealth account for only 5 percent of income in Sweden, and as such would have a minor effect on the distribution of income. The statistics are based on tax assessment data.*

The average income for all adult Swedes included in the study was 4,400 kronor in 1951 and 15,800 kronor in 1969—an average increase of 7.5 percent a year. The average income for men increased from 10,900 kronor to 23,000 kronor, and the average income for women increased from 3,200 kronor to 8,800 kronor. These statistics are based on the inclusion of all persons over 20 years of age as income receivers, whether they received income or not. All persons not included in the income tax statistics were assigned an income largely corresponding to half the minimum taxable income. In 1967 income earners assessed as having a nontaxable income were registered as having zero incomes, but were assigned an estimated income.

---

*The methodology is contained in the study. Obligations to declare income exist if the gross income is above a certain amount (1951: 600 kronor, 1952-61: 1,200 kronor, and 1962-66: 2,400 kronor.) Thus for any year 7 to 17 percent of the adult population receiving income may be excluded. Minimum income applies to both single persons and persons filing jointly. The study includes all persons over 20 whether they earned income or not.

TABLE 3.4

Distribution of Income in Sweden for the Top 10 Percent and 1 Percent, and the Concentration Coefficient for the Years 1951-69

Years	Percent of Income Received by Top 10 Percent	Percent of Income Received by Top 1 Percent	Concentration Coefficient
1951	34.2	8.5	.557
1952	33.3	7.9	.550
1953	33.5	8.0	.550
1954	33.0	7.9	.544
1955	32.8	7.8	.542
1956	32.9	7.6	.543
1957	33.0	7.8	.544
1958	33.0	7.9	.543
1959	33.5	8.1	.544
1960	33.3	7.5	.541
1961	33.0	7.4	.539
1962	32.7	7.3	.532
1963	32.6	7.2	.529
1964	32.2	7.1	.525
1965	31.9	7.1	.520
1966	31.7	6.9	.520
1967	32.1	7.1	.519
1968	32.1	7.1	.516
1969	31.4	6.9	.505

Source: Unpublished study prepared for the Swedish Low-Income Commission by Pebbe Selander and others of Uppsala University. Tables 1 and 3 are used.

The Effect of Income Taxation
on the Distribution of Income

Swedish personal income taxes have an important impact upon the distribution of income in that they divert a part of the flow of personal income away from savings and private consumption, and thus alter the distribution of money income that results from the play of market forces. In Sweden, as a result of the extensive use of income taxes, the upper-income groups have to pay more for government services and transfers than do the lower-income groups. The end result is that there is a substantial equalization of both money and real income. But Swedish taxes, given their nature, must inevitably reduce the total volume of investment, partly by reducing the volume of savings that would normally come from the upper-income groups, and partly by reducing the level of consumption and thus the profitability of additional investment.

In apparent confirmation of the above statement, household savings in Sweden declined from 8.5 percent of disposable income in 1960 to 5.6 percent in 1969.[20] Savings, exclusive of insurance saving, declined from 6.4 percent of disposable income in 1960 to 2.7 percent in 1969. On the other hand, household payments of state income taxes rose from 11.2 percent to 14.1 percent of factor income for the same time period, while payments of local income taxes increased from 8.8 percent to 15.7 percent of household factor income.[21] Despite increases in social security payments and other income transfers, disposable income decreased from 92 percent of household factor income in 1960 to 87 percent in 1969.[22] It is important to note, however, that rising income taxes are not necessarily the key factor contributing to a decline in household savings. One can hypothesize, for example, that an increase in transfer payments creates a higher marginal propensity to consume than earned income in that the recipients are more likely to be low-income earners.

Table 3.5 presents the marginal tax rates for the combined local and national income taxes for 1972. Excluded from the table are old-age pension contributions, which are also withheld along with the income taxes from taxable income. The contribution amounts to 5 percent of taxable income of up to 30,000 kronor. In 1972 the average rate of the local income tax was 22.5 percent. Included in the table are the marginal rates for a single person and for a family with one income earner and no children. As can be seen in the table, the marginal rate on an income of 75,000 kronor ($15,000) is 66.5 percent.

It has already been mentioned that an income equalization policy has high priority in the Palme government. One manifestation of such a policy is the very heavy burden of the personal income tax. As the following tables will indicate, it is rather apparent that inequality in the distribution of income is reduced through the use of income taxation. In Table 3.6 the number of taxpayers in Sweden in 1970 and net

TABLE 3.5

Income Classes and Marginal
Income Tax Rates for Swedish Taxpayers

Income Classes	Marginal Rate (single)	Marginal Rate (married)
6,000 kronor	32.5%	—
10,000	32.5	32.5
15,000	38.5	38.5
20,000	44.5	44.5
30,000	53.4	53.4
50,000	60.5	60.5
75,000	66.5	66.5
100,000	71.5	71.5
125,000	71.5	71.5
150,000	76.5	76.5
300,000	76.5	76.5

Source: Rates computed by the author based on Swedish tax tables.

income before taxes is presented. It is to be emphasized that a number of these taxpayers belong to family units and were in 1970 permitted to aggregate their income for tax purposes. In 1971, as a result of reforms of the income tax, all married persons were taxed individually on earned incomes, but their income from capital could have been combined to some extent for tax purposes. Net income in the table refers to that part of Swedish personal income that is subject to the national and local income taxes. The term can be identified with the concept of pre-redistributional income. It corresponds to the U.S. concept of adjusted gross income for income tax purposes.

The distribution of income before taxes is one measure of inequality in the distribution of income. In Table 3.6 before-tax income distribution is presented. Income in the sense used here includes wages and salaries, income of unincorporated enterprises, rent, interest, dividends, and income from agriculture. In 1970 the breakdown of income from each of these sources was as follows: employee income, 84.4 billion kronor; income of self-employed persons, 10.6 billion kronor; income of unincorporated enterprises, 4.8 billion kronor; rent, interest, and dividends, 2.9 billion kronor; and income from agriculture, 2.1 billion kronor. Excluded from the table are transfer payments of all types, which would also have an impact upon the redistribution of income. It is also necessary to point out the fact that many income earners in the table are students and other persons

TABLE 3.6

Before-Tax Distribution of Income
in Sweden for 1970

Income Classes (millions of kronor)	Income Earners	Total Income (millions of kronor)
1,000 - 4,999 kronor	409,672	1,206.7
5,000 - 9,999	985,869	7,347.4
10,000 - 14,999	696,209	8,598.7
15,000 - 19,999	610,223	10,685.3
20,000 - 24,999	654,376	14,730.9
25,000 - 29,999	598,154	16,383.9
30,000 - 39,999	619,108	21,092.4
40,000 - 49,999	203,535	8,992.0
50,000 - 59,999	84,429	4,588.9
60,000 - 99,999	91,253	6,710.0
100,000 and over	25,836	3,834.3
Total	4,978,764	104,170.5

Source: Statistiska Centralbyran, "Inkomst och Förmögenhets-fordelningen Ar 1970," Statistiska Meddelanden 1971 (Stockholm, 1971), p. 11.

who work for part-time incomes and older persons who are also in the labor force. Swedish income taxes are applicable to almost anyone who earns an income in Sweden.

The median income of all income earners subject to taxation in Sweden was 18,258 kronor, and the mean or average income was 20,923 kronor. The first quintile value was 7,950 kronor and the fifth or highest quintile value was 33,700 kronor. The average income of the lowest quintile of income earners was 5,940 kronor and the average income of the highest quintile of all income earners was 43,520 kronor. The before-tax ratio between the highest and lowest quintile averages was approximately 7.2 to 1.*

---

*The computations are based on those persons who had income above the minimum tax assessment level. The formula for the median is $L + i (N/2-F)/f$, where L = lower limit of the median class, i = class interval, N = number of frequencies, F = cumulative number of frequencies down to the median class, and f = number of frequencies in the median class. Quintiles are computed the same way, except for $N/5$ and $4N/5$. All data should be accepted as simply based on tax data.

Income distribution in Sweden for 1970 can also be examined from the standpoint of sex. On the basis of this criterion, the approximately five million income earners can be divided into 2.8 million males and 2.2 million females—a ratio of 56 percent to 44 percent. However, the majority of female income earners is in the lower-income brackets, reflecting a pattern of incomes similar to that in the United States. In the highest income bracket of 100,000 kronor and above, approximately 94 percent of the income earners were male; in the next highest income category, 60,000 to 99,999 kronor, males still accounted for 93 percent of the income earners.[23] On the other hand, in the two lowest income brackets females accounted for 70 percent of all income earners. Based on a recent low-income study using 1966 data, 80 percent of all men between the ages of 25 and 55 earned 20,000 or more kronor a year, while 70 percent of all women in the same age category earned 20,000 kronor or less.[24]

Age and geography also have an effect upon income distribution. The bulk of all income earners in the three highest income categories was in the age categories 35 to 49 and 50 to 66, while the bulk of low-income earners was concentrated in the age categories of 19 and under and 67 and over. One-third of all income earners in the major Swedish cities—Gothenburg, Malmo, Stockholm, and Uppsala—had incomes in excess of 30,000 kronor, compared to 13 percent of income earners in the rural areas.[25] Forty percent of all income earners with incomes in excess of 100,000 kronor were located in Stockholm.

Table 3.7 presents income distribution in Sweden before and after taxes for the tax year 1970. In the table all Swedish income earners are grouped into taxpaying units. Basically, there are three categories of taxpayers—single taxpayers, jointly assessed taxpayers, and taxpayers who are subject to special tax treatment (for example, persons from other countries who work in Sweden under special conditions and who are not subject to the Swedish census). In 1970 this last category amounted to around 1.5 percent of all Swedish taxpayer units. Taxes in the table are the local and national personal income taxes and contributions for old-age pensions, all of which are withheld from income. In 1970 the local income tax accounted for 18.9 billion out of the 36.3 billion kronor total in taxes levied against Swedish taxpayers.[26] The national income tax accounted for 14.1 billion kronor, and the contributions for old-age pensions amounted to 3.2 billion kronor.

It is apparent that inequality in the distribution of income is reduced through income taxation. The reduction in the number of upper-income taxpayers is particularly significant. Referring to Table 3.7, approximately 10 percent of all taxpaying units had net incomes of 50,000 kronor ($10,000) or more before taxes in 1970, but less than 2 percent had after-tax incomes of 50,000 kronor or more. The upper 1 percent of all taxpayers was reduced to 0.15

TABLE 3.7

Income Distribution in Sweden Before and After Taxes, 1970

(millions of kronor)	Taxpayers	Income Before Taxes	Taxpayers	Income After Taxes (millions of kronor)
0 - 4,000 kronor	39,489	98.7	135,215	334.5
5,000 - 9,999	576,457	4,171.2	824,745	6,089.2
10,000 - 14,999	522,364	6,385.0	860,812	10,636.9
15,000 - 19,999	437,945	7,530.3	693,538	12,073.1
20,000 - 24,999	455,811	10,131.9	479,209	10,760.6
25,000 - 29,999	426,011	11,612.6	337,599	9,277.2
30,000 - 34,999	587,634	20,516.6	306,342	10,709.4
40,000 - 49,999	345,665	15,536.4	82,894	3,724.0
50,000 - 59,999	178,500	9,806.8	29,783	1,635.1
60,000 - 99,999	172,931	12,953.5	25,082	1,877.9
100,000 and over	38,554	5,427.5	5,142	769.5
Total	3,780,361	104,170.5	3,780,361	67,887.4

Sources: Statistiska Centralbyran, "Inkomst och Förmögenhetsfördelningen År 1970," Statistiska Meddelanden, 1971 (Stockholm, 1971), pp. 16 and 18; Statistiska Centralbyran, Statistisk Arsbok För Sverige 1972 (Stockholm, 1973), pp. 333 and 334.

percent after taxes. On the other hand, at the other end of the income scale, 40 percent of all taxpayers had before-tax incomes of 20,000 kronor or less, compared to 66 percent after taxes. Although single and married taxpayers were combined in the table, the shifts in before- and after-tax incomes were more pronounced for single taxpayers than for married.

It is necessary to stress the point that Table 3.7 does not reflect the changes that were made in the Swedish income tax system in 1971. Probably the most important change was the discontinuation of deductibility of the local income tax from income for purposes of the national income tax. Currently neither tax is deductible for any purpose. Another important change was made in the system of personal allowances. Before 1971 a standard deduction of 2,250 kronor for single persons and 4,500 kronor for married persons was permitted. This meant that the Swedish tax system to some extent redistributed income toward those persons with more dependents, because a married man was taxed more lightly than a bachelor. In 1971 the personal allowance was changed to 4,500 kronor for every person, married or single. The system of joint assessment for purposes of income taxation was also discontinued in 1971. Now both husband and wife have to file separate income returns on earned income. Finally, the system of personal allowances starts to decrease as income increases, reaching a vanishing point at a taxable income level of 52,500 kronor ($10,500). On the basis of these changes, it can be assumed that a further redistribution of income occurred after 1971.

The impact of the local and national income taxes and the old-age pension contribution upon the redistribution of income can be measured. For example, the average income of the highest quintile or one-fifth of all taxpayers before taxes was 68,669 kronor, and the average income of the lowest one-fifth of all taxpayers before taxes was 8,041 kronor—a ratio of 8.5 to 1. The highest quintile average for all taxpayers after taxes was 36,991 kronor, and the lowest quintile average was 6,297 kronor—an after-tax ratio of 6 to 1. The highest quintile value before taxes was 39,854 kronor, and the lowest quintile value was 11,580 kronor—a ratio of 3.6 to 1. After income taxes and the social security contribution had been taken into account, the highest and lowest quintile values were 25,629 kronor and 8,935 kronor—a ratio of 2.9 to 1.

In Table 3.8 Swedish income is expressed as a percentage for each quintile before and after taxes for 1970. There are some shifts for each quintile, with the sharpest shift occurring for the highest quintile—a reduction from 42.5 percent of income to 34.0 percent. The share of the top 5 percent of income earners was reduced from 17.1 percent of before-tax income to 10.8 percent of after-tax income. Income distribution at the lower end of the income scale is affected to some extent by the fact that a number of workers are employed either part time or are females who head families and who are employed in low-paying jobs. Age is also a factor in analyzing

TABLE 3.8

Percentage Distribution of Swedish Income Earners
by Quintiles Before and After Taxes in 1970

Quintiles	Percent of Total Before Taxes	Percent of Total After Taxes
Lowest quintile	5.4	7.2
Second quintile	9.9	13.2
Third quintile	17.6	21.4
Fourth quintile	24.6	24.2
Highest quintile	42.5	34.0
Total	100.0	100.0

Note: It is to be emphasized that the data are based on the number of persons who were singly or jointly assessed for income taxes. When judging the information, Swedish income statistics include many persons with low incomes—women who work part time, university students, and pensioners. In fact only 40 percent of all Swedes who filed income tax returns in 1970 worked full time. There is a greater degree of income equality when only full-time employment is concerned.

Source: Computations based on Table 3.9.

the causes of low incomes in Sweden.[27] For example, in 1970, 45 percent of all workers who were 67 or older were in the two lowest income categories. These persons accounted for 19 percent of all taxpayers and 43 percent of the income earners in the two lowest income categories. Women represented approximately 70 percent of those persons 67 or older who earned less than 10,000 kronor ($2,000) a year in 1970.

The Lorenz Curve and Gini Coefficient

The Lorenz curve and Gini coefficient both measure the extent of departure from complete income equality. The Lorenz curve indicates the percentage of the cumulative number of income earners; the Gini coefficient measures the extent to which the Lorenz curve deviates from the diagonal line of complete income equality. Based on tables 3.8 and 3.9, it is possible to develop Lorenz curves showing before- and after-income-tax distribution of income in Sweden for 1970 (see Figure 3). It is also possible to compute the Gini coefficients before and after income taxes through the following steps: (1) Find the sum of the areas corresponding to quintiles beneath the Lorenz curve.

FIGURE 3

A Before- and After- Income Tax
Lorenz Curve for Sweden, 1970

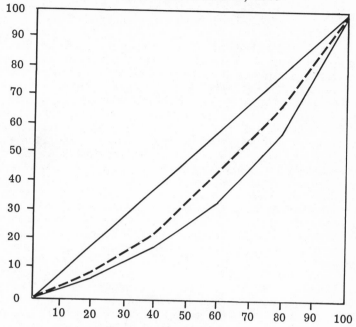

Solid line represents before taxes
Dashed line represents after taxes

(2) Subtract this sum from the area under the diagonal of equal distribution of income, which is always equal to 5,000. (3) Divide the
result by 5,000.

The before- and after-tax Gini coefficients for 1970 are .3556
and .2584 respectively. A very rough comparison can be made with
the coefficient of .3350 for the United States.28 The Swedish calculations are based on income tax data in which the concept of net income (the American equivalent of adjusted gross income) is used.
Excluded are all transfer payments. The American income data includes income from both labor and property as well as transfer payments—money earnings and income other than earnings. The calculations for Sweden combine all taxpayers, single and jointly assessed,
for the purpose of comparing before- and after-tax incomes; the
American data involve incomes received by families and have no
relation to before- and after-tax income distribution. The main point

that really is developed is the fact that Swedish personal income taxes do have a rather significant impact on income distribution in that inequality is narrowed considerably.

The Burden of Taxation in Sweden

When direct and indirect taxes and social security contributions are compared to gross national product, it is evident that a considerable part of the latter is diverted from the private to the public sector of the Swedish economy. The 44 percent relationship indicates the magnitude of the economic flows that are affected directly by public policy. The impact of taxation is felt by both individuals and corporations, even though a large part of the public sector's income is returned to the private sector in the form of transfer payments and the provision of free goods and services. To some persons, the benefits will counterbalance or exceed the cost of the taxes; to others, the costs of taxes will exceed the benefits received.

Table 3.9 presents a general idea of the impact of taxation in Sweden for various income classes. Included in the tax calculations are the local and national income taxes, social security contributions, and the value-added and sumptuary taxes. Income receivers are divided into two categories, single persons and families with one income earner. Transfer payments, which normally would redound to the financial advantage of those persons with low incomes, are not included in the table. The impact of indirect taxes is felt in particular by both single and married persons in the lower-income classes. For the three highest income classes, beginning with 75,000 kronor, the total tax take amounts to 60 percent of income.

One stated goal of Swedish economic policy is a more equal distribution of income. Other stated goals are full employment, stable prices, and rapid economic growth. However, given the fact that the Swedish economy is oriented toward foreign trade, there is the question of whether or not these goals can be maintained or achieved if an equilibrium in foreign trade is not re-established. Swedish industry's competitive power has to be strengthened in order that the balance of trade compensate for a deficit in the overall payments balance and, most particularly, in transfer payments. In order to restore balance in foreign trade, it is estimated that industrial investments would have to increase by 6.5 percent annually during the next few years.[29]

There is, then, a conflict between the necessity for growth in the industrial sector and the objective of a more even distribution of income. To achieve an improved rate of growth of industrial investments, higher profits are necessary in order to provide the funds for internal financing of investments. To restore external balances and to stimulate economic growth requires the increase of financial

TABLE 3.9

Burden of Swedish Taxation
for Various Income Classes, 1973

Taxes	Income Classes (kronor)			
	8,000	15,000	20,000	40,000
Local income tax	650	2,330	3,530	8,770
National income tax	190	680	1,030	5,430
Social security levies	480	925	1,195	2,095
Indirect taxes (single)	1,670	2,765	3,560	5,925
Total single	2,990	6,700	9,315	22,220
Percent	37	45	47	56
Direct taxes (married)	—	2,135	3,955	14,495
Indirect taxes (married)	2,000	3,215	4,010	6,375
Total married	2,000	5,350	7,965	20,870
Percent	25	36	40	52
	50,000	75,000	100,000	200,000
Local income tax	11,650	17,810	23,810	47,810
National income tax	8,790	18,525	30,275	81,720
Social security levies	2,095	2,095	2,095	2,095
Indirect taxes (single)	6,865	9,140	10,955	17,095
Total single	29,400	47,570	67,135	148,720
Percent	59	63	67	74
Direct taxes (married)	20,735	36,630	54,380	129,825
Indirect taxes (married)	7,315	9,590	11,405	17,545
Total married	28,050	46,220	65,785	147,370
Percent	56	62	66	73

Source: Skattebetalarnas Forening, Fakta för Skattebetalare
(Stockholm, 1973), p. 7.

resources, particularly in the industrial sector, through higher profits. But the goal of higher profits comes into conflict with the goal
of a more equal distribution of income, which in essence means a
rising share of national income accounted for by wages. It would
appear that an impasse has been reached that is difficult to resolve.
With a deterioration in her financial strength caused by declining profits in the 1960s, and with little prospect for a general improvement
of industry's profits in international competition in the 1970s, Sweden
may well find it necessary to increase the share of profits in national
income at the expense of wages.

The Effect of Transfer Payments
on Income Distribution

Large sums of money are redistributed through the medium of
transfer payments in Sweden. As mentioned previously, there are
those transfers that are designed to benefit certain sectors of society,
such as family allowances and old-age pensions. Then there are also
grants to certain sectors of the economy, such as agricultural subsidies, which result in lower prices for goods and services. Finally,
there are some services provided by the government that are, in
effect, nonmonetary transfers, such as free education. The analysis,
however, is limited to direct monetary transfers to households, which
amounted to 28 billion kronor in 1972, or around 18 percent of personal
income. The extent to which incomes are redistributed through income
transfers is going to depend on a taxpayer's position on the income
ladder.

Swedish studies on income redistribution tend to confirm the
following points: [30]

1. Major gains in redistribution through transfer payments and
other forms of government expenditures are confined primarily to the
lowest income groups. A break-even point, where taxes counterbalance gains from expenditures, is reached rather rapidly. For
example, in 1967 this break-even point was around 11,000 kronor on
a per capita basis. What this means is that taxes more than counterbalance gains for the majority of taxpayers, who received more than
80 percent of total income. It is not only the upper-income groups,
but the average-income groups as well, who defray the cost of income
redistribution.

2. Distribution of transfer payments among income groups
favors the nonactive segment of the Swedish population over the active
segment. For example, the average annual income of all persons who
were fully employed was 24,800 kronor in 1967.[31] Average taxes
amounted to 7,900 kronor, while average income from various transfers amounted to 1,200 kronor—a net loss, so to speak, of 6,700
kronor.[32] On the other hand, those who were partially employed or
who were receiving old-age pensions showed a net gain in terms of
income. For low-income earners, typically those receiving 5,000
kronor or less in 1967, transfer payments accounted for around 60
percent of total income. But again it is necessary to reinforce the
point that on balance the loss in terms of redistribution hits the active
segment of society. In 1967 the average annual income in agriculture
was 7,000 kronor. Direct taxes amounted to 3,300 kronor, while income from government transfers amounted to 3,000 kronor—a net
loss of 300 kronor.[33]

3. Government expenditures tend to have an equalizing effect
on the standard of living. Family and housing allowances illustrate
this point. The family allowance, which is not taxable, results in a

lateral transfer of income among families in the same income group. Families with identical taxable incomes of 20,000 kronor would have different disposable incomes based on the number of children each has. For example, income taxes would take approximately 20 percent of income, but a family with three children would receive approximately the same percentage back in family allowances, while a childless family would receive no allowance. Moreover, the family with three children would be eligible for a housing allowance, while the childless family would be ineligible. Education is free for the family with children. Inequality in the initial distribution of income is modified by the system of family and housing allowances, the bulk of which is directed to households in the lower-income ranges.

In summary, it can be said that the distribution of transfer payments in Sweden is heavily skewed in favor of households and individuals in the lower-income brackets, hence the major effect of the system of transfers is to reduce inequality in the money distribution of income among the income classes. In particular, it is the basic pensions, including old-age pensions, widows' benefits, and housing allowances, that contribute the most to a more uniform distribution of income. It is estimated that the basic pensions increase the uniformity of total income distribution by 12 percent, with old-age pensions accounting for around 70 percent of the greater uniformity in distribution.[34]

There are also secondary effects upon income distribution. It has been pointed out that a part of old-age pensions is financed by contributions from employers. It can be assumed in part that the burden of contributions is passed on to wages, that is, wages become lower than they would have been without the contributions. Such a development would lower the incomes of economically active groups relative to the inactive groups, with a more uniform distribution of income the end result. However, the above assumption may not conform to the realities of the Swedish labor market, given the existence of a prolonged period of full employment, inflationary pressures, and a strong trade union movement.

It is also necessary to point out that about one-half of all social security income transfers are financed by the national government from general tax revenues. These revenues come from income taxation as well as from indirect taxes on expenditures. Given the fact that the corporate income tax constitutes one source of general tax revenues, it can be said that a part of transfer payments is financed from corporate profits. This would lead to a reduction in dividends to stockholders or a reduction in undistributed profits. The groups primarily affected in either case would be those with the greatest wealth in both the active and passive segments of the population. Since there is a strong correlation between high incomes and the ownership of stock, the effect of corporate income taxation would be to promote uniformity in the distribution of income.

91

DISTRIBUTION OF WEALTH IN SWEDEN

Distribution of wealth in Sweden in 1970 is presented in Table 3.10. Property as used in the table refers to real estate, bonds, stock, and other tangible assets. All properties in excess of 150,000 kronor are included in the table. The number of property assessments rather than the number of persons is used. In Sweden property may be assessed for a single person or jointly assessed, with one or both persons subject to the tax. In 1970 the number of properties of 150,000 kronor and over amounted to 176,394, and the value of the property amounted to 57.7 billion kronor. Less than 1 percent of the properties accounted for 12 percent of the value of property, and the top 10 percent accounted for 35 percent of total property value.

There is a direct relationship between property size and the size of personal incomes. Three-fourths of the property assessments of two million kronor or more also had incomes for 1970 of 100,000 kronor or more, while only eight assessments had related incomes of 10,000 kronor or less. A total of 17,300 properties had related incomes of 100,000 kronor or more. On balance, however, it would appear that there is not an overwhelming concentration of property in the hands of a few persons. Capital incomes and the yield from other forms of wealth generally account for around 5 percent of total personal income in Sweden. As a contributor to inequality in the distribution of income, it appears that income from property is less

TABLE 3.10

Distribution of Property Income in Sweden by Size of Property, Value of Property, and Number of Assessments for 1970

Size of Property	Number of Assessments	Value of Property (millions of kronor)
150,000 - 199,999	71,171	12,251
200,000 - 249,999	36,371	8,093
250,000 - 299,999	20,529	5,598
300,000 - 399,999	20,833	7,144
400,000 - 499,999	9,945	4,420
500,000 - 599,999	12,754	8,523
1,000,000 - 1,999,999	3,666	4,495
2,000,000 and over	1,425	7,175
	176,394	57,699

Source: Statistiska Centralbyran, Statistik Arsbok För Sverige (Stockholm, 1972), p. 339.

important than other factors such as age, sex, and number of hours worked. As a matter of fact, there has been a decline in importance of capital income during the period from 1950 to 1969. It is estimated that the influence of capital income on income distribution was 25 percent greater in 1958 than in 1969. In particular, stock dividends have increased at a lower rate than the rise in total personal income.

SUMMARY

The initial distribution of income in Sweden probably corresponds to income distribution in the United States in that the lowest and highest quintiles of income recipients receive approximately the same income shares. Unlike the United States, however, the trend in Sweden has been toward greater equality in the distribution of income. This has been achieved in part through progressive income taxation and trans- fer payments, both of which have a massive redistributive effect on personal income. The end result is a distribution of both money and real income that appears to be more equal in Sweden than in other Western countries. A negative factor is a tax burden that is the highest of any major country in the world. This burden may have caused a slower increase in the rate of economic growth for the country, although such an effect would be difficult to prove.

Income distribution in Sweden is affected by such factors as age, sex, and the number of hours worked. There are a large number of low-income earners, primarily women who work part time. Capital income and other yields from wealth constitute a small fraction of total income, but accrue primarily to upper-income groups. However, this income from wealth contributes a very small part to the total dispersion in income distribution. More important factors explaining variations in income are the total number of hours worked, age, sex, and education. Another factor, which is more subjective, is the high rate of employment that has been maintained in Sweden for almost three decades. A tight labor market is bound to have some effect on income distribution.

NOTES

1. Marquis Childs, Sweden: The Middle Way (New Haven: Yale University Press, 1961).

2. Gunnar Adler-Karlsson, Functional Socialism—A Swedish Theory for Democratic Socialization (Stockholm: Bokforlaget Prisma, 1969).

3. Cited in Social Goals in National Planning (Stockholm: Bokforlaget Prisma, 1972).

4. For a comprehensive study of the Swedish economy, see Martin Schnitzer, The Economy of Sweden: A Study of the Modern Welfare State (New York: Praeger, Publishers, 1970).

5. Statistiska Centralbyran, Taxeringsutfallet, 1971 (Stockholm, 1972), p. 12.

6. Ibid., p. 13.

7. Ministry of Finance, The Swedish Budget, 1973-1974 (Stockholm, 1973), p. 60.

8. Ibid., p. 67.

9. Skandinaviska Enskilda Banken, The Tax System in Sweden (Stockholm, 1972), pp. 79-99.

10. Ibid., pp. 79-80.

11. Ibid., p. 85.

12. Ibid., pp. 22-25.

13. Ibid., pp. 141-144.

14. Skattebetalarnas Forening, Fakta för Skattebetalare (Stockholm, 1973), p. 5.

15. The Tax System in Sweden, pp. 94 and 97.

16. National Institute of Economic Research, The Swedish Economy 1972 (Stockholm, 1972), p. 167.

17. Ibid., p. 167.

18. The Swedish Budget, 1972-1973, p. 58.

19. Unpublished study prepared for the Swedish Low Income Commission by Pebbe Selander of Uppsala University and translated into the English by the author.

20. Statens Offentliga Utredningar, Svenska Folkets Inkomster (Stockholm, 1970), p. 38.

21. Ibid., p. 40.

22. Ibid., p. 41.

23. Statistiska Centralbyran, "Inkomst och Förmögenhetsfördelningen År 1970," Statistiska Meddelanden 1971 (Stockholm, 1971), p. 14.

24. Ibid., p. 15.

25. Ibid., p. 36.

26. Taxeringsutfallet, 1971, p. 43.

27. Royal Commission on Low Incomes, The Structure of Incomes in Sweden, August 1970, pp. 19-21.

28. U.S. computation is based on Table 4, page 25, in U.S. Bureau of the Census, "Current Population Reports, Consumer Income," December 1972.

29. Villy Bergstrom and Jan Sodersten: "Industrial Growth and the Distribution of Incomes—A Conflict of Goals for Economic Policy," Skandinaviska Enskilda Banken Quarterly Review 3 (1972): 98-108.

30. The studies used were Lars Soderstrom, Laginkomstproblemet (Stockholm: Statens Offentliga Utredningar, 1972); and Lars Soderstrom, Den Svenska Kopkraftsfordelningen, 1967 (Stockholm: Statens Offentliga Utredningar, 1971).

31. Den Svenska Kopkraftsfordelningen, 1967, p. 52.
32. Ibid., p. 78.
33. Ibid., p. 80.
34. Selander, op. cit., p. 7.

4

INCOME DISTRIBUTION
IN WEST GERMANY

The first comprehensive program of social security was developed in Germany when Bismarck sponsored the health insurance law of 1883. Bismarck was a political pragmatist of the first order who realized that concessions to the working classes had to be made to check the rise of socialism. He sponsored social legislation in order to alleviate the causes upon which socialism was developing. The national health insurance law was designed to cover most industrial workers. Workers contributed two-thirds and employers one-third of the cost. The coverage of the law was constantly widened. By 1911 when the Insurance Consolidation Act brought all German insurance systems under one statute, a majority of all workers was insured against sickness and invalidity. Benefits included medicine, hospitalization, maternity benefits, and payments of 50 percent of the wages lost by illness.

The health insurance program was followed in 1884 by legislation that sponsored employment-injury insurance, or workmen's compensation as it is called in the United States. The workmen's compensation law was also the first of its kind in the world and provided benefits regardless of the circumstances of the injury. The cost of compensation was placed entirely on the employer. In 1889 the Old Age and Invalidity Law was passed, providing an old-age pension payable to wage earners who had been regularly employed and who had reached the age of seventy. It was financed by a tax on both the employer and employee, each paying half; the national government granted additional subsidies. The law was extended to cover salaried workers in 1911. The final component of social security, unemployment compensation, was introduced in 1927.

Germany was also the first major country to utilize income taxation. The personal income tax has its origins in the Prussian income tax of 1820, which assigned liabilities for tax payments on the basis of social classes, with burdens increasing with the descent of the social order. The Prussian tax was amended in 1851 to include everyone beyond a certain minimum income regardless of social status. In 1891 the income tax was made progressive, with rates reaching a maximum of 4 percent on incomes above 100,000 marks. The income tax remained a state tax until the creation of the Weimar Republic, when there was a shift in power from the states to the federal government. In 1920 both the personal and corporate income taxes became federal taxes, with both taxes being levied on net worth. In 1925 the concept of taxable income was redefined and income taxation took on the form it has today.

State social legislation met with relatively less resistance in Germany than in most other industrialized countries. Almost with the very inception of industrialization in Germany, socialists, liberals, religious leaders, and political pragmatists, such as Bismarck, began to call attention to the adverse effects of industrial development and to push for government action. There was, however, a tradition of state cameralism and paternalism that extended back for many centuries. This fact was reflected in the development of social legislation under Bismarck, who once made the statement, "No doubt the individual can do much good, but the social problem can only be solved by the state." As mentioned previously, though, social reform legislation was undoubtedly spurred on by the rapid rise of the socialist and labor movements.

There is, then, a rather distinct difference in the development of social welfare legislation in Germany as compared to Sweden and the United Kingdom after the end of World War II. Perhaps this can be explained in part by the fact that the socialist tradition, which has long been represented by the Social Democratic party, runs deep in Germany. In addition, there was a favorable climate for the development of Marxian socialism. A situation developed where during the period of the Weimar Republic, the combined votes of the socialists, as represented by the Social Democrats, and the communists amounted to 45 percent of the popular votes in national elections.

THE WEST GERMAN ECONOMY

In spite of partition from its eastern part, West Germany has emerged as a world power. After the war the German economy relied on market forces instead of controls to accomplish recovery from the devastation caused by the war. To channel profits into investment and savings, income tax rates were modified to favor savers and investors. These measures were especially beneficial to persons in the upper-income brackets. Since capital formation was a prime desideratum of economic policy, preferential treatment was given to the receivers of high incomes, who, according to empirical studies, have a much greater marginal propensity to save than people in the lower-income brackets. So the larger part of newly created capital during the postwar period accumulated in the hands of an entrepreneurial class, thereby raising the degree of inequality in the distribution of income and wealth.

The West German economic system is a mixed system in which there is both private and public ownership of the agents of production. A large nationalized sector exists with a market economy. The bulk of German industry is in private hands, and pricing decisions are determined in the marketplace. Nevertheless, there is a traditional German reliance on state intervention in economic affairs that goes back well into the nineteenth century. Under Bismarck a paternalistic government developed to set the pattern that still exists in Germany. During the Bismarck era, the railroad system was nationalized and foundations were laid upon which the war economy of a later period could be built. Bismarck was also the chief architect of most of the social legislation that exists in West Germany today.

The role of the public sector, which includes the federal, state, and local governments, can be emphasized by presenting the total volume of receipts and expenditures for 1972 (see Table 4.1). A frame of reference is the 1972 gross national product figure of DM 828.5 billion and a national income figure of DM 634.4 billion.[1] Current government receipts from all sources amount to 39 percent of gross national product. The two main government expenditures, government consumption of goods and services and transfer payments, amount to around one-third of the gross national product. It is to be noted that direct taxes account for less than one-third of total current receipts of the public sector.

National Income

West German national income for 1972 amounted to DM 634.4 billion. This income can be broken into two categories—income from employment, which amounted to DM 438.9 billion, and income from property and entrepreneurship, which amounted to DM 195.5 billion. Income from wages and salaries (employment income) amounted to 69.2 percent of national income in 1972, while property and entrepreneurial income amounted to 30.8 percent.[2] Over time there has been a decided shift in the distribution of national income toward wages and salaries. In 1960 income from employment amounted to DM 142.8 billion, compared to DM 92.9 billion in property and entrepreneurial

TABLE 4.1

West German Public Sector Receipts and
Expenditures for 1972
(billions of DM)[a]

Current Receipts		Current Expenditures	
Property and entrepre-			
neurial income	11.7	Government consumption	147.1
Indirect taxes	112.0	Subsidies	11.2
Direct taxes	89.7	Interest	8.0
Social security			
contributions	102.9	Transfers to households	110.6
Transfers	6.1	Other transfers	8.1
Total	322.4	Total	285.0[b]

[a]The West German currency unit is the Deutsche Mark (DM).
[b]Saving (surplus on current account) is 37.3.

Source: Deutsche Bundesbank, Monatsberichte der Deutschen
Bundesbank (Frankfurt am Main, March 1973), p. 22.

income. Most of the shift in factor costs came during the period from
1967 to 1971 when wage increases really accelerated for the first
time during the postwar period. In this five-year period, wages and
salaries increased at an average annual rate of 17.7 percent, compared
to 9.7 percent for property and entrepreneurial income.[3] Total enterprise profit increased at an average annual rate of 4.5 percent.

Personal Income

Personal income in West Germany amounted to DM 618.7
billion in 1972.[4] Included in the personal income total are several
elements that are not factor costs. There are the transfer payments
of government and business, which are incomes for individual use but
are not necessary to elicit factor contributions toward total output.
Both corporate income taxes and retained earnings are factor income
not allocated to persons. Dividends, rent, and interest (excluding
public debt interest) are both factor income and personal income.
West German personal income data are divided into three main
categories—wages and salaries, net of employer contributions to

social security; property and entrepreneurial income, net of retained earnings and direct taxes; and transfer payments from government and business. The values of these three categories were DM 382.0 billion, DM 132.0 billion, and DM 104.7 billion respectively. Transfer payments are a large component of West German personal income, accounting for 16.1 percent of the total in 1972.

PUBLIC FINANCE

No analysis of income distribution is possible without a prior presentation of the tax-transfer payment mechanisms, which obviously have an impact upon income distribution. Taxes divert resources from the private to the public sector of an economy, and the level of taxation relative to gross national product indicates the extent to which the influence of the state exists. In Germany the combined federal, state, and local governments control about 39 percent of the gross national product. A considerable part of gross domestic investment is financed out of tax revenues, and income redistribution is facilitated by one of the most comprehensive social welfare programs in the world. The social security system is similar to that of the Swedes in that the tax-transfer payment arrangement is largely independent of the federal budget.

The West German Tax System

The West German tax system is characterized by a multiplicity of taxes. Altogether some 50 different types of taxes, most of which are excises, are used in West Germany. The bulk of tax revenues, however, is derived from a half-dozen major taxes, the most important of which are the value-added and income taxes. Direct taxes, indirect taxes, and social security contributions are evenly balanced with respect to their overall contribution to total public sector revenues. In 1972 direct taxes amounted to DM 89.7 billion, of which DM 72.7 billion came from taxes on individuals and DM 17 billion came from taxes on businesses.[5] Indirect taxes, most of which are broad-based taxes on consumption, amounted to DM 112.0 billion, and social security contributions amounted to DM 102.9 billion. These contributions came from three sources: levies on employers, on employees, and on self-employed persons.

The Value-Added Tax

The value-added tax (Mehrwertsteuer) was introduced in January 1968. It was developed in accordance with a EEC harmonization

directive that called for a value-added tax in all EEC countries by
January 1, 1970. The tax is levied primarily on sales at the production
and wholesale levels. The tax is collected in a series of fractional
payments; each taxpayer making a taxable sale is liable for the tax,
not on the full sales price he receives but only on the portion of the
price that represents the value added by him in the course of the
manufacturing and distribution process. Each taxpayer in the production and distribution process chain contributes only a fraction of the
total tax due—a fraction based on his contribution to the final value
of the product.

The value-added tax, as now utilized by West Germany, is levied
at a general rate of 11 percent of value added at each stage of the
production process.6 There are, however, numerous items to which
a lower rate is applied. For example, many food and agricultural
products are taxed at a rate of 5.5 percent, and exports and certain
items and services are exempt from the tax. In the case of imports,
the importer pays an equalization tax equal to the value-added tax.
Since the value-added tax is fully passed onto and borne by the ultimate
consumer, it is not an element of cost or expense to the manufacturer
or trader and does not appear as such on his financial statements.

Personal Income Tax

The German personal income tax (Einkommensteuer) is progressive. For single persons the rates vary from 19 percent on
taxable income of DM 8,009 or less to 53 percent on taxable income
in excess of DM 110,039. Married persons are entitled to income
splitting and pay the same rates on taxable incomes of DM 16,018 or
less to DM 220,079 or more. In addition, there is a special 3 percent
surcharge on taxable incomes in excess of DM 16,020 for single
persons and of DM 32,040 for married persons. This surcharge, however, is gradually being phased out. The rates of the personal income
tax are reduced for taxpayers who are residents of West Berlin;
reduced rates also apply to income of other taxpayers from sources
in West Berlin.

For income tax purposes, it is necessary to mention the fact
that income is divided into two categories—income from wages and
salaries, which is subject to a wage tax (Lohnsteuer), and income
from self-employment and other sources, which is subject to an income tax (Einkommensteuer). The wage tax is levied on employment
income and is characterized by the fact that the responsibility for
collection is on the employer. The employer must withhold the wage
tax on the full amount of the employee's compensation based on a
wage tax card issued to each employee. In most cases, the employee's
tax liability is fully satisfied with the payment of the withholding tax.

But regardless of whether a wage or income tax is used, the rates of the West German income tax are the same for all persons receiving income.

Exemptions and deductions under the personal income tax are somewhat similar to those permitted in the United States. There are general exemptions of DM 1,680 for the taxpayer and his wife. There are additional exemptions of DM 1,200 for the first child, DM 1,680 for the second child, and DM 1,800 for the third and subsequent children. Single persons over 50 years of age with no children receive a further exemption of DM 840. Single persons and couples over 65 years of age receive additional exemptions of DM 720 and DM 1,440 respectively. Wage and salary earners are entitled to a special DM 240 exemption; this amount is to be doubled in the future.

There are a number of deductions that are permissible under the German tax system. First, depreciation is deductible, as in the United States. Expenditures designed to acquire and maintain income are deductible. These include certain types of interest payments, real estate taxes, transportation to and from work, and expenses for tools and clothes required for work. Specified insurance premiums, deposits with building and loan associations, property and church taxes, and contributions for charitable, religious, or political purposes are also deductible. There is an automatic lump-sum deduction of such outlays up to a maximum of DM 936 for every employed person. Then there are special allowances for extraordinary expenses incurred through unusual circumstances. The typical example results from an accident or a prolonged illness of the taxpayer or a member of his immediate family. The taxpayer can reduce his taxable income by the amount which the extraordinary expenditure exceeds the amount he could be reasonably expected to bear himself.

Income from dividends, with some exceptions, is subject to a 25 percent withholding tax that can be applied to the taxpayer's total income tax. Income from interest, also with some exceptions, is subject to the regular income tax. Capital gains, as a general rule, are not taxed; however, capital losses cannot be deducted. As an exception to this rule, gains from speculation are subject to taxation at regular tax rates. There is, however, a holding period of two years for real property and six months for personal property. If these periods are exceeded, the capital gain is not taxed. Losses from speculative transactions can be offset against gains from the same source realized within the same taxable year.

Corporate Income Tax

The corporate income tax (Körperschaftssteuer) applies to corporations, limited liability companies, mutual insurance companies, associations, societies, foundations, institutions, and enterprises owned by public corporations operated for profit. If the corporation operates within the confines of the Federal Republic, its entire income is subject to the tax, regardless of where it is earned. For corporations not located in the Federal Republic, only income derived from German sources is subject to the tax. In computing the corporate income tax, contributions for charitable, religious, and political purposes are deductible up to 5 percent of total income, or 0.2 percent of total turnover plus wages and salaries paid during the calendar year. Contributions for scientific purposes are deductible up to 10 percent of total income. Dividends from corporate subsidiaries are not taxable when received by a parent corporation subject to unlimited tax liability if it owns at least one-fourth of the stock of the subsidiaries. Property and income taxes are not deductible, but tax deferments may be granted for investments in developing countries.

The rate of the corporate income tax is 51 percent of undistributed profits for corporations with unlimited tax liability and 49 percent for corporations with limited tax liability. Distributed profits of corporations with unlimited tax liability are taxed at a rate of 15 percent. Graduated tax rates apply to the undistributed profits of small commercial entities owned primarily by individuals, including certain credit institutions. The 3 percent surcharge mentioned in the discussion of personal income taxes is also applicable to the corporate tax. Corporations located in West Berlin are entitled to a reduction of their income tax under the provisions of the Berlin Aid Law. Consequently, the regular corporate income tax rates are reduced from 15 percent to 8.8 percent for distributed profits and from 51 percent to 37.6 percent for retained earnings.

The Trade Tax

The trade tax (Gewerbesteuer) is an important source of revenue to local governments. It is levied on all business enterprises and is a combined tax on business income and capital and payrolls. The tax is regulated by federal law but is collected by the municipalities. Federal law defines the taxpayers and the basic rates of the tax. The trade tax on business profits is based on the taxable income as computed for the purpose of the income tax. Taxable business capital is the assessed value of the business as most recently determined prior to the end of the taxable year. Although the trade tax must always be computed on the basis of business profits and capital, the use of the payroll base is optional with the localities. The payroll tax is based on monthly salaries and wages paid by an enterprise to its employees. While rates differ from locality to locality, the average trade tax comes to about 14 percent of income and payrolls subject to the tax.

103

Excise Taxes

One characteristic of the West German tax system is the reliance on a wide variety of excise taxes (Verbrauchsteuern) as a source of revenue. These taxes, with the exception of the beer tax, which is a state tax, are levied by the federal government on a wide variety of articles, including tobacco, salt, tea, coffee, matches, electric bulbs, alcohol, petroleum, and playing cards. The producer, manufacturer, or importer is expected to shift the tax to the buyer by including the amount in the purchase price of the article. The impact of excise taxes on the individual taxpayer is very heavy, as may be gathered from the fact that the revenue from the two principal excise taxes, tobacco and gasoline taxes, has been almost as much as the federal share of income taxes. In 1969, for example, the federal share of personal and corporate income taxes amounted to DM 18.4 billion, compared to a take of DM 16.4 billion for the tobacco and gasoline taxes. In 1971, however, the respective amounts were DM 29.9 billion and DM 19 billion. The bases of the various excise taxes vary with the taxable products. In some cases, the measure of the tax is the weight or liquid volume of the product; in others, it is the sales price of the product.

Inheritance Taxes

The inheritance tax is a state tax. It has special rates based on the consanguinity of the inheritors to the person who is deceased. There are five rates, which are levied upon inheritances and also gifts. The lowest rate is paid by those inheritors who were closest to the deceased, including the children and surviving spouse. The rates range from 2 percent on taxable property of DM 10,000 or less to 15 percent on taxable property of DM 10 million and over. Exemptions are quite generous. For example, the surviving spouse is not taxed on the first DM 250,000 in value of taxable property if children are living at the time the liability for the tax originates. Other exemptions also serve to reduce the effective rate of the tax. The highest tax rate for inheritances, as well as gifts, ranges from 14 percent on taxable property of DM 10,000 or less to 60 percent on taxable property of DM 10 million and over. This rate applies to cousins and friends of the deceased or donor.

Social Security Contributions

In West Germany the bulk of social security contributions is kept in the social budget (Sozialbudget), which is administered separately from the federal budget. The social budget, however, is under the jurisdiction of the federal government. Basically, the bulk of the German social security system is financed by payroll taxes and other contributions, which are in the social budget, and from the general revenues of the federal budget. The family allowance, which is typical of most European social security systems, is financed primarily from general government revenues.

In looking at the financing of the West German social security system, it is necessary to make the following observations. First, social security taxes account for around one-third of government revenues from all sources—a very high ratio in comparison to other countries. Second, the bulk of the cost of social security is financed by taxes levied directly on the beneficiaries of the system. The revenues, however, are not adequate to cover all outlays of funds by the system. A part of the cost must be covered by the general revenues of the federal government. Thus, some portion of all taxes paid by individual income recipients is used to finance the welfare expenditures of the social security system. With respect to direct taxes, it is difficult to determine what portion of taxes on individuals is allocated to social security expenditures. There is also the parallel problem of the incidence of the taxes. These problems would not be especially difficult to solve if all government expenditures were financed by direct taxation, which is far from the actual case.

Old-Age, Disability, and Survivors' Insurance

Old-age and survivors' benefits, including disability pensions, are provided by an insurance scheme that is compulsory and covers all wage earners and salaried employees. Special systems are provided for miners, civil servants, self-employed persons, artisans, and farmers. There is also the option of private insurance, which is open to persons provided their premiums equal their contributions under the public programs. In either case, employers and employees generally each pay half of the cost of the premiums. In 1972 the general public old-age and survivors' insurance scheme was financed by a tax of 8 percent of payrolls levied on the employer, a tax of 8 percent of earnings levied on the employee, and an annual subsidy provided by the federal government out of general revenues, which usually amounts to around one-third of the cost of the program. As of 1972, the monthly ceiling for the assessment of contributions was DM 1,900 or DM 304, which was equally shared by the employer and employee.

Sickness Insurance

Sickness insurance is an important component of the West German social security system. It is financed by contributions from employers, employees, and from general revenues of the federal budget. This system is fragmented into a number of insurance funds, all of which are under the general supervision of the Federal Ministry of Social Affairs (Bundesministerium für Arbeit und Sozialordnung). Employee and employer contributions range from 4 to 5.5 percent of earnings and payrolls, depending on the sickness fund. Maternity grants, which are payable under sickness insurance schemes, are financed entirely by grants from the federal government.

Unemployment Compensation

Unemployment compensation in West Germany is almost an anomaly. With some exceptions, notably during the 1967 recession, unemployment rates have been generally less than 2 percent of the total labor force. Benefits are financed by a tax on all insured persons of 0.65 percent of earnings up to DM 1,300 a month and by a tax of 0.65 percent on the payrolls of employers. As is true of the other components of the West German social security system, financing takes place mainly through payroll taxes shared 50-50 between employers and employees, with the federal government financing any deficit through general revenues from the budget.

Transfer Payments

In 1972 transfer payments in the form of direct cash payments to individuals and households amounted to DM 110.6 billion or 16.1 percent of personal income. This amount actually understates the role of the West German public sector in the distribution of income, for some of the services provided by the government are, in effect, nonmonetary transfers. This would be true for such expenditures as free medical care, since the recipients of this service benefit by obtaining it at a cost below its real cost, as measured by the government expenditures for the resources necessary to provide the service. Further analysis, however, involves only the actual cash payments that flow from the public to the private sector in the form of income transfers.

The bulk of West German transfer payments is contained in the social budget. In Table 4.2 expenditures for all forms of social assistance are presented. Included are the standard social security expenditures, family allowances, war pensions, equalization of burdens, rent subsidies, and other forms of assistance. The total amount of DM 126.5 billion includes actual cash payments of DM 90.7 billion, which represent direct transfers to individuals and households. The remainder includes payments for services performed, such as medical

106

TABLE 4.2

Expenditures and Revenue Sources in the West German Social Budget, 1972
(DM in billions)

Expenditures		Revenues	
Social insurance			
(private)		Source	
Old-age and sur-			
vivors' benefits	55.7	Levies on employees	37.6
Health insurance	28.2	Levies on employers	39.4
Accident insurance	4.3	Government revenues	51.1
Unemployment			
compensation	3.3	Property	4.9
Total	91.5	Surplus on account	5.2
Other Services			
(private)			
Family allowances	3.5		
Rent allowances	1.7		
Other services	6.9		
Total	12.1		
Public sector pensions			
and services			
Pensions	18.0		
Family allowances	1.8		
Other	.9		
Total	20.7		
Compensation payments			
War pensions	8.1		
Other	1.9		
Total	10.0		
Total Expenditures	134.5	Total income	138.2

Source: Bundesministerium für Arbeit und Sozialordnung, Sozialbericht 1972 (Bonn, 1972), p. 215.

costs, and payments in kind, together totaling DM 27.4 billion, and other payments, including administrative expenses, amounting to DM 8.4 billion. Also presented in the table are the sources of revenue to finance the social assistance programs.

The largest single expenditure in the social budget is for old-age and survivors' pensions and benefits. Old-age pensions amount to 1.5 percent of a worker's assessed wage multiplied by the years the worker was insured.[7] A worker credited with 45 years of coverage whose compensation during the period of insurance equaled the national average is entitled to a pension of 67.5 percent (1.5 percent multiplied by 45) of the national average earnings of employees during the three calendar years prior to the date of his retirement. In addition to the old-age pension, there is an invalidity pension computed in the same manner; children's supplements, which when added to the widow's pension amount to 100 percent of the regular pension; and funeral grants of a lump sum of 20 to 40 days' earnings or three month's pension, if a pensioner.

Sickness insurance is also an important expenditure component. Benefits involve the payment of medical expenses and the payment of an allowance to compensate for the loss of earnings during the period of sickness. Persons covered by sickness insurance are reimbursed for the cost of hospitalization, drugs, and the fees of physicians and dentists in an amount usually equal to 100 percent of the cost or fee. Physicians and dentists are not, as in the case of England, employees of the state. A scale of fees is established by consultation between the appropriate social security administration and the organization representing doctors or dentists. Doctors are not legally obligated to observe the scale of fees, so the actual extent to which a patient is compensated for the cost outlay in a particular illness may vary. Patients are required to pay a maximum of DM 2.5 for medicine.

Cash benefits paid to persons who are sick include an amount equal to 65 percent of weekly earnings during the first six weeks of confinement and 75 percent of weekly earnings thereafter up to a period of 78 weeks. During the first six weeks, employers must pay the difference between the cash benefit and the regular wage. In addition to the regular sickness benefit there is a supplementary benefit of 4 percent of weekly wages for the first dependent and 3 percent for the second and third dependent. Maternity benefits include a payment of 100 percent of earnings for six weeks before and eight weeks after childbirth; and a maternity grant of DM 100 per birth. Nonworking wives of insured persons are also eligible for maternity grants.

The family allowance, or children's allowance as it is commonly called, is a regular cash payment to families with children. The West German family allowance system is fairly unique in comparison to systems in other countries in that the first child is excluded from the allowance. A monthly allowance of DM 25 is paid for the second child provided that the annual family income is less than DM 13,200 or when a family has three or more children. The allowance for the third and fourth child is DM 60 each, and for the fifth and subsequent children DM 70 each. The allowance is paid for all children under the age of 18. In addition, education allowances are paid to families with two or more children.

In addition to the family allowance, there are other general social welfare measures. There is social assistance (Sozialhilfe), which includes welfare and charitable expenditures for such things as aid to the aged and infirm, medical care for the insane, and grants to tubercular persons. In general, such assistance is directed to persons who, for one reason or another, are not eligible for benefits or assistance under the regular social security programs. A second form of assistance is aid to youths (Jugendhilfe). This assistance primarily takes the form of education grants to enable students to attend school. Rent subsidies are also included under general social measures. In Germany rental allowances are paid to low-income families that spend a certain proportion of their income for rent and live in residences that meet certain minimum conditions of health and sanitation. Rent subsidies are typically provided for persons with low fixed incomes.

There are many other types of income transfers. Work-injury compensation includes provisions for medical expenses arising from the injury plus a pension that is generally equal to 65 percent of weekly earnings. If the injury is permanent, a pension of 66.66 percent of weekly earnings is payable for life. There are supplemental incomes of 10 percent of the pension for each child under 18. For unemployment compensation, benefits ranging from 40 percent to 90 percent of earnings are paid for a period of from 13 to 52 weeks, plus cash supplements for dependents. War and war-related pensions and financial assistance, as might be expected, are also important transfers. There are a variety of forms of assistance to war veterans and their dependents, including not only pensions, but such things as medical care, homes for the aged and disabled, financial aid for vocational training, scholarship, and the care of war orphans. Then, too, there is the Equalization of Burdens Fund, which is designed to redistribute equitably among the population of West Germany war and postwar losses, which have affected the citizens to an uneven degree.

INCOME DISTRIBUTION IN WEST GERMANY

Given the components of the West German tax-transfer payment system, it is now possible to proceed to the next step, namely, an analysis of income distribution and the extent to which both taxes and transfer have an effect upon the alteration of the distribution. Data on income distribution in West Germany come from several sources, the most important of which are the various publications of the Federal Statistical Office (Statistisches Bundesamt), including the Statistical Yearbook, and the publications of the prestigious German Institute for Economic Research (Deutsches Institut für Wirtschaftsforschung).

Trends in Income Distribution

In June 1973 the Deutsches Institut für Wirtschaftsforschung published a very significant study of income distribution by households for the period from 1950 to 1970.[8] Included as income was income from wages and salaries, self-employment, and property. The study indicates that despite a shift in the relative share of wages and salaries from about 59 percent of national income in 1950 to 67 percent in 1970, there has been very little change in the distribution of income. In 1950, for example, the highest 20 percent of all households received 45.2 percent of total income; in 1970 the highest 20 percent of all households received 45.6 percent of total income. Although a shift toward a greater equality in the distribution of income did occur during the period from 1955 to 1964, a reversal occurred from 1964 to 1970, primarily because the incomes of self-employed persons, including incomes of unincorporated enterprises, increased more rapidly than wages and salaries and other income sources. During the period from 1960 to 1970, average monthly income for self-employed persons increased by DM 1,850, compared to an increase of DM 800 for wage and salary earners.

The results of the study can be summarized in three tables. The first table (Table 4.3) presents the distribution of monthly net incomes by household income classes for various years, including the three main years, 1950, 1960, and 1970. The number of households is also presented. In 1950 four-fifths of all households received a monthly net income of less than DM 500; only 3 percent received an income of DM 1,000 or more. In 1970 only 12 percent of all households had a monthly net income of less than DM 500, while 61 percent had incomes of DM 1,000 or more. One factor contributing to shifts in income distribution was a 300 percent increase in the number of married women in the labor force.

The distribution of income is net of income taxes, but includes transfer payments. In the second table (Table 4.4), distribution of net income is presented by quintiles for the same time periods. Also presented in the table are the Gini coefficients. In 1950 the top 20 percent of income recipients received 45.2 percent of income; in

110

TABLE 4.3

Distribution of Monthly Net Incomes of Private
Households in West Germany by Income Classes, 1950-70

Year	Number of Households (millions)	Under DM 500	DM 500- 1,000	DM 1,000- 1,500	DM 1,500- 2,000	DM 2,000- 3,000	DM 3,000 and Over
1950*	15,250	80.6%	15.9%	2.5%	0.6%	0.4%	
1955*	16,230	53.3	34.2	8.4	2.4	1.7	
1960	18,905	34.6	37.5	17.4	6.0	2.9	1.6
1964	20,370	23.9	33.9	22.1	10.6	6.1	3.4
1968	21,550	17.0	30.9	22.8	13.2	9.7	6.4
1970	22,400	11.9	27.0	22.4	15.1	13.2	10.4

*Excludes Berlin and the Saarland.

Source: Deutsches Institut für Wirtschaftsforschung, "Einkommen-sverteilung und -schichtung der privaten Haushalte in der Bundesrepublik Deutschland 1950 bis 1970," Wochenbericht 25/73 (West Berlin, June 21, 1973), p. 223.

1970 the top 20 percent received 45.6 percent. There was little change in the share of incomes received by the bottom 40 percent of income recipients. The Gini coefficients also reflected very little change toward equality during the period, with the exception of the two time periods 1960 and 1964.

A general comparison can be made of income distribution in the United States and West Germany for the two time periods 1950 and 1970. In the United States family income is used, and in West Germany household data are used.* It is apparent that income in West Germany

*Household income in West Germany consists of the sums of the various incomes of all household members from work, property and income transfers. It is net of income taxes. The term "household" needs clarification. It covers both families and single persons. A single person living alone but employed is considered a household.

Family income, as used in the U.S. Bureau of the Census income data, refers to income received by a group of two or more persons related by blood, marriage, or adoption and residing together; all such persons are considered as members of the same family. Unrelated individuals are treated separately. An unrelated individual may be treated as a one-person household, and would be included in West Germany under household income totals, but not in the U.S. under family income.

is more unevenly distributed, particularly when taking into consideration the fact that West German income data are net of income taxes. In both countries there was very little change in income distribution patterns during the 1950-70 period. This fact is somewhat surprising, since West Germany has had full employment during most of the twenty-year period. In a tight labor market, it is normal to expect shifts to occur in favor of labor income, and this is actually what has happened in West Germany. However, there have been only minor shifts in the distribution of income by quintiles. United States and West German comparisons are shown in Table 4.5

Another set of income data provides information pertaining to the distribution of income for the three time periods 1960, 1965, and 1971. Income is presented on a net monthly basis for five classes of recipients—white-collar workers, blue-collar workers, government employees, self-employed persons, and persons who received incomes from pensions and other income sources. The data are not for households, but are expressed in terms of net incomes of all workers in the West German labor force. The most significant shift that occurred during the three time periods was the increase in the percentage of the number of self-employed persons in the highest income bracket. The data are presented in Table 4.6

TABLE 4.4

Distribution of Net Monthly Incomes of All Households in
West Germany by Quintiles and the
Gini Coefficient, 1950-70

Year	Quin-tile 1	Quin-tile 2	Quin-tile 3	Quin-tile 4	Quin-tile 5	Gini Coefficient
1950	5.4%	10.7%	15.9%	22.8%	45.2%	.396
1955	5.8	10.7	16.2	23.2	44.1	.384
1960	6.0	10.8	16.2	23.1	43.9	.380
1964	6.1	10.8	16.1	22.9	44.1	.380
1968	6.2	10.5	15.7	22.5	45.1	.387
1970	5.9	10.4	15.6	22.5	45.6	.392

Source: Deutsches Institut für Wirtschaftsforschung, "Einkommensverteilung und -schichtung der privaten Haushalte in der Bundesrepublik Deutschland 1950 bis 1970, "Wochenbericht 25/73 (West Berlin, June 21, 1973), p. 233.

TABLE 4.5

A Comparison of Income Distribution in the United States
and West Germany by Quintiles, 1950 and 1970

| | United States | | West Germany | |
	1950	1970	1950	1970
First Quintile	4.5%	5.5%	5.4%	5.9%
Second Quintile	12.0	12.0	10.7	10.4
Third Quintile	17.4	17.4	15.9	15.6
Fourth Quintile	23.5	23.5	22.8	22.5
Fifth Quintile	42.6	41.6	45.2	45.6
Total	100.0	100.0	100.0	100.0

Source: U.S. Bureau of the Census, "Current Population Reports, Consumer Income," Series P-60, No. 85 (Washington, December 1972), p. 38; Deutsches Institut für Wirtschaftsforschung, "Einkommensverteilung und -schichtung der privaten Haushalte in der Bundesrepublik Deutschland 1950 bis 1970," Wochenbericht 25/73 (West Berlin, June 21, 1973), p. 223.

Income Redistribution Through Taxes

The basic West German taxes have been presented. The one tax that would have the most obvious impact on incomes is the personal income tax. It is through the progressiveness of the West German income tax, with its minimum rate of 19 percent and maximum rate of 53 percent plus a surcharge, that some amount of income redistribution is achieved. However, it is necessary to examine the income tax carefully, for there are certain features, as follows, that reduce its potential progressiveness.

1. The use of income splitting provides an important rate modification under the West German personal income tax rate structure. Married couples filing a joint return compute their joint liability by applying the statutory tax rates on one-half of their combined taxable income and multiplying. The German income tax rates are in actuality applied to two sets of taxable income. The lowest marginal tax rate of 19 percent is applied to incomes exceeding DM 8,009, or DM 16,008 for taxpayers entitled to income splitting, while the maximum marginal rate of 53 percent is applied to any income in excess of DM 110,039, or DM 220,078 in the case of income splitting.

TABLE 4.6

Income Distribution in West Germany, 1962, 1967, and 1971

Income Groups	Number of Recipients	Under DM 150	DM 150-300	DM 300-600	DM 600-800	DM 800-1,200	DM 1,200-1,800	DM 1,800 and Over	Not Listed
				September 1962					
Self-employed	2,129	3.0%	7.4%	22.7%	18.5%	18.6%	10.2%	8.8%	10.8%
Government	1,280	0.2	1.9	27.2	29.4	28.4	9.2	1.2	2.4
White-collar	6,483	9.3	11.6	39.7	18.9	11.5	3.6	1.0	4.5
Blue-collar	12,981	9.0	15.5	58.5	12.6	1.3	0.0	0.0	3.4
Pensioners	8,011	18.8	40.0	27.7	4.2	1.6	0.3	0.1	7.3
Total	30,884	10.8	19.9	42.8	12.8	5.8	1.9	0.9	5.0
				March 1967					
Self-employed	2,061	1.6	3.8	11.7	15.2	23.3	16.2	17.6	10.1
Government	1,360	0.1	0.9	8.4	21.5	40.5	21.7	6.0	0.9
White-collar	7,248	6.4	7.0	26.3	22.5	24.0	8.5	3.2	2.2
Blue-collar	12,266	6.6	9.5	36.4	35.6	10.5	0.4	0.0	1.2
Pensioners	8,971	12.0	26.3	41.3	9.7	4.2	1.0	0.4	7.3
Total	31,874	6.9	12.9	32.6	23.4	13.9	4.4	2.2	3.7
				March 1971					
Self-employed	1,896	1.2	2.0	6.6	8.9	18.7	20.3	31.0	11.3
Government	1,458	0.0	0.3	2.2	7.2	33.9	36.6	18.7	1.1
White-collar	8,124	2.2	6.8	14.9	17.4	29.0	20.0	7.9	1.8
Blue-collar	12,176	3.2	7.3	18.0	27.0	37.4	5.5	0.2	1.6
Pensioners	9,896	7.3	14.4	37.2	16.9	9.6	2.5	0.8	11.2
Total	33,550	3.9	8.7	21.6	19.8	26.0	10.3	4.8	4.9

Source: Statistisches Bundesamt, "Einkommensschichten nach Stellung und Höhe des Monatlichen Nettoeinkommens," (Wiesbaden, March 1971)

2. To some extent unearned income, including income from capital gains, is taxed more lightly than earned income in West Germany. Capital gains, with the exception of gains from specific transactions involving property not held for a specific period of time, are exempt from taxation. Dividends are taxable at the source, and the tax is credited against an individual's total tax liability for the tax year. Interest from certain government bonds and securities is tax exempt, and rent income is taxed separately from regular income.

3. Regular income tax rates are reduced for so-called extraordinary income. This income is taxed at one-half of the average tax rate applied to the entire taxable income. Extraordinary income includes, among other things, gain from the sale of an unincorporated enterprise or partnership.

4. The family size of the West German taxpaying unit also has an important impact upon the effective rate of tax progression under the personal income tax. The right of married couples to file a joint return, along with the ability to add additional exemptions for each child in a family, greatly reduces the marginal tax rate bracket of taxable income for the family as opposed to that of the single unmarried taxpayer. It can be said that there is an element of regressiveness in the tax system through the use of exemptions for children.

The West German income tax is proportional through a wide income zone that includes approximately 50 percent of all wage and salary earners. In this zone, which extends from a minimum of DM 6,000 to a maximum of DM 20,620, the minimum tax rate of 19 percent is applicable. The zones of progression really begin with a taxable income of DM 15,000 for single persons and a taxable income of DM 30,000 for a married couple. By the time taxable income reaches DM 30,000 for singles and DM 60,000 for marrieds, the marginal tax rate has jumped from 24 to 40 percent. When taxable income has reached DM 110,000 for singles and DM 220,000 for marrieds, the maximum rate of 53 percent has been reached. After these levels, the income tax is proportional.

An example of the mechanics of the West German personal income tax is presented in Table 4.7. There are two assumptions—first, a married couple with two children are involved in the tax payment and, second, a 10 percent increase in earnings is used at certain income levels. The table involves a wage earner, thus the wage tax (Lohnsteuer) is used. The marginal rate of the income tax is presented. In the last column, the yield elasticity of the personal income tax has been computed. This shows the percentage change in wages (10 percent) divided into the percentage change in income taxes. The yield elasticity of the tax is much higher at the lower income scale and becomes progressively lower as income increases.

TABLE 4.7

Income Elasticity of the West German Income Tax
for Various Income Levels

Income	10 Percent Increase	Tax on Income	Tax on 10 Percent Increase	Marginal Rate	Elasticity of the Tax
DM 8,400	DM 840	DM 78	DM 160	19%	20.5%
9,600	960	306	184	19	6.0
10,800	1,080	534	206	19	3.8
12,000	1,200	762	228	19	3.0
15,000	1,500	1,332	286	19	2.1
18,000	1,800	1,902	342	19	1.8
21,000	2,100	2,474	422	20	1.7
27,000	2,700	3,766	664	25	1.7
30,000	3,000	4,508	800	27	1.8
150,000	15,000	55,932	7,480	50	1.3
200,000	20,000	81,274	10,314	52	1.3

Source: Institut Finanzen und Steuern, Zur Verteilungenspolitischen Wirkung der Besteuerung (Bonn, 1973), p. 6.

The effect of the West German personal income tax upon income redistribution is presented in tables 4.8 and 4.9. The tables show income distribution by taxpaying classes before and after the imposition of the income tax. Each table presents income data for 1968; however, income is divided into two categories—income from wages and salaries and income from self-employment and property. Although the personal income tax rates are the same regardless of the source, there is a definite delineation in that the wage tax (Lohnsteuer) applies to wages and salaries and the income tax (Einkommensteuer) applies to other income. The basic difference is that the wage tax is assessed, or, in other words, actually withheld by employers and paid to the Ministry of Finance, while the income tax is nonassessed and based on returns filed at the end of the tax year. Each employee has a wage tax card to which the assessed tax is applied. Table 4.8 is based on data obtained from wage cards turned into the Ministry of Finance. It is necessary to mention the fact that the number of income earners and the amount of income and taxes tend to be understated by about 10 percent for the reason that the data are based only on wage tax cards returned to the Ministry of Finance.

TABLE 4.8

Before- and After-Income-Tax Distribution
Of Wages and Salaries in West Germany for 1968

Income Groups	Number of Persons (millions)	Total Income (billions)	Taxes (billions)	Net Income (billions)
Under DM 5,000	3,698	7,865	80	7,785
5,000 - 12,000	6,959	61,347	3,854	57,493
12,000 - 16,000	3,852	53,306	4,096	49,210
16,000 - 25,000	3,422	66,448	6,545	59,903
25,000 - 50,000	764	23,429	3,235	20,194
50,000 - 100,000	43	2,718	589	2,129
100,000 and over	6	1,030	352	678
Total	18,744	216,143	18,751	197,392

Source: Statistisches Bundesamt, "Bruttolohn und Lohnsteuer," Fachserie L, Reihe 6 II (Wiesbaden, 1972).

The average income for wage and salary earners in 1968 was DM 11,531 ($2,850), and the average rate of the income tax was 8.7 percent. The average before-tax income of the lowest one-fifth (lowest quintile) of all wage and salary earners was DM 2,311, and the average before-tax income of the highest one-fifth (fifth quintile) of all wage

TABLE 4.9

Distribution of Income by Quintiles
for Wage and Salary Earners in West Germany for 1968
(in percent)

Quintiles	Before Taxes	After Taxes
First quintile	3.8	4.2
Second quintile	15.3	15.7
Third quintile	16.7	17.0
Fourth quintile	25.3	25.4
Fifth quintile	38.9	37.7

Before-tax Gini coefficient .3208   After-tax Gini coefficient .3068

Source: Compiled by the author, and based on Table 4.8.

and salary earners was DM 22,530—a ratio of approximately 9.6 to 1. The after-tax average income of the lowest and highest quintiles of wage and salary earners was DM 2,187 and DM 19,840 respectively—a ratio of approximately 9 to 1.

Before- and after-tax distribution of income is also presented by quintiles. The shifts are rather minor, particularly for the first through the fourth quintile of income earners. The Gini coefficient is also computed, and it, too, indicates a small redistributional effect toward greater income equality.

Tables 4.10 and 4.11 represent a different group of income tax payers, namely, those who are subject to tax assessments at the end of the tax year. This group files its own tax returns. Income may come from wages and salaries not subject to a withholding tax, property, self-employment, agriculture, and other sources, and is subject to an income tax (Einkommensteuer). In 1968 4.8 million taxpaying units filed returns. This, of course, is substantially less than the total of 8.3 million persons who received an income, but married persons are combined into single taxpaying units. Out of the total income of DM 119.5 billion, income from self-employment amounted to DM 11.2 billion, entrepreneurial income was DM 45.2 billion, income from interest, dividends, and rent was DM 7.8 billion, and wages and salaries amounted to DM 57.7 billion.[9]

TABLE 4.10

Before- and After-Income-Tax Distribution of Income
from Self-Employment and Property in West Germany

Income Classes	Taxpayers (millions)	Gross Income (billions)	Income Tax (billions)	Net Income (billions)
Under DM 5,000	305.6	1,071.5	13.3	1,058.2
5,000- 12,000	1,357.6	11,864.2	604.4	11,249.8
12,000 - 16,000	718.7	9,976.4	817.0	9,159.4
16,000- 25,000	1,231.4	25,101.8	2,833.4	22,268.4
25,000- 50,000	896.9	29,506.0	4,367.3	25,138.7
50,000-100,000	221.1	15,066.2	3,438.9	11,627.3
100,000 and over	111.0	26,905.3	10,263.0	16,642.3
Total	4,842.3	119,491.4	22,337.3	97,154.1

Source: Statistisches Bundesamt, "Bruttolohn und Lohnsteuer," Wirtschaft und Statistik, Reiche 6, Fachseries L (Wiesbaden, 1972).

TABLE 4.11

Distribution of Income by Quintiles from
Self-Employment and Property in West Germany for 1968
(in percent)

Quintiles	Before Taxes	After Taxes
First quintile	5.7	6.7
Second quintile	8.3	9.5
Third quintile	14.1	15.6
Fourth quintile	19.3	20.7
Fifth quintile	52.6	47.5
Total	100.0	100.0
Before-tax Gini coefficient .4192		After-tax Gini coefficient .3712

Source: Compiled by the author, and based on Table 4.10.

The average income from self-employment, property, and other income not subject to a withholding tax was DM 24,677 ($6,150), and the average tax was DM 4,613.* The overall effective rate of the tax was 18.7 percent. The average before-tax income of the lowest one-fifth of all income earners was DM 5,793 and the average before-tax income of the highest one-fifth of income earners was DM 64,952—a ratio of approximately 11 to 1. The average after-tax income of the lowest one-fifth of income earners was DM 5,498, and the average after-tax income of the highest one-fifth of income earners was DM 47,605—a ratio of approximately 8.5 to 1.

Before- and after-income-tax distribution of income from self-employment and property can be broken down into quintiles. The before- and after-tax Gini coefficients can also be computed. The overall impact of the West German income tax upon the distribution of income from self-employment and property appears to be moderately progressive, with certainly nowhere near the impact of the Swedish personal income tax. The highest quintile of income recipients received DM 62.9 billion before taxes, paid DM 16.8 billion in taxes, for an effective tax rate of approximately 27 percent, and ended

---

*The West German-U.S. exchange rate of DM 4 to $1.00, which was in effect in 1968, is used.

119

up with DM 46.1 billion. The Gini coefficient of income equality, which includes all quintiles, was reduced from .4192 before taxes to .3712 after taxes.

Based on the wage tax and income tax statistics, 22.6 percent of wage-tax obligated persons earned 43.3 percent of total gross wages and paid 57.2 percent of the wage tax, while 2.3 percent of income-tax obligated persons received 22.5 percent of total income and paid 46 percent of the total income tax. The bottom one-third of income earners received 10.8 percent of gross income and paid 2.8 percent of total income taxes. The bulk of income earners (those with incomes between DM 16,000 and DM 100,000) received 58.3 percent of total income and paid 47.7 percent of the income tax. It would appear that the West German income tax, both withheld and assessed, satisfies one objective of income taxation, namely, equity, while having a rather low redistributional effect, except perhaps on the upper 1 percent of West German taxpayers. This statement is confirmed by West German studies.

A 1973 West German study analyzes the effect of the wage tax (Lohnsteuer) on wages and salaries.[10] The study indicated a yield elasticity of 1.8 percent for the wage tax—a change in the tax divided by a change in wages and salaries. In 1972, for the first time since the creation of West Germany, the wage tax replaced the value-added tax (before 1968 the turnover tax) as the single most important tax revenue source. The distributional effect of the wage tax yield of DM 49.8 billion can be measured by dividing taxpayers into approximately three equal groups. Tax-obligated persons in the lowest one-third of all taxpayers received 12 percent of wage and salary income and paid 5 percent of all taxes.[11] The middle one-third received 28 percent of wages and salaries and paid 25 percent of income taxes. The highest one-third received 60 percent of wage and salary income and paid 70 percent of the total tax. The average take of the tax from each income group was 6.1 percent for the lowest, 10.5 percent for the middle, and 13.9 percent for the highest. The average take from all incomes was 11.8 percent, compared to 8.7 percent for 1968.

In summary, it can be said that the redistributional effect of the personal income tax shows a modest shift in favor of the lower-income groups.[12] On the other end of the income scale, there is no drastic shift in the after-tax position of the higher-income groups. In this connection it is necessary to remember that progression is accomplished by the "bracket" method, whereby each successive higher rate applies only to income in excess of the previous bracket maximum. Furthermore, continuing exemptions reduce somewhat the overall burden of the scheduled rate. Actually, therefore, the overall effective rates on total incomes are much less than the maximum bracket rates applied to these incomes.

Indirect Taxes

The so-called "indirect taxes," the most important of which is the value-added tax, accounted for 54 percent of West German tax revenues (excluding social security contributions) in 1972.[13] These taxes, in terms of their redistributional effects, are normally considered to be regressive and are passed on to the consumer in terms of higher prices. However, indirect taxes in West Germany, in particular the value-added tax, appear to be more proportional than regressive for the reason that not all consumer goods are equally burdened by the tax. As mentioned previously, lower rates of the value-added tax are applied to basic consumer goods, such as food, while drugs are exempt. A study based on 1971 data indicates that 55.7 percent of the consumer expenditures of social security recipients was subject to the lower, more favorable rate of the value-added tax, compared to 35.4 percent of consumer expenditures of the highest one-third of income earners.[14] The effective rate of the value-added tax on all consumer expenditures in 1971 was 6.9 percent, compared to 6.0 for pensioners and social security recipients.

Another study made by the Deutsches Institut für Wirtschaftsforschung (German Institute for Economic Research) indicates somewhat similar results for 1972.[15] On the basis of consumption expenditures at all levels of income, indirect taxes were found to be mildly progressive. The favorable treatment of basic consumer goods created less of a tax burden on lower-income households. There was a close relationship of the value-added tax to consumption expenditures, as indicated by a yield elasticity of 1.1—a 10 percent increase in consumption was accompanied by a 11 percent increase in the value-added tax. The yield elasticity of the gasoline tax was 1 percent, while the yield elasticity of excises on beer and tobacco was .8 percent.

The Impact of Social Security Contributions

Several points can be made with respect to the income redistribution effect of social security contributions in the German economy. First, social security taxes account for around one-third of government revenues from all tax sources—a high ratio in comparison to other countries. For example, in 1969 German social security contributions amounted to 30 percent of total tax revenue in that year, compared to 17 percent for the United States and 16 percent for Japan. This means that social welfare expenditures in Germany are comprehensive, although the cost of financing these expenditures is also comprehensive.

121

Second, it is possible to advance ideas about the incidence of the social security levies. Unlike France, where the cost of social security is borne almost exclusively by the employer, German employees and employers share the cost about equally. That part of social security payroll taxes that is levied on the employee is very much like an income tax. The major difference is that personal exemptions and exemptions for dependents are lacking. The tax normally is not shifted forward either to the employer or to the consumer. The effect is that of an addition to withholding under the personal income tax. Given, however, a shortage of labor and a high level of aggregate demand, both of which have characterized the German economy, and given the high rate of 8 percent on a ceiling of DM 1,900 a month, which is well above average monthly earnings, it is possible that labor is in a position to try to force a rise in wage rates. The tax would then be pushed forward to the employer, who would try to shift as much as possible to the consumer. That part of the payroll tax levied on the employer would be shifted in all likelihood to the consumer. Given the high level of demand that has prevailed in Germany, most or all of the tax would be shifted forward to the consumer.

The redistribution effects of social security are complicated by the fact that if benefits are not subject to income taxation, they are worth more to a man with a high taxable income than they are to a poorer man. Given the broad coverage of the German social security system, it is obvious that the major part must be paid by those who benefit. It is also probable that the social security system has involved some income redistribution downward, particularly from younger, able-bodied, and employed workers to the aged, the ill, and the unemployed. For the most part, this productive group receives less in benefits than it pays in taxes. It is also necessary to point out that a part of this whole redistributive process is covered by taxes on beer, tobacco, food, gasoline, and other indirect taxes.

Redistributional Effects of Transfer Payments

As mentioned previously, transfer payments are an important component of West German personal income. Given the magnitude of income transfers (DM 110.6 billion in 1972), it is necessary to get some idea of the extent to which incomes are altered for various income groups by transfer payments. In Table 4.12 monthly household incomes for various income groups are presented for 1969. Household income in the table is the source of various incomes of households from work, property, and transfer payments. Household incomes are presented as averages for each income class. For example, average

TABLE 4.12

Household Income by Sources in West Germany for 1969

Monthly Income	Number of Households (in thousands)	Average Income	Work Income	Property	Transfers	Other*
Under DM 300	457	254	23	19	202	—
300- 600	2,555	477	72	31	338	36
600- 800	2,065	773	309	49	380	35
800- 1,000	2,398	1,034	620	57	322	35
1,000- 1,200	2,572	1,285	931	70	245	38
1,200- 1,500	3,385	1,584	1,225	92	223	45
1,500- 1,800	2,421	1,932	1,451	125	237	49
1,800- 2,500	2,946	2,446	1,964	177	245	60
2,500-10,000	1,742	4,129	3,359	404	283	83

*Extraordinary income, including the sale of property.

Source: Statistisches Bundesamt, "Zusammensetzung und Verteilung der Einkommen privater Haushalte 1969," Wirtschaft und Statistik (Wiesbaden, September 12, 1972), pp. 708-710.

monthly income in the income group DM 2,500-DM 10,000 was DM 4,129. Property income, as used in the table, includes all income from property ownership, in particular rent, but excludes interest on savings accounts in credit institutions, which is difficult to impute on a monthly basis. Given the exclusion of interest, a comparison of property income by income groups shows that income from this source is twenty times larger in the highest income group than in the lowest income group.

The redistributional effects of transfer payments can be examined when income recipients are divided on the basis of occupation, age, and marital status. In Table 4.13 occupational categories reflect a broad social stratum—farmers, self-employed persons, government employees, white-collar workers, blue-collar workers, and persons who are retired. As might be expected, transfers are most important to the last category of persons. Table 4.13 also presents income recipients on the basis of age categories, with transfer payments presented as a comparison to total income. Finally, sex, marital status, and number of children constitute a third category of income

TABLE 4.13

West German Household Incomes Including Transfer
Payments Based on Occupation, Age, and Marital
Status in 1969

Categories	Average Monthly Income	Work Income	Pro-perty	Trans-fers	Other
Occupational					
Farming	DM 1,884	DM 1,513	DM 207	DM 148	DM 17
Self-employed	2,969	2,585	267	90	27
Government	2,117	1,880	113	40	85
White-collar	2,103	1,860	111	75	56
Blue-collar	1,617	1,404	82	97	34
Retired	949	159	101	636	53
Age					
Under 25	1,145	937	22	65	121
25–35	1,731	1,544	68	53	66
35–45	2,044	1,778	129	91	46
45–55	2,052	1,701	145	164	41
55–65	1,503	1,058	121	288	36
65 and over	1,015	218	107	646	43
Marital Status (households)					
One person	753	307	59	345	42
Two persons	1,505	950	113	400	43
Three persons	1,970	1,612	123	181	55
Four persons	2,111	1,708	137	116	50
Five persons	2,334	1,896	182	214	42

Source: Statistisches Bundesamt, "Zusammensetzung und Verteilung der Einkommen privater Haushalte 1969,"Wirtschaft und Statistik (Wiesbaden, September 12, 1972), p. 709.

recipients. The table indicates that transfer payments have the greatest redistributional impact on retired persons, older persons in general, and one-person households where a female is the sole income earner.

Determination of the pattern of income redistribution through transfer payments cannot, of course, be separated from the general question of the incidence of taxation. The whole matter hinges, in a sense, on identification of the groups that pay the taxes that finance the various income transfers. This would present no particular problem provided that the taxes are direct taxes, for then a comparison can be made of the taxes that fall on the beneficiaries of the income transfers and the amount of income transfers received. However, in West Germany there are two difficulties involved in comparing costs to benefits. First, taxes levied on the beneficiaries of various income transfers do not cover the cost of the transfers. As mentioned previously, a part of the West German social security system is covered by general government revenues. Second, difficulties also arise since the West German government depends on indirect taxes for the larger part of its revenue.

In Table 4.14, however, it is possible to get some idea of the relationship between direct taxes, social security contributions, and transfer payments for households in each income class for 1969. The data are expressed in terms of averages for each income class. The data on tax payments lead to conclusions concerning the West German tax structure similar to those reached in the preceding section on taxation, in that the income tax is proportional through much of its range, achieving some progressivity in the upper-income classes. However, included in the tax category are taxes on property, the effects of which are discussed in the section on wealth distribution. Social security contributions are listed separately in the table. Both taxes on income and property and social security contributions are expressed in terms of averages per income class and also as a percentage of average monthly income. Finally, average transfer payments for each income class are presented, and the average gain or loss, which is found by subtracting income and property taxes and social security contributions, is recorded. For example, the average gain in the income class DM 300 and under is DM 196. Thus a comparison of tangible tax contributions to income transfers received is facilitated by the table.

Based on tables 4.12, 4.13, and 4.14, it is possible to arrive at the following conclusions pertaining to the tax-transfer system in West Germany.

1. Inequality in the initial distribution of income is modified to some extent by the system of income taxes and transfer payments. Referring to Table 4.14, taxes and social security contributions amount to about 16 percent of the highest average monthly income of DM 4,129,

TABLE 4.14

A Comparison of Monthly Income, Tax Payments,
and Transfer Payments by Income Classes for West Germany, 1969

Income Classes	Average Monthly Income	Taxes	Income and Property		Social Security		Transfers	Gain/ Loss
Under DM 300	DM 254	DM 6	DM 0	.0%	DM 6	2.5%	DM 202	DM +196
300– 600	477	18	6	1.2	12	2.5	338	+320
600– 800	733	72	30	3.9	42	5.3	380	+308
800– 1,000	1,034	133	62	6.0	71	6.9	322	+189
1,000– 1,200	1,285	185	91	7.1	94	7.3	245	+ 60
1,200– 1,500	1,584	242	128	8.1	114	7.2	223	– 19
1,500– 1,800	1,932	292	166	8.6	126	6.5	237	– 55
1,800– 2,500	2,446	355	229	9.4	126	5.1	245	–110
2,500–10,000	4,129	654	870	13.8	85	2.1	283	–371

Source: Statistisches Bundesamt, "Zusammensetzung und Verteilung der Einkommen Privater Haushalte 1969,"Wirtschaft und Statistik (Wiesbaden, September 12, 1972), p. 709.

while transfer payments account for only 7 percent of total income. On the other end of the income scale, taxes represent 2.5 percent of the average income of DM 254, while transfer payments amount to 80 percent of income.

2. Distribution of transfer payments among social classes favors the nonactive segment of the West German population at the expense of the active segment. This can be attributed to the fact that old-age pensions constitute one of the major parts of the West German social security system. In 1969 persons aged 65 and over had an average monthly household income of DM 1,015, paid income taxes and social security contributions of DM 65, but received average monthly transfers of DM 646. The tax-transfer relationship is 6 percent to 64 percent. However, the age group 25-35 received an average monthly income of DM 1,731, including DM 53 in transfer payments, but paid average monthly taxes of DM 286. This group paid out 16.5 percent of its income in the form of taxes, but received back only 3.1 percent of its income in the form of transfer payments.

3. Farmers also benefit from transfer payments under the West German tax-transfer system. In 1969 farmers received average monthly transfer payments of DM 148, which was 7.8 percent of average monthly income of DM 1,884, while paying out a monthly average of DM 80, or 4.3 percent of income, in the form of income and property taxes and social security contributions.

4. Wage earners benefit more from the tax-transfer arrangement than other active groups. In 1969 they received 6.0 percent of their total income in the form of transfer payments, while paying out 18.7 percent of their income in the form of income and social security taxes.

5. Social security contributions are progressive, proportional, and regressive within income ranges. For incomes up to DM 1,200 a month, social security contributions are a greater burden than income and property. So approximately 50 percent of all West German households pay out more in social security contributions than they do in income taxes.

Table 4.15 substantiates some of the points presented above. In the table, households are divided into occupational and age classes, and comparisons are made of average monthly incomes, taxes, and transfer payments.

DISTRIBUTION OF WEALTH IN WEST GERMANY

The distribution of wealth in West Germany also has an impact on the distribution of income.[16] Through available data, which are presented in Table 4.16, it is possible to get some idea of the

TABLE 4.15

A Comparison of Monthly Income, Tax Payments,
and Income Transfers on the Basis of Occupation and
Age in West Germany, 1969

Groupings	Average Monthly Income	Income and Property Taxes	Social Security Contributions	Transfer Payments
Occupational				
Farmers	DM 1,884	DM 51	DM 29	DM 148
Self-employed	2,969	426	20	90
Government	2,117	235	18	40
White-collar	2,103	239	137	75
Blue-collar	1,617	139	163	97
Retired	949	35	20	636
Age				
Under 25	1,145	101	92	65
25-35	1,731	167	119	53
35-45	2,044	200	118	91
45-55	2,052	211	119	164
55-65	1,503	140	76	288
65 and over	1,015	46	19	646

Source: Statistisches Bundesamt, "Zusammensetzung und
Verteilung der Einkommen privater Haushalte 1969," Wirtschaft und
Statistik (Wiesbaden, September 12, 1972), pp. 709-711.

distribution of wealth. As might be expected, there is a much more
uneven distribution of wealth than income. In 1966, 78.2 percent of
all property owners had property valued between DM 50,000 and DM
500,000 while 3.6 percent of all property owners had property valued
at more than DM 1 billion. One-tenth of 1 percent of all property
owners owned 16.3 percent of all property. Also presented in the
table are property tax yields for 1966.

TABLE 4.16

Distribution of Property in West Germany for 1966

Property Groups		Property Owners (thousands)	Taxable Property (millions of DM)	Property Tax Yield (millions of DM)
	under DM 30,000	13,311	59	1
30,000	- 40,000	17,944	219	2
40,000	- 50,000	24,792	372	4
50,000	- 60,000	57,306	1,298	12
60,000	- 100,000	74,972	2,866	28
100,000	- 250,000	149,817	15,381	150
250,000	- 500,000	50,008	14,775	145
500,000	- 1,000,000	21,470	13,672	134
1,000,000	- 2,500,000	10,738	15,566	153
2,500,000	- 5,000,000	2,852	9,591	95
5,000,000	- 10,000,000	1,065	7,298	72
10,000,000 and over		596	15,751	156
Total		424,867	96,849	952

Source: Statistisches Bundesamt, Statistisches Jahrbuch 1969 (Wiesbaden: Verlag W. Kohlhammer, 1969), p. 408.

The Effect of Property and Inheritance on Distribution of Wealth

Property taxes are of two types: the general property tax (Vermögenssteuer) and the real estate purchase tax (Grunderwerbsteuer). The general property tax is a revenue source for local government units. Real property, with certain exemptions, is subject to an annual tax rate of 1 percent on its assessed value. This basic rate is fixed by federal law. It may, however, be reduced to 0.75 percent of the value if real property does not exceed an amount stipulated in the Equalization of Burdens Law. The real estate purchase tax is imposed on the transfer of property. The rate of the tax is usually 7 percent, based on the sales price of the property or, in some cases, on the assessed value of the property. The purchase tax is a joint tax because both state and local governments use it.

The effect of the property tax on wealth appears to be minimal. As Table 4.16 indicates, the yield is 1 percent of the value of the property subject to taxation. Many German property owners escape the property tax entirely. For example, there is a personal exemption of DM 20,000 per taxpayer unit for housing and a tax-free amount of DM 10,000 for capital property. There are also special evaluations and debt deductions available for owners of houses and apartments. The property tax is also deductible for purposes of the personal income tax. Personal property, including cars and other consumer durables, generally is not included in the property tax.

The inheritance tax accounted for 0.3 percent of all tax revenues in 1971. This low percentage is attributable to the fact that most inheritances are less than the maximum exemption levels. Inheritance tax rates depend upon the consanguinity of the decedent, with five brackets or classes available, with rates ranging from 2 percent to 14 percent in the first tax class and 14 percent to 60 percent in the fifth tax class. As a device for the redistribution of wealth, the inheritance tax appears to have a very minor impact. Table 4.17 presents the most current (1962) information available concerning the impact of the inheritance tax. Even after combining the five tax classes, only 44,852 taxpayers paid an inheritance tax in 1962. Taxable inheritances of DM 1.5 billion amounted to around 1.5 percent of all wealth in West Germany in 1962. In comparing the inheritance tax to taxable inheritances for each inheritance class, the tax appears to be more proportional then progressive. Even for the highest inheritance class, the effective tax rate was 13 percent.

SUMMARY

The objective of this chapter has been to examine income distribution in West Germany and the extent to which it has been altered by taxes and transfer payments. The most important findings that have resulted from the data available on West Germany have been presented. In concluding the chapter it is appropriate, perhaps, to restate some of these findings. Insofar as income distribution is concerned, the picture is one of relative inequality among various social groups. This inequality is mitigated to some extent by the tax-transfer mechanism. Transfer payments in particular serve chiefly to bolster the income position of persons in the nonactive segment of the population and certain other groups, including farmers and households headed by a single person.

It appears, however, that taxes have little redistributional effect upon incomes. The personal income is both proportional and progressive through various income zones, with true progressivity tending to hit only the highest income zone. Some redistributional effect does occur, particularly on incomes from self-employment and

TABLE 4.17

The Impact of Inheritance Taxes on Wealth Distribution
in West Germany in 1962

Inheritance Classes	Taxable Inheritance (in thousands of DM)	Inheritance Tax (in thousands of DM)	Taxpayers
Under DM 5,000	43,288	4,293	14,359
5,000 - 10,000	63,599	5,763	9,330
10,000 - 20,000	73,113	7,714	5,422
20,000 - 30,000	45,265	5,403	2,226
30,000 - 40,000	40,839	4,358	2,970
40,000 - 50,000	49,052	4,457	2,242
50,000 - 100,000	198,815	16,316	4,475
100,000 - 150,000	134,267	11,063	1,408
150,000 - 200,000	103,016	9,297	710
200,000 - 300,000	131,915	12,232	686
300,000 - 400,000	112,858	11,317	422
400,000 - 500,000	67,241	7,012	192
500,000 - 600,000	47,290	4,649	98
600,000 - 700,000	40,776	4,843	75
700,000 and over	349,947	45,856	237
Total	1,501,281	154,574	44,852

Source: Statistisches Bundesamt, "Erbschaftsteuer 1953-1962," Fachserie L, Reihe 6 V (Wiesbaden, 1972).

property. Taxes on property have the characteristic of an additional tax on top of the income tax and have some redistributional effect in that they are paid by the recipients of high incomes. The value-added tax, which is the most important indirect tax in West Germany, is proportional rather than regressive.

NOTES

1. Deutsches Institut für Wirtschaftsforschung, Wochenbericht (West Berlin, March 8, 1973), p. 86.

2. Deutsches Bundesbank, Monatsberichte der Deutschen Bundesbank (Frankfurt am Main, March 1973), p. 18.

3. Ibid., p. 60

4. Deutsches Institut für Wirtschaftsforschung, Wochenbericht, p. 86.

5. Monatsberichte der Deutschen Bundesbank, p. 22.

6. All tax data were obtained from August Lethe, Steuerlehre (Bad Homburg: Verlag Dr. Max Gehlen, 1970). Updates were obtained from the West German Embassy.

7. All data on social security were obtained from Bundesministerium für Arbeit und Sozialordnung, Sozialberich 1972 (Bonn, 1971), p. 13.

8. Deutsches Institut für Wirtschaftsforschung, "Einkommensverteilung und -schichtung der privaten Haushalte in der Bundesrepublik Deutschland 1950 bis 1970," Wochenbericht 25/73 (West Berlin, June 21, 1973). One other study on income distribution that was utilized is Josef Körner, Struktur und Personelle Verteilung von Lohn und Lohnsteuer in der Bundesrepublik Deutschland seit 1950 (Munich: Ifo-Institut für Wirtschaftsforschung, 1970).

9. Statistisches Bundesamt, "Bruttolohn und Lohnsteuer," Fachserie L. Reiche 6, 11 (Wiesbaden, 1972).

10. Deutsches Institut für Wirtschaftsforschung, "Lohnsteuer wird zur ergiebigsten staatlichen Einnahmequelle," Wochenbericht 17/73 (West Berlin, April 26, 1973), pp. 144-145.

11. Ibid., p. 145.

12. See also the study by the Institut Finanzen und Steuern, Zur Verteilungenspolitischen Wirkung der Besteuerung, (Bonn, 1973).

13. Statistisches Bundesamt, Statistisches Jahrbuch, 1972 (Wiesbaden: 1972), p. 492.

14. Deutsches Institut für Wirtschaftsforschung, "Wirken indirekte Steuern, regressiv? Die Belastung der privaten Haushalte mit indirekten Steuern," Wochenbericht 21/72 (West Berlin: May 18, 1972) pp. 188-189.

15. Lohnsteuer wird zur ergiebigsten staatliche Einnahmequelle, Wochenbericht.

16. The following studies on property and inheritance were used: Jürgen Siebke, "Die Vermögensbildung der privaten Haushalte in der Bundesrepublik Deutschland," Forschungsauftrag des Bundesministeriums für Arbeit und Sozialordnung (Bonn, May 1971), unpublished paper; Deutsches Institut für Wirtschaftsforschung, Die Vermögenseinkunfte der privaten Haushalte in der Bundesrepublik Deutschland, Wochenbericht 11/73 (West Berlin, March 15, 1973), pp. 89-91; and Institut Finanzen und Steuern, Zur verteilungspolitischen Wirkung der Besteuerung (Bonn, March 1973), pp. 21-26.

Income distribution in a socialist economy, such as East Germany
(German Democratic Republic), is determined by the state rather than
by the marketplace. Income distribution policy has several clear-cut
aims within the broader framework of the national economic plan. It
determines, on the one hand, the total volume of wages in the economy
and their distribution into sectors, industries, and branches, and
regulates, on the other hand, principles for setting the absolute level
and relative position of rewards of individual workers. In particular,
income distribution policy is responsible for the efficient allocation
of manpower resources and for rewarding workers systematically,
so that desired behavior is differentially rewarded and thus incentives
provided are related to the success criteria of an economic unit. Last,
but not least, income distribution aims at balancing the total volume
of wages and other income to the total value of consumer goods to
insure price stability.

In a socialist country income is primarily limited to wages and
salaries. It has been a socialist article of faith, which has been subject to question only recently, that labor is the only factor of production endowed with the capability of creating value. Therefore, labor
should be remunerated to the exclusion of land and capital. The total
amount of wages to be paid, and the production counterpart to support
wages, depends on the division of socialist national income between
accumulation and consumption, and further, of consumption between
the social consumption fund and the wage fund. It stems from this
that there would be as a matter of necessity a high degree of centralization and control over the determination of wages and salaries.

However, income may also take other forms. In East Germany,
for example, a private sector continues to operate even after two
decades of a state policy of appropriating private industry. In Poland
a private sector is dominant in agriculture, and in Yugoslavia private
industry as well as private agriculture is allowed to exist, so a private
sector consisting of individual enterprises, artisans, craftsmen,

retailers, wholesalers, and innkeepers provides both profit and entrepreneurial income. Moreover, interest also figures in the national income of socialist countries to some extent, as a part of income received by individual producers may be considered as interest on the relatively small amounts of capital they own. Interest is also used as a device to encourage personal savings, which are regarded as necessary to put a brake on excess consumer demand, and interest rate differentials exist in favor of long-term savings deposits.

Also, in a socialist economic system goods are produced and services provided for money, although some goods, and to a greater extent services, are provided free of charge by the state. This leads to the problem of relating the total volume of wages to the total value of consumer goods and services. The maintenance of balance between incomes from work and the resources allocated to personal consumption is therefore yet another part of income distribution policy and especially of wage planning. As prices of consumer goods and services may change, this also involves the problem of maintenance of the purchasing power of wages and the relationship between nominal and real wages. There is no assurance that these different aspects of income policy will always be in harmony with one another.

The economic reforms of the 1960s, which had an impact on the socialist economies of Eastern Europe, inaugurated new and far-reaching changes in policies governing the distribution of wages. Emphasis is now placed on the relation between rewards and the economic performance of state enterprises. While retaining the system of central determination of basic wage scales and also some of the traditional forms of incentive payments, including piece-rates, bonuses, and premia, actual overall earnings are now directly linked to the economic results of enterprises. There is one essential difference in comparison to previous attempts in this direction. The yardstick of success is no longer the implementation of centrally determined planned targets, but the actual income of an enterprise earned by producing and selling commodities in controlled markets within the framework of a macroeconomic plan.

Income distribution and economic planning are interrelated in a socialist system. Economic planning represents an attempt to balance the supply of and demand for resources in order to achieve a balance or equilibrium. As such, planning is an instrument of economic strategy used to achieve an optimum growth of national income. A series of material or interbranch balances are used to reconcile planned targets with the limiting constraints of existing resources. These balancing arrangements are expressed in both physical and financial terms and comprise the following flows, which have to be harmonized: production, consumption, and accumulation; the distribution of national income; personal money income and expenditures and utilization of labor resources.

National income in a socialist economy begins with the concept of the net material product, which can be defined either as the net contribution of the productive sectors of the economy, that is, gross production, less the value of intermediate products and depreciation charges, or as the total income realized by the productive sectors. To put it more simply, the concept of socialist national income is that of national income produced and national income distributed. National income produced covers those activities that create material goods or help in the productive process, for example, gathering raw materials and processing them into finished products. National income distributed refers to the process of primary distribution of the income of the labor force, enterprises, and society by financial flows. This income can be divided into two categories. The first category of income is distributed to individuals and consists of gross money income before taxation of workers employed in the production process, money income and income in kind of farmers, and the value of net production from private activity of a productive character. The second category of national income distributed consists of gross profits before taxation of production enterprises, the turnover tax, and contributions of enterprises to social insurance.

A schematic presentation of national income distributed may be presented as follows:

Primary incomes of individuals
1. Wages and salaries of the state sector of productive industries
2. Wages and salaries of producer cooperatives
3. Income of cooperative farmers from cooperative activities
4. Income of cooperative farmers from private plots of land
5. Incomes of individual farmers
6. Incomes, private or otherwise, from other activities of a productive nature

Primary incomes of the social sector
1. Gross profits before taxes of productive enterprises
2. Turnover taxes
3. Contributions of enterprises to health insurance

Socialist income accounting differentiates between productive and nonproductive sectors. As these primary incomes of individuals and firms are generated only in the productive sectors, this flow of distribution gives no account of incomes of individuals working in the nonproductive spheres of activity, of unearned incomes of individuals with claims to transfer payments from public funds, and of enterprises operating in the nonproductive sectors. All of these incomes are included under the category of personal income, along with the primary incomes of individuals employed in the productive sectors.

A system of income balancing is also used to relate personal income to personal outflows. Personal income comes from two main sources—wages and salaries and other types of labor income, and various transfer payments. Personal income can be regarded as

135

income generated in the process of redistributing the socialist national income. This process is effected by transfers between the state and society, between different sectors of society, and by transfers between different units of a public character. These transfers are realized mainly through the state budget, which is the most important instrument in modifying income flows in a socialist economy, and through a system of credits. Many transfers are payments by the state for which no service is provided in return, but which redistribute income to various groups. Examples are old-age pensions and family allowances. Personal outlays include personal consumption on goods and services, taxes, and other payments. The end result is an economic balance that relates total money income of the population to their total outlays. An example of this balance is presented below.

Personal Income and Outlays in a Socialist Economy

Income	Outlays
Wage fund (wages and salaries)	Consumption goods
Income of cooperatives and individual farmers	Services
	Consumption of goods in kind
Other income from enterprises (supplements)	Consumption of services in kind
	Total private consumption
Imputed rent	Personal contributions
Other labor and rental income	Personal tax payments to institutions
Total income from work and property	
Government transfer payments	
Total income	Total outlays

As mentioned before, wages constitute the great bulk of personal income distributed in a socialist economic system. Although labor itself enjoys some freedom from central planning, there is a high degree of centralization and control over the determination of wages. The total amount of wages to be paid is set in the wage fund, which provides gross payments for all work done, including basic wage rates, payments based on piece-rate norms, basic salaries, premia and bonuses of all kinds, payments for overtime, and payments for night work and work on Sunday and holidays. The former refers to outlays that provide for the collective or societal consumption of such goods and services as housing, education, and cultural activities. The wage fund is linked to private consumption. Consumption, both collective and private, has to be planned in advance because it constitutes an integral part of the national economic plan, which cannot be constructed and balanced unless the size and structure of consumption are laid down. The planning of consumption necessitates the planning of the wage fund.

136

THE EAST GERMAN ECONOMY

East Germany (German Democratic Republic) has a highly developed industrial economy with the highest per capita income and living standards of all of the Soviet bloc countries. The economy is run by the allocation of resources by administrative decisions rather than by a market mechanism; its operations are governed by a priority system that over the years has given preference to capital goods and military and scientific goods over consumer goods. The key economic questions concerning production and resource allocation are decided by economic planning. Predetermined tasks govern the operations of both industrial and agricultural enterprises. The state, through the economic plan, not only prescribes the objectives to be followed by all economic units but also the success criteria for evaluating performance.

The organization of the East German economy is easy to present. Industry can be divided into four categories: state-owned, semistate-owned, cooperative, and private. The state-owned enterprise is dominant both in terms of the number of persons employed and the value of total output. Private enterprises exist but contribute a small part of total output. They are used for the gratification of many varied consumer needs and for the procurement of foreign exchange. Agriculture, with minor exceptions, is concentrated into two basic production units—the state farm and the collective farm. Trade is primarily controlled by state retail and wholesale units; there is, however, some private ownership of retail stores and various service enterprises, such as restaurants and inns. There are also some self-employed persons in the GDR—artisans, craftsmen, commission brokers, engineers, and so forth.

National Income

National income in the GDR for 1971 was 113.6 billion Ostmarks. As has already been mentioned, the basic concept of socialist national income includes material production only. This can also be called national income produced. Only those industries directly involved in material production are included in national income data. It has also been pointed out that national income may also be viewed from the standpoint of an income flow to all persons and enterprises involved in material production. Finally, national income may be divided into accumulation and consumption. Accumulation is that part of national income that is produced but not consumed during the year in question. It consists of productive and nonproductive investments, stocks of producer and consumer goods, and the balance of trade. National income by this division may be represented by the equation $Y = C + I$ where Y equals national income, C equals consumption, and I equals investment in its broadest sense (accumulation).

Depreciation is excluded, but indirect taxes are included in the equation, so East German national income compares somewhat to the national accounts concept of net national product used in the United States and other Western countries (see Table 5.1).

National income in the East German income accounts is considerably lower than the value of the gross product, which in 1971 was 289.7 billion Ostmarks. The gross product is derived from the sum of total gross outputs of all enterprises belonging to the productive sector of the economy. The difference between gross product of 289.7 billion Ostmarks and national income of 113.6 billion Ostmarks is due to materials used in the production process. The total amount of material expenditures of all productive enterprises includes depreciation and the consumption of materials.

Personal Income

It is to be emphasized that the main difference between national income and personal income in a socialist system of national income accounts lies in the fact that only incomes of individuals and firms generated in the productive sectors—industry, agriculture, and others listed in Table 5.1—are counted in national income, while personal income takes into account income earned in the nonproductive sectors as well. These sectors are education, health, justice, finance, and public administration. These sectors are considered nonproductive, not because they are not useful, but because they don't contribute directly to the creation of material production. Therefore, personal income in a country such as East Germany would consist of wages and salaries of all workers employed in both productive and nonproductive industries, incomes of workers employed on cooperative farms, incomes of self-employed persons and independent entrepreneurs, and income from other sources including, for example, the income from the sale of agricultural products grown on private plots of land. Personal income would also include transfer payments of various types— family allowances, old-age pensions, and other types of direct income transfers. Excluded from personal income are various direct taxes.

The remainder of the chapter is devoted to the determination and distribution of income in East Germany. The first part is concerned with the determination of wages and the types of wage systems used in the GDR. The last part considers the distribution of East German income by income categories. In this respect a similar arrangement to that used in the previous chapters will be adopted, namely, the distribution of income into quintiles, with some comparisons made of average incomes in the highest and lowest quintiles. But this, in itself, is incomplete, for it is also necessary to examine the effect of taxes and transfer payments on personal income. The

TABLE 5.1

Production and Distribution of East German
National Income for 1971
(billions of Ostmarks)

National Income by Productive Sectors		Accumulation and Consumption	
Industry	72.5	Accumulation	25.1
Construction	9.9	Productive	13.2
Agriculture and forestry	12.6	Nonproductive	9.1
Transportation and		Reserves	2.8
communications	6.2	Consumption	88.5
Trade	14.9	Individual	77.6
Other material production	1.9	Collective	10.9
Net product	118.0		
Less: Depreciation	- 4.4	National	
National income	113.6	income	113.6

Source: Staatliche Zentralverwaltung für Statistik, Statistisches Jahrbuch der Deutschen Demokratischen Republik, 1972 (East Berlin: Staatsverlag der Deutschen Demokratischen Republik, 1972), pp. 37-42.

tax-transfer payment system in the GDR follows a pattern similar to other socialist countries in that both account for a relatively large proportion (in relation to capitalist countries) of state revenues and expenditures.

WAGE SYSTEMS

In the socialist economy of East Germany, with its social owner- ship of almost all of the means of production, the role of wages must of necessity be spread out wider than in a country of private entrepre- neurship. Income from employment accounts for by far the bulk of East German household income. Thus it is necessary to examine the control of the formation and distribution of income from employment, that is, of wages and salaries. Outside of the subject of systems re- mains the determination and distribution of income from other sources, such as cooperative farming and private activity. Also outside of the scope of wage determination, although influenced by it, are incomes derived from government transfer payments and other minor sources of income.

The Leistungsprinzip

The basis for the East German wage system is codified in the Gesetzbuch der Arbeit in which the principle of performance (Leistungs- prinzip) is formally recognized as the main determinant of wage pay- ment.[1] Stated simply, the Leistungsprinzip means that wage payments are tied to the quality of work. Differences in wages are based on the quality of work done by each worker. Piecework pay, wage differen- tials, and bonuses to outstanding workers have always been a part of the East German reward system. According to the constitution of the GDR, only work and its results can determine a person's material and social position.[2] Work is a duty and a matter of honor for every able-bodied citizen, in accordance with the principle, "He who does not work, neither shall he eat."

In looking at the wage system in East Germany, it is obvious that considerable reliance is placed upon the use of material incentives to stimulate worker productivity. Wages in East Germany are re- garded as remuneration for work in proportion to its quantity and quality. In addition to wages, bonuses are also used to stimulate worker performance. One result of the economic reforms in East Germany was the tying of enterprise profit to performance. To stimu- late performance, material incentive funds were created for each enterprise and are distributed to the workers on the basis of both individual and collective performances. These bonuses are treated separately from regular income in that they are not subject to income taxation.

Industrial Wages

Wages are set by the government within the framework of the national economic plan. The wage system is based on the total wage funds (Gesamtlohnfonds), which are a part of the national economic plan. The computation of the funds is based on the number of em- ployees of the GDR in one plan year; the average rate of increase intended for the average wage earner is figured according to the planned increase in production and productivity for the planning year.[3]

The total wage fund is partitioned into wage funds for all eco- nomic fields (Wirtschaftsbereich). Important considerations are national economic policies and enlargement or reduction in importance of certain industrial fields. For example, the plan may call for an increase in chemical output and a decrease in mining output. Then the wage fund of the chemical industry will be increased and the wage fund of the mining industry decreased. This influences the manage- ment of both industrial fields; the chemical industry can create new jobs and the mining industry has to reduce them. The wage levels of the two industries are also influenced. In the chemical industry wages will be raised, and in the mining industry they will be lowered. The purpose of this procedure is to redirect the movement of labor to the chemical industry and also to increase worker productivity.

The wage funds for the various economic fields are then divided into funds for the individual firms. The wage fund for a particular firm consists of the following components:[4]

1. The basic wage including payments for overtime;
2. Wages for workers who are not directly involved in the production process;
3. Extra wages based on the difficulty of the work, including payments for night, holiday, and Sunday work; and
4. Additional wages for state holidays, vacations, and participation in public duties.

The unions have little influence upon the development of the wage fund, for procedures are worked out by the state planning commission in the development of the economic plan. The total system of the wage funds is organized from the national level down to the individual firm. This excludes pressure that can be exerted by the unions at the local, county, or district level. The unions can influence the form the wage fund takes at the firm level, particularly with respect to piece rates.

The wage fund actually takes two basic forms—piece wages and time wages. Both are based on work-output indicators (Leistungskennziffern), which include a minimum work effort.[5] Then technically based wage standards (Technisch Begrundete Arbeitsnormen, or TAN) are computed, forming the basis of the wage computation. Fulfillment of the TAN is necessary to receive piece and time wages. The work-output indicators and TAN are the responsibility of enterprise management rather than central authority. In this respect trade unions can have some influence over the wage structure, particularly with respect to piece wages. Usually the unions will attempt to lower output standards so that overfulfillment is made easier.

One characteristic of the wage system in the GDR is the extensive reliance on the use of piece rates. It is estimated that piece-rate payments comprise 50 to 70 percent of the total wages of all industrial workers in East Germany.[6] The merit of the piece-rate system is that it can be used to stimulate worker productivity and to distinguish between good and bad workers. Under this system a base rate is set for performing a given task; for example, workers assembling carburetors in a factory making automobile parts may be paid 1 Ostmark for each carburetor assembled. A slow worker may assemble only 5 carburetors a day, and his wage would accordingly be 5 Ostmarks. An average worker, assembling 8 carburetors a day, would receive 8 Ostmarks, and a superior worker, completing 12, would receive 12 Ostmarks. Each is paid according to his productivity, and the purpose behind this system is to get the workers to produce as large a daily output as possible.

Actually, there are a number of piece-rate arrangements. The arrangement used in East Germany is to establish a normal daily output for the average worker.[7] For example, the average worker may be expected to assemble 5 carburetors a day. The minimum payment is 5 Ostmarks. If a superior worker exceeds the norm, he receives payment in proportion to his productivity in excess of the norm. In addition to the regular piece rate, there is a premium piece rate that is tied to factors other than quantity of output. For example, premium piece rates are paid when output meets special quality requirements. The purpose of the premium piece rate is to prevent concentration on quantity of output at the expense of quality.

The most important element of an East German worker's income is his wage, which is paid from the wage fund of each enterprise.[8] In addition to piece wages and time wages, however, there are also bonuses. In fact, piece rates or time rates plus bonuses cover most industrial wage earners. The rationale of the bonus is to tie personal interests of workers more closely to the interests of production. The bonuses are not paid from the wage funds but from incentive funds that are tied to enterprise earnings. Bonuses may be awarded on the basis of individual or collective performance. Individual bonuses are based on the performance of each worker as measured against other workers, while collective bonuses reward a group of workers as a whole and are divided uniformly among the workers. In East Germany incentive funds have averaged about 4 percent of the wage funds in production firms since they were first introduced in 1967. The bonus has ranged from one-third to twice a worker's monthly wage.[9]

Wage Groups

Wages are determined by government fiat. In the GDR the main state agency responsible for wage determination is the State Office for Work and Wages (Staatlichen Amt fur Arbeit und Lönne). This office is responsible for examining prevailing wage structures and practices within East Germany. It has to approve all collective agreements between unions and management. It participates in the calculation of wages that are a part of the national economic plan, and it is responsible for the classification of workers into wage groups, which are as follows:[10]

1. For production workers, there are eight wage classifications. Classes 1 and 2 are for unskilled and part-time workers; classes 3 and 4 are for semiskilled workers; class 5 is for skilled workers who have passed a special examination but who have no work experience; classes 6 and 7 are for skilled workers with work experience; and class 8 is for workers with extensive specialized knowledge and work experience. Thus East German workers are paid according to a multiple wage-grade scale differentiated according to variations in skill from unskilled to highly skilled workers. There are also wage scales within classes. Wage scales by class are also differentiated

by branch in line with the East German regime's priorities for differential industrial development.

A standard wage payment pattern is used as the basic pay mechanism for both piece- and time-rate workers in various industries. Each worker is classified by class according to skill and function. Overall satisfactory performance entitles the worker to the standard wage rate for his category. Wage differentials between the highest and lowest wage classes vary according to the branch of industry. Industries with high priorities have a wage differential as much as 5 to 1 in standard wage payments. This excludes bonuses, superior work performance, and overtime. Wage differentials within classes are much narrower than between class differentials, averaging around 20 percent for the wage scales.

2. There are also eight wage classifications for white-collar workers. Straight time rates, usually monthly, are paid to workers in the white-collar category. A standard wage for each class is set, which depends upon education, years of service, and other qualifications. There are wage scales within a class.

3. There are five wage classifications for management and members of the scientific and technical intelligentsia. The standard wage payment for each class depends on education and work experience. A college education or its equivalent is a basic requisite. Included in the wage groups would be commercial and technical firm managers, branch managers, managers and assistant managers of laboratories and research branches of a firm, directors of institutes and educational institutions, and any type of person who performs some sort of managerial function.

4. There are four wage classifications for master workers. Included in this category would be electricians, carpenters, construction workers of different skills, and craftsmen of various types.

There are also those workers who would fall outside of the regular classification system. Public service workers have their own wage system, which is set by the state. There are also self-employed persons and workers who are employed by the few remaining private enterprises in the GDR. In this case wages also have to conform to standards set by the state. Wage agreements are concluded between these enterprises and the state.

In total there are twenty-five wage groups into which all workers with the exception of public service employees, self-employed persons, and scattered other workers are classified. The wage system is developed and determined by the state. The German Confederation of Free Trade Unions (Freier Deutscher Gewerkschaftsbund, or FDGB) participates in the administration of wages but has little impact on their actual determination. It can make recommendations, but the decisions made by the State Office for Work and Wages are final and must be followed. There is a reason for central planning and decision-making concerning wages. The economic plan has to

take into consideration all supply and demand factors and regulate
the distribution of wages, investment, and social income. There has
to be a balancing of resources, which is the function of the national
economic plan and its planning organs. Interference over wage matters
on the part of unions would detract from the necessary balancing of
resources.

Agricultural Wages

There is a distinct similarity between agricultural and industrial
wages in the GDR in that both are directly tied to performance standards. The State Norm Commission sets the amount to be paid for the
various kinds of jobs. Minimum yearly work standards are established
at a general meeting of all members of an agricultural unit. Work is
evaluated by various evaluation groups, depending on the type and
responsibility of the job, and is calculated in terms of work units.
The work unit is computed through the use of the following equation:[11]

$$\frac{(\text{actual work performed}) \times (\text{rating factor})}{\text{daily work norm}} = \text{work unit}$$

For example, the weeding of turnips may contain a rating factor of
1.2, the daily work norm may be 2,000 meters of turnips weeded a
day, and the actual work performance may be 3,000 meters of turnips
weeded a day. The work unit would be computed as follows:

$$\frac{3,000 \times 1.2}{2,000} = 1.8 \text{ work units per day}$$

The calculated work units are then adjusted according to the
quality of work. There are three quality standards, which are as
follows:[12]
1. Quality standard 1: not only has the work norm been ful-
   filled, but the quality of work is flawless.
2. Quality standard 2: the work is satisfactory. The quality
   of work is up to 80 percent of perfect performance.
3. Quality standard 3: a generally poor performance in terms
   of the quality of work.
Wages, then, are based on both the quantity and quality of work.
The calculation of wages is as follows:[13]
1. The full wage is paid if the work performance falls within
   quality standard 1.
2. Eighty percent of the full wage is paid if the work performance falls within quality standard 2.
3. Fifty percent of the wage is paid if the work performance
   falls within quality standard 3.

Wages are paid out of the wage funds of agricultural enterprises. In addition, there are bonus funds that are distributed among the workers. These funds have assumed increasing importance during recent years. Bonuses are also based on performance and are distributed as follows:[14]

1. A type 1 bonus pays up to 60 percent per 100 work units and up to 40 percent of land shares.
2. A type 2 bonus ranges up to 70 percent per 100 work units and up to 40 percent of land shares.
3. A type 3 bonus amounts to at least 80 percent per 100 work units and up to 20 percent of land shares.

Income Differentials

Income differentials in the GDR exist to a considerable degree. Although, from an ideological standpoint, the East German regime would like to see productivity and economic growth based on the revolutionary fervor and enthusiasm of the masses, from a practical standpoint it finds it necessary to rely upon traditional methods of motivation.

Income differentials primarily take the form of wages. There are wage differentials based upon skills. As has been pointed out previously, there are eight skill grades for industrial workers, which are differentiated according to variations in skill from unskilled to highly skilled. The use of piece rates and bonuses also automatically causes considerable variations in earnings among workers, even in the same grade. Income disparities tend to be accentuated by the new role of material incentives. Salary differentials based on the skill requirements and complexity of the job and the importance of the industry relative to the national economy exist for white-collar workers, engineers, and managers. As one would expect, average wages are higher in those industries where higher skills are required and work is difficult. Hazardous work commands a higher premium than less arduous work.

It is difficult to be specific about the exact extent of wage differentials in the GDR. There is obviously a considerable disparity between high and low incomes. One indication of this disparity is revealed in the scale of union membership dues. For one thing, union dues range from 0.5 Ostmarks on monthly incomes of 100 Ostmarks or less to 35 Ostmarks on incomes of 2,600 Ostmarks or more.[15] This would indicate a minimum wage disparity of at least 26 to 1. The lower and upper ranges of monthly income, however, may represent extreme situations, as, for example, the minimum monthly wage was 300 Ostmarks a month in 1970 and was raised to 350 Ostmarks a month in 1971. Unquestionably, income disparity is also reduced by taxes and transfer payments that redistribute income from one group to another. The extent of the redistribution may well

145

be overrated, however, for the reason that the GDR relies extensively on consumption taxes. Moreover, there are certain privileges, expressed in nonmonetary terms, that redound to the advantage of the party elite, professional workers such as managers and engineers, and members of the intelligentsia. For example, special priorities are given for housing, automobiles, and travel.

Another measure of income differentials can be obtained by using the range of incomes subject to income taxation. The income tax in the GDR starts at a base yearly income of 1,200 Ostmarks and ends at a flat rate of 90 percent on yearly incomes of 500,000 Ostmarks or more.[16] This only indicates a range of incomes, however, and tells nothing about the actual distribution of incomes within income classes. The range does indicate that a wide latitude in earnings potential exists. It is certainly true that successful enterprise managers and professional people and persons with special skills in short supply do earn large incomes in the GDR. The income tax range indicates that an income differential of at least 20 to 1 is probable.

Average monthly incomes by industrial classification also indicate wage variations. These averages do not show the difference between the highest and lowest wage in each industrial field, however, nor do they reflect the effect of bonuses on income. These bonuses may vary considerably from worker to worker and from one industry to another. Table 5.2 presents the average monthly income for industrial fields in the GDR for 1971.

It is obvious, then, that the socialist system of the GDR has not succeeded in eliminating the privileged class, nor have any moves been made to equalize all wages and salaries effectively. To the contrary, an elite group consisting of the intelligentsia, scientists and technicians, and highly placed party members enjoys a very high standard of living. The difference between the income of the average worker and that of someone in the privileged strata is striking and is enlarged by special contributions from the state, including such special benefits as private villas and personal limousines (also a common practice in other socialist countries). In spite of such subsidies as extremely low rents and utility costs, the wages of the typical worker are insufficient to enable him to afford many of the consumer durable products that are taken for granted by his industrial counterpart in West Germany.

This situation is changed, however, when the income amounts to several times the average wage, as would be the case for middle-echelon party and state functionaries, engineers, plant managers, and scientists, who frequently have a take-home pay of between 2,000 and 4,000 Ostmarks a month. These individuals also enjoy special economic advantages over lower-income workers, such as being able to take their leaves in cheaper vacation homes and being able to shop

TABLE 5.2

Average Monthly Incomes for Industrial Groups, East Germany, 1971
(Ostmarks)

Industrial Groups	Average Monthly Incomes*
Energy and fuels	848
Chemicals	821
Metallurgy	892
Building materials	793
Machinery	828
Electronics and instruments	825
Light industry	691
Textile	648
Food	741
Average	796

*The average is for all industrial workers.

Source: Staatliche Zentralverwaltung für Statistik, Statistisches Jahrbuch der Deutschen Demokratischen Republik, 1972 (East Berlin: Staatsverlag der DDR, 1972), p. 140.

in special stores. Such bonuses, which are not apparent in the actual salaries, result in increasing the standard of living of such persons to a level far beyond that of the average worker.

Moreover, there is a category of wage earners in the GDR whose incomes are at least ten times that of the average worker. For these persons, the state introduced in 1952 so-called individual contracts, which were to be concluded primarily with scientists, artists, and other persons who possessed special talents.[17] In part these individual contracts were designed to keep persons with the talents needed by the state from fleeing to West Germany. When the decree was issued, an average number of fifty individual contracts with salaries ranging between 7,000 and 15,000 Ostmarks a month and an average number of twenty individual contracts with salaries of more than 15,000 Ostmarks a month were to be issued each year.[18] Since 1952 there has been an increase in the number of contracts as well as in the amount of the salaries granted.

In addition to their exceptionally high salaries, selected persons also receive premiums and special awards that provide additional income. Walter Ulbricht, former chairman of the SED, has been awarded one Lenin Order, two Karl Marx orders, three Hero of Work titles, and various other awards. The Lenin Order included an award of 10,000 rubles, each Karl Marx Order carried a gift of 100,000 Ostmarks, and each Hero of Work award amounted to 10,000 Ostmarks.[19] The National Prize First Class, valued at 25,000 Ostmarks, is granted to various scientists, actors, and writers. Writers, actors, engineers, and scientists are therefore able to increase their incomes considerably. Long-time members of the SED can also be counted among the elite class of East Germany. Not only do they frequently receive two or three times the normal pensions, but they are also given special awards that range from 1,000 to 25,000 Ostmarks.

It should be pointed out, however, that the education system in the GDR does provide considerable upward mobility for any talented person. The SED and the state have both provided substantial incentives for those persons who are capable of attending universities or technical colleges. A new elite social group has been created that consists of the managers and technicians who run the state enterprises. This group is a product of the educational system. Thus it can be said that to a considerable extent income differentials are based on merit and performance in the GDR.

General education in the GDR is free and obligatory. It begins at the age of six and is based on a ten-year polytechnical school system. From the general educational system the student may elect, if he is qualified, to proceed to further schooling. The majority of students go on to vocational schools; the remainder go on to universities and technical schools. Professional and social advancement is the end result of a university education. Career-oriented subjects, particularly the applied sciences, are emphasized as opposed to the liberal arts "frill" subjects in vogue in many Western universities. As is true in other aspects of East German life, the performance principle underlies the system of education, with monetary incentives being directly tied to performance in the classroom.

THE EFFECT OF TAXES AND TRANSFER
PAYMENTS ON INCOME DISTRIBUTION

Wages and other types of income payments constitute only one side of the coin as far as income distribution is concerned, for the state can add to the income of some citizens through transfer payments and reduce the income of others through taxation. The mechanism for the redistribution of national income is the East German state budget. The state budget governs a much wider area of activity in East Germany than is governed in the United States or other capitalist countries by the national budgets. About 70 percent of the East German national income passes through the state budget in the form of receipts and expenditures. The state budget is the financial cornerstone of the national economic plan in that it provides the finances for the bulk of the financial and social tasks expressed in the plan. The almost all-inclusive functioning of the East German state is thus naturally reflected in the extensive area covered by its budget.

The East German Tax System

Given the magnitude of the East German state budget, it would stand to reason that taxes would have to be utilized to provide the basic source of revenue. However, taxes are levied not only to provide needed revenue, but also to help accomplish political and social goals of far wider importance than mere fiscal objectives. The use of personal income taxes is an example. In East Germany, as in other socialist countries, material incentives play a very important role in stimulating worker productivity. It is felt that a truly progressive income tax would have a more negative impact on work incentives than indirect taxes. An indirect tax, such as a sales tax, is more invisible than the income tax and would not have the effect of reducing the take-home pay of the worker. So for the great majority of East German income earners, the personal income tax is less progressive than income taxes in Sweden or the United States are on their income counterparts.

Total government revenues in the GDR are obtained from several sources—deductions from profits, which is not considered a profits tax but is regarded as a form of deduction from the surplus product created in the state sector by state enterprises, turnover taxes, income taxes, and various other taxes, including excise taxes on tobacco and alcohol and property taxes. State enterprises provide the bulk of the receipts to the state budget. This is understandable since the state is the owner of the enterprises and contributes to their support out of the state budget. Thus it is necessary to examine taxes and levies that would have more effect on income earners. Included in this category are the turnover tax, the personal income tax, and social security contributions.

The Turnover Tax

The turnover tax (Umsatzsteuer) is the most important source of tax revenue in the state budget. The tax represents the difference between the total cost of production of a commodity and the price it brings as an article of general expenditures on the market. It represents a firmly fixed portion of the price and is delivered to the state budget in accordance with sales of goods on which the tax is levied. The tax is collected by wholesalers, retailers, individual enterprises, and procurement organizations dealing with consumer goods and foodstuffs. As a rule the following procedure is used: If enterprises making goods subject to the tax sell them directly to buyers or to trade organizations, then the turnover tax is paid by the enterprises themselves according to the place of production of such goods; if, however, goods are sold through wholesale organizations, then the turnover tax is paid by the latter at the place of sale of the goods. The burden of the tax ultimately falls on the East German consumer, so that it can be considered to represent a part of the flow of funds between the state and households.

The turnover tax is in actuality a broad-based sales tax, since it applies, on a gross basis, to all transactions through which a tangible economic good passes. The basic rate of the turnover tax is 3 percent.[20] This rate is levied on the retail price of most consumer products. Rates in excess of 4 percent are levied on products that have an inelastic demand schedule—beer, cosmetics, tobacco, and articles made of precious metals. A minimum rate of 1.5 percent is levied on the retail price of basic foodstuffs.[21] The tax is complex, and rates vary from city to city and region to region. The rates may be expressed as an absolute sum per unit of a commodity, as a percentage of the full retail sales price of a commodity, or as a difference between retail sales less the retail markup and the enterprise wholesale price.

In its basic features the turnover tax bears some resemblance to a value-added tax, and as such would have some influence on the distribution of income in East Germany. This is true because of its regressivity to income as a tax base. Since the marginal and average propensities to consume tend to be lower at higher income levels, the purchase of items subject to the turnover tax is ordinarily a smaller proportion of the higher incomes. It also should be remembered that the turnover tax is a "cascade" tax. the amount getting larger as the number of transactions increases. Therefore, the final market price of consumer goods could contain a number of turnover taxes.

Income Taxation

Unlike most socialist countries, East Germany places considerable reliance on income taxation as a source of revenue. The personal income tax is levied on the following sources: wages of individuals, income from agriculture or forestry, capital income, income from independent work, and income of small businesses.[22] Certain income is exempt from taxation, including social security payments, welfare payments, stipends for students paid from public sources, and payments to "fighters against fascism." There are also special forms of income exemptions. National prizes and awards are exempt from taxation. Interest on savings accounts and on the bonds of the local and national governments is also exempt. Maternity payments and special benefits are not taxed.

In addition to personal exemptions there are deductions for various types of expenses.[23] Debt interest is deductible. Other deductions include property taxes, fees for professional associations, expenditures for travel between the home and the job, expenses for professional improvement, and expenses for tools and working clothes. Family deductions are also permitted. There are deductions of 300 Ostmarks for each child and 500 Ostmarks for the spouse. Support of parents is also deductible, provided that they are unable to work. Special provisions are also made for older workers. A man is entitled to a special deduction of 120 Ostmarks a year if he is 64 years or over, and a woman is entitled to the same deduction if she is 49 years or over. All of the family deductions are permitted only for taxpayers whose incomes are less than 20,000 Ostmarks a year.

The income tax is progressive, the rates depending on the source and size of income. Discriminatory rates are so designed as to inhibit the accumulation of excessive profits by nonstate enterprises and to prevent private enrichment. The degree of tax progression on incomes earned by free professionals, that is, individuals not directly employed by state enterprises, is markedly greater than the progression on the income of wage and salary earners. For example, the tax schedule for certain occupational groups, including lawyers, artisans, engineers, architects, commercial artists, advertising experts, and other freelance operators, was amended in 1971 through the introduction of a progressive tax scale starting with an income of more than 20,000 Ostmarks a year up to a maximum rate of 60 percent.[24] The existing tax system is maintained for all freelance individuals with an income of up to 20,000 Ostmarks per year. The degree of progression is actually much greater for private craftsmen and entrepreneurs, extending to 90 percent of incomes in excess of 500,000 Ostmarks a year.[25] Personal income taxes are also levied on farmers selling privately grown produce directly to consumers and on the private owners of buildings, rooms, and equipment.

The discussion of the East German income tax rate structure can be enhanced by comparing the average and marginal rates of tax. The average tax rate is computed by dividing the tax liability by the tax base. The marginal tax rate is computed by dividing the change in total tax liability by the change in the total tax base. If the tax rate structure is proportionate, the marginal rate must be equal to the average rate as the tax base increases in size. If the tax rate structure is progressive, the marginal rate must be higher than the average rate as the tax increases. If the tax rate structure is regressive, the marginal rate must be less than the average rate as the tax base increases. In Table 5.3 the marginal and average rates for single persons and married persons with one child are compared.

Social Insurance Taxes

Taxes to finance the East German social security system are levied as a percentage of wages and salaries. The revenue is paid into a state social insurance budget, which is consolidated with the state budget. Disbursement of social insurance funds is the responsibility of the trade unions. The financing of the social insurance system is as follows:[26]

1. Old-age pensions, health care, and maternity benefits are financed by a tax of 10 percent of earnings up to 600 Ostmarks a month on the workers and a payroll tax of 10 percent on employers. Self-employed persons pay a tax of 14 percent of monthly earnings up to 600 Ostmarks a month, and mining enterprises pay a payroll tax of 20 percent. There are special tax rates for members of co-operatives. Any deficit is supported by funds from the state budget.

2. Work-injury and unemployment compensation are financed by a tax on payrolls of employers, which range from 0.3 to 3 percent a month. Maximum earnings upon which contributions are based amount to 600 Ostmarks a month. Any deficit is supported by funds from the state budget.

3. Family allowances are financed entirely from the funds of the state budget. There are no contributions from employers and employees.

It is significant to note that a major part of social insurance expenditures in East Germany are financed out of the general tax revenues of the state budget. The apportionment of these expenditures, however, varies for the different types of social welfare service. The cost of the family allowance is borne entirely by the state out of general tax revenues. Old-age pensions and sickness insurance benefits are financed by employee and employer contributions, with the state making up any deficit. Unemployment compensation is financed by employers, with the state financing any deficit.

Social Insurance

The social insurance system in East Germany provides benefits in money and kind to augment the wages of industrial and agricultural

TABLE 5.3

Comparison of Marginal and Average Income Tax Rates, East Germany
(percent)

Monthly Income (Ostmarks)	Single Person		Married with One Child		Married with Three Children	
	Marginal	Average	Marginal	Average	Marginal	Average
400- 500	24.0	9.5	20.0	4.5	15.0	0.8
500- 600	30.0	12.4	24.0	7.6	20.0	3.6
600- 700	34.0	15.3	30.0	10.3	24.0	6.3
700- 800	22.5	18.0	34.0	13.1	30.0	8.9
800- 900	22.5	18.6	22.5	15.8	34.0	11.5
900-1,000	22.5	19.0	22.5	16.5	22.5	14.0
1,000-1,260	22.5	19.4	22.5	17.1	22.5	14.9
1,260-1,500	20.0	20.0	21.0	18.2	22.1	16.4
1,500-2,000	20.0	20.0	20.0	18.7	20.0	17.3
2,000-3,000	20.0	20.0	20.0	19.0	20.0	18.0
3,000-4,000	20.0	20.0	20.0	19.3	20.0	18.7

Source: Deutscher Bundestag, Materialen zum Bericht zur Lage der Nation 1971 (Bonn-Bad Godesberg: Dr. Hans Heger Verlag, 1971), pp. 338-339.

workers. Under its provisions, workers are covered for sickness, injury, and disability; death and maternity; retirement; and miscellaneous other benefits. The system is contributory, with workers and employers contributing a fixed percentage of earnings and payrolls for the various social insurance categories. The state finances deficits out of general budgetary revenues. The social insurance funds are administered by the trade union organizations and, in some cases, by insurance agencies of the state. There is a built-in incentive element in the social insurance system in that most benefits are graded according to wages. There are also negative incentives in that eligible workers who are not members of trade unions usually receive lower benefits during sickness and old age. The purpose is to keep the number of nonunion members low.

A series of social security reforms occurred in the spring of 1968.[27] These reforms concerned all forms of payments made under social security laws. Minimum social security benefits were raised, and changes were made in voluntary supplementary social security contributions. Benefits were set at a minimum of 150 Ostmarks a month, including cost-of-living supplements. Old-age pensions were increased by 21 Ostmarks a month and widows' pensions by 31 Ostmarks a month. Additional changes were made in other types of benefits in an effort to raise the amounts paid to some groups up to a national average.

The GDR actually has several social security organizational arrangements. In this respect it is somewhat similar to France and other European countries in that it is fragmented in terms of its operation. There is the social security system proper, which is administered by the trade unions and which covers the vast majority of white- and blue-collar workers. There is also a national insurance organization, which covers the self-employed and small-scale private enterprises with five or fewer employees. In addition, there are several special social security groups, such as the ones for the people's police, customs administration, employees of the state railways, and the postal service. Additional old-age pensions and other benefits are given to the academic intelligentsia, artists, scientists, engineers, and members of medical establishments through insurance contracts with the national insurance organization of the GDR.

The social security system is financed by employer and employee contributions of 10 percent on payrolls and earnings up to 600 Ostmarks a month. These rates, as of 1972, had been unchanged for a period of twenty-two years. Self-employed persons pay a rate of 14 percent and members of collective farms (Landwirtschaftliche Produktionsgenossenschaft or LPG) contribute 9 percent. The share of state funds necessary to finance the difference between contributions and expenses was estimated to be around 50 percent in 1969.

In this connection it is necessary to point out that family allowances are financed out of general state revenues. The framework of benefits payable in the East German social insurance system is outlined below.28

Old-Age and Invalidity Benefits

Old-age pensions are provided to males 65 and over and females 60 and over. Miners are allowed to draw pensions at the age of 50. Workers must be insured for a minimum of fifteen years to draw a full pension. The amount of the pension is calculated by multiplying 1 percent of average monthly earnings times years of insurance, plus 30 Ostmarks a month. There are dependents' supplements, which amount to 39 Ostmarks a month for the surviving spouse and 40 Ostmarks a month for each child under the age of 15. Disabled workers receive 1 percent of average monthly earnings times years of insurance, plus 30 Ostmarks a month. There are also dependents' supplements of 39 Ostmarks a month for a spouse of 60 years or over, or one who is caring for small children, and 40 Ostmarks a month for each child under 15. In the event of accidental death there is a widow's pension which amounts to 60 percent of the base pension of the insured. There are also orphans' pensions, which amount to 25 percent of the base pension of the insured for each person under 15. Maximum survivors' pensions can amount to 100 percent of the pension of the insured. A lump sum payment of twenty days' earnings is available for funeral expenses.

Sickness and Maternity Benefits

Sickness benefits involve the cost of medical expenses and the payment of an allowance to compensate for the loss of earnings during the period of illness. Persons covered by sickness benefits are reimbursed for the cost of hospitalization and drugs and the fees of physicians. Sickness benefits amount to 50 percent of average earnings for the calendar year, payable from the first day of confinement and extending for six weeks. This base payment continues for 39 weeks; however, after the six weeks additional payments are provided for dependent children. Workers with two or more children receive from 65 to 90 percent of average earnings for the calendar year for the seventh to thirteenth week of confinement. Benefits are paid up to the thirty-ninth week of confinement, but only if recovery is assured. Medical benefits, including general and specialist care, hospital and laboratory services, and appliances, are also covered under the social insurance system.

155

Maternity benefits are available to all women covered by social insurance proper; they are to be distinguished from other maternity benefits that are a part of the system of family allowances and are paid to all women after a pregnancy. Maternity benefits for women covered by the social insurance system include coverage of all medical expenses plus payment of all or part of earnings lost as a result of pregnancy. Working women are entitled to 100 percent of earnings for six weeks before birth and eight weeks after birth. Nonworking women receive lesser amounts that are based on the extent of social insurance contributions. Nursing mothers receive 10 Ostmarks a week additional assistance for a period of six months. Moreover, there is additional financial support based on the number of children in the family. For example, two children would provide a lump sum grant of 600 Ostmarks for home care.

Employment-Injury Benefits

The third facet of the East German social insurance system consists of a program designed to provide care for the victims of industrial accidents or occupational disease. The coverage of this program extends to all employed persons. Four types of benefits are provided for those eligible under the program—payments for medical care, allowances in lieu of wages for temporary disability, pensions in the event of permanent disability, and annuities for the dependents of the victim of a fatal accident. All medical expenses incurred as a result of work injury are covered. Temporary disability benefits are similar to sickness benefits. Pensions for permanent disability amount to two-thirds of average monthly earnings for a calendar year, plus supplements for children of 10 percent of the pension. For partial disability, pensions are prorated on the basis of loss of work capacity. Widows and other dependents of workers killed in an accident receive survivors' pensions that range from 40 percent to 100 percent of the earnings of the insured.

Unemployment Compensation

Unemployment compensation is similar to employment-injury compensation in terms of financing. Each is financed by a payroll tax on employers. On an a priori basis it can be concluded that the rate of unemployment in the GDR is extremely low. In the past it was generally assumed that the only unemployment that can be tolerated is of the frictional type, which, owing to economic planning, should not exceed 1 percent of the total work force. In recent years, however, economists have argued that optimal employment is below maximum employment, as the latter may in fact lead to lower national income. Unemployment benefits in the GDR amount to 10 percent of earnings, based on 26 weeks of coverage during the last 12 months before unemployment. There are also supplements for dependents. Benefits are payable after a seven-day waiting period for a period up to 26 weeks.

Family Allowances

The family allowance system differs from other social insurance programs in that the benefits do not depend upon the actual wage or salary of the worker, and all benefits are in the form of cash payments. Family allowances consist of a monthly cash payment to each family with dependent children. The monthly payment is 20 Ostmarks a month for the first and second child, 50 Ostmarks for the third, 60 Ostmarks for the fourth, and 70 Ostmarks for the fifth and subsequent children. The allowance is limited to children under 15 and to students. In addition to the family allowance there are birth grants that rise progressively from 500 Ostmarks for the first birth to 1,000 Ostmarks for the fifth and subsequent births.

Other Welfare Expenditures

The welfare expenditures referred to above are all made within the framework of the East German social insurance system. In addition to these expenditures, however, there are several other types of expenditures for welfare purposes that are financed out of budgetary expenditures. Housing subsidies are provided for families with low fixed incomes. Welfare and charitable expenditures are made by local governments for such things as aid to the aged and infirm, medical care for the insane, and aid to children. In general such assistance is directed to persons who, for one reason or another, are not eligible for benefits or assistance under the existing social security programs. There are also a variety of forms of assistance to war victims and "fighters against fascism" and their dependents. These include not only special pensions but such things as medical care, homes for the aged and disabled, financial aid for vocational training, scholarships, and the care of war orphans.

The magnitude and composition of the items coming under the category of social security and other social welfare measures reflects the tremendous social service functions of the East German state. Social security expenditures provide for payments for persons unable to work because of illness, accident, or related causes; for funeral expenses; and for maintenance of sanatoria, rest homes, and so on. Then there are various expenditures of a social and cultural type that would cover the cost of museums, expositions, theatres, and orchestras. All of these benefits, which are difficult to measure in monetary terms, would add to both the real income and the psychic income of East German workers. However, the benefits are not free of cost, as might be supposed, for in the final analysis someone has to pay for them. The someone is the consumer of the services.

INCOME DISTRIBUTION IN EAST GERMANY

Data on income distribution in East Germany must be carefully defined. First, the persons included in Table 5.4, on household incomes, are all blue- and white-collar workers employed in state enterprises, administrative organs, producer cooperatives, trade organizations, and as independently employed professionals. Second, the data involve average monthly wages, which include all amounts paid from wage funds and bonuses from enterprise bonus funds. Excluded from the latter category is income in the form of special bonuses and rewards. Third, the data include some transfer payments, in particular the family allowance, but is net before income taxes. In other words, the data presented in Table 5.4 involve household personal income before taxes. Personal income includes wages and salaries, family allowances, bonuses not related to plan fulfillment, pensions, and special payments for overtime or night work.

There are also other problems involved in the use of East German income data. For one thing, there are certain privileges that redound to the advantage of certain groups—the party elite, professional workers such as managers and engineers, and some highly skilled workers—that are difficult to qualify in money terms. These groups, to whom John Dornberg refers in his book on Russia as the "New Tsars,"[29] are characteristic of other socialist countries. It is also necessary to point out that certain income is excluded from the table. For example, income of individual entrepreneurs is excluded. Income from various other sources, interest, rent, and the sale of agricultural produce grown on private plots, is also excluded. It is logical to assume that the table may well understate incomes in the upper-income groups.

One factor that has had an effect on income distribution in East Germany is the large percentage of women in the labor force. The fact that East Germany has one of the lowest birth rates in Europe, coupled with a labor shortage, has forced the state to recruit, as a matter of public policy, as many women as possible for work. Just under one-half (46 percent) of the labor force is comprised of women. In particular, the percentage of married women in the labor force is quite high (80 percent). There is some variation by income groups, with women working in 92.3 percent of the lowest-income households, compared to 76.3 percent in the highest-income households.[30]

TABLE 5.4

Distribution of Household Monthly Income in East Germany for Selected Years (in percent)

Incomes (in Ostmarks)	1960	1967	1970
0 and under 400	10.4	4.9	3.1
400 and under 600	23.8	16.0	11.9
600 and under 800	25.2	19.1	14.3
800 and under 1,000	21.9	24.1	19.0
1,000 and under 1,200	10.8	19.8	22.0
1,200 and under 1,500	5.6	11.6	19.2
1,500 and over	2.4	4.5	10.6
Total	100.0	100.0	100.0

Source: Staatliche Zentralverwaltung für Statistik, Statistisches Jahrbuch der DDR (Berlin: Staatsverlag der DDR, 1972), p. 360.

This distribution of income may also be divided into quintiles for the years 1960, 1967, and 1970. The results obtained from Table 5.4 are presented in Table 5.5. It is necessary to point out that there is some difficulty in making comparisons between the GDR and other countries. For one thing, the table is applicable to wage and salary earners. Incomes of self-employed persons, persons working on co-operatives, and individual entrepreneurs are excluded, as are incomes in the form of premiums and special rewards.

Based on available data, using the Gini index of equality, it would appear that income distribution is more equal in East Germany than in the other countries used in this study. There is, however, a wide disparity between the incomes of scientists, technicians, and members of the intelligentsia on one hand, and unskilled workers and collective farmers on the other. The increased role recently assigned to material incentives also militates against the socialist egalitarian principle. Nevertheless, there are not the extremes in incomes that prevail in a country such as the United States. Efforts are constantly made to improve the position of the unskilled worker through minimum wages and through education and vocational training. A shortage of labor has also contributed to the uplifting of wages of the least skilled workers.

TABLE 5.5

A Comparison of Distribution of Net Income
by Quintiles for East German Households,
1960, 1967, and 1970
(in percent)

Quintiles	1960	1967	1970
First Quintile	10.4	10.7	10.4
Second Quintile	15.3	15.9	15.8
Third Quintile	19.2	20.0	19.8
Fourth Quintile	23.4	22.9	23.3
Fifth Quintile	31.7	30.5	30.7
Total	100.0	100.0	100.0
Gini coefficient for 1960	.2008		
Gini coefficient for 1967	.1864		
Gini coefficient for 1970	.1924		

Source: Calculations made by the Deutsches Institut für Wirtschaftsforschung of Berlin and by the author.

Taxes and Transfer Payments

Wage payments constitute only one side of the coin as far as income distribution is concerned. Taxes and income transfers alter the initial distribution of income. In East Germany both taxes and transfers have a redistributive effect on income distribution. Then, too, it is important to point out that the price structure in East Germany, particularly for food and basic services, is maintained at a low level to favor low-income consumers. The use of subsidies to maintain low prices for certain foodstuffs, transportation, and services is common. The prices charged by the state to consumers bear little relationship to the different production costs or the procurement prices paid to farms. Many consumer goods are priced below costs, but, on the other hand, prices for such luxury items as coffee and fruit are maintained at high levels. Price subsidies are a factor to consider when income distribution is examined.

Table 5.6 gives a very rough idea of the total effect of taxes and transfer payments upon income distribution. The table presents the average monthly income for white- and blue-collar workers in East Germany from all sources for 1970. There is no available data for various income groups that permits an analysis of the effects of taxes and transfers on each group.

TABLE 5.6

Real Income of White-Collar and Blue-Collar Workers in East Germany for 1970
(in Ostmarks)

Gross work income	1,095
Money income	1,076
Other income	
From social funds	389
Health and social welfare	146
Sick pay	22
Pensions	32
Children's allowances	32
Education and culture	146
Housing	21
Banks, insurance	27
Nonmonetary services	49
Gross yield—total	1,484
Gross monetary yield	1,208
minus: deductions	158
Wage taxes	82
Social security contributions	76
Usable real income	1,326
Net money income	1,050
minus: other taxes	64
savings	64
Consumption	1,198

Source: Staatliche Zentralverwaltung für Statistik, Statistisches Jahrbuch der DDR 1972 (Berlin: Staatsverlag der DDR, 1972), p. 364.

The personal income tax is levied on individuals in the form of wages and salaries or from self-employment. A separate scale of tax rates is established for various occupational groups, with workers directly employed by state enterprises favored with lower rates than self-employed persons and persons who receive an independent income from private employment. The rates of the personal income tax, at least as they apply to the vast majority of income recipients, are more proportional than progressive. Moreover, they reach down to the lower income levels, so that it would appear that few persons avoid paying at least some income taxes. The social security tax is also paid by the workers and is levied at a flat rate on monthly incomes up to 600 Ostmarks. This rate is also differentiated on the basis of occupational categories. When the personal income and social security taxes are combined, it is possible to get some idea of the burden of direct taxes in the GDR. It is necessary, however, to make the following observations.

First, the actual burden of the income tax is far less than the rates would indicate. Although it is true that the rates begin at a rather low level of income, there are many deductions and exemptions that reduce the size of the tax base. It is also true that certain income, that is, prizes and pensions, are also free from taxation or taxed at reduced rates.

Second, social security taxes are set at proportional rates and stop when a certain level of income is reached. Incomes above the level of 600 Ostmarks a month are not subject to a tax. This means that a considerable part of total income is untaxed. Moreover, as incomes have risen, the amount not subject to the tax has also increased.

There is strong presumption that the incidence of indirect taxation is primarily on the consumer. Although it has been argued that the turnover tax is derived from the surplus product created in the state sector of production and does not come from personal income, and is thus not a tax, the generally accepted view is that it is a tax that does indeed fall on the consumer. This is so because the consumer will pay for a particular quantity of a commodity a price that is higher by the amount of the tax than he would pay for the same quantity in the absence of the tax.

The turnover tax is the most important source of tax revenue in the East German state budget, accounting for around two-thirds of revenue. It can be said that the state depends upon indirect taxation not only for the bulk of general expenditures but a considerable part of welfare expenditures as well. Although no simple statement about the relationship of the turnover tax to the redistribution of income is possible, the implication is fairly clear. There is at best a very limited vertical redistribution of income between social and economic classes in the GDR. Whatever progressivity there is in direct taxation is counterbalanced by the turnover tax. With respect to social welfare payments, which are financed to a large extent out of general budgetary revenues, a considerable part of the real cost of these payments is borne, in the final analysis, by those who benefit by them.

SUMMARY

Income distribution in the GDR takes primarily the form of wages, which are regarded as a part of the social product, the distribution of which is the business of the state. The basis for distribution is performance. For the worker's work and his wages, the basic socialist principle holds good: "From each according to his ability, to each according to his performance." This means that there is considerable difference in incomes among workers, which tends to be accentuated by the important role assigned to the use of material incentives. The purpose of material incentives is to provide a further stimulus to output. The incentives are tied closely to the performance of enterprises as measured in terms of profits. A part of profits is channeled into a material incentives fund, from which bonuses are paid to workers to reward them for performance. Thus profits and bonuses are tied together; the larger the one, the larger the other.

The tax-transfer payment system in the GDR follows a pattern similar to other socialist countries. Income and social security taxes, however, account for a larger proportion of state revenue than is usually the case. Nevertheless, the turnover tax is the single most important source of state tax revenue. Transfer payments are distributed primarily through the social security system, which has as its objective to guarantee all citizens some minimum standard of material well-being. Compulsory insurance against sickness, accident, and old age is normally extended to cover all workers, all self-employed persons who do not employ more than five workers, members of co-operatives, and special categories of professional persons. Responsibility for the administration of social security benefits for the masses of industrial workers falls on the unions affiliated with the FDGB, while the National Insurance Institution is responsible for the insurance of self-employed persons and business and professional men.

NOTES

1. Gesetzbuch der Arbeit der Deutschen Demokratischen Republik (East Berlin: Staatsverlag der DDR, 1969), pp. 37-39.
2. Verfassung der Deutschen Demokratischen Republik (Berlin: Staatsverlag der DDR, 1968), p. 17.
3. Löhne, Preise, Gewerkschaftsrechte, Vergleiche Zwischen Beiden Deutschen Staaten (Bonn: Neue Gesellschaft Verlag, 1971), p. 14.
4. Ibid., pp. 14-15.
5. Ibid., p. 15.
6. Deutscher Bundestag, Materialien zum Bericht zur Lage der Nation 1971, Drucksache VI/1690 (Bonn-Bad Godesberg: Dr. Hans Heger Verlag, 1971), p. 89.
7. Löhne, Preise, Gewerkschaftsrechte, p. 16.
8. Ibid., p. 27.
9. Ibid., p. 28
10. Ibid., pp. 17-19.
11. H. Jorg Thieme, Die Sozialistische Agrarverfassung (Stuttgart: Gustav Fischer Verlag, 1969), p. 62.

12. Ibid., p. 62.

13. Ibid., p. 63.

14. Ibid., p. 64.

15. Satzung des Freien Deutschen Gewerkschaftsbundes, 1968, p. 32.

16. Gesetzblatt Der Deutschen Demokratischen Republik, Einkommensteuergesetz, Sonderdruck Nr. 670 (East Berlin, Staatsverlag der DDR, December 15, 1970), p. 368.

17. Dorothy Miller, "The Upper Ten Thousand in the GDR," Radio Free Europe (Munich, October 1969), p. 1. (Unpublished paper.)

18. Ibid., p. 2.

19. Ibid., p. 3.

20. Gesetzblatt der Deutschen Demokratischen Republik, Umsatzsteuergesetz, Sonderdruck Nr. 673 (East Berlin: Staatsverlag der DDR, November 2, 1970), p. 2.

21. Ibid., p. 3.

22. Einkommensteuergesetz, op. cit., p. 4.

23. Ibid., p. 12.

24. Gesetzblatt der Deutschen Demokratischen Republik, I, 23 (East Berlin: Staatsverlag der DDR, December 15, 1970), p. 368.

25. Einkommensteuergesetz, op. cit., p. 4.

26. Materialien zum Bericht zur Lage der Nation 1971, op. cit., pp. 122-131.

27. Ibid., p. 141.

28. Bundesministerium für Gesamtdeutsche Fragen, Zahlenspiegel, Ein Vergleich, BRD-GDR (Bonn, 1970), pp. 39-41.

29. John Dornberg, The New Tsars: Russia Under Stalin's Heirs (Garden City: Doubleday & Co., Inc., 1972).

30. Staatliche Zentralverwaltung für Statistik, Statistisches Jahrbuch der DDR (Berlin: Staatsverlag der DDR, 1972), p. 362.

6

INCOME DISTRIBUTION
IN THE UNITED KINGDOM

The year 1945 is often represented as a line of demarcation in British history. The welfare state, as the phrase has come to be used, stems from the victory of the Labour Party in the general election of that year. The phrase is really tied to the publication of the Beveridge Report of 1942 and is roughly descriptive of government activities that are redistributive in character. The welfare state developed in the United Kingdom partly as a result of the deprivations sustained during World War II and partly as a remembrance of prewar British capitalism, in particular the high rate of unemployment and excessive and widespread inequalities in the distribution of wealth and income. In 1924, for example, two-thirds of the total wealth in the United Kingdom was owned by 1.6 percent of all wealth-owners.[1] Also, the United Kingdom, being one of the older capitalistic countries, had had more time for the institution of inheritance to do its work.

The modern British social welfare system began with the Beveridge Report.[2] The report was the most comprehensive survey of the British system of social insurance ever made, and it provided a carefully reasoned scheme, the Beveridge plan, for the abolition of wants as they had been known during the prewar period. The Beveridge plan was essentially an insurance scheme, giving, in return for contributions, benefits up to a subsistence level as a right and not based on a means test. In return for contributions that all would pay, a minimum income sufficient to meet basic needs would be guaranteed for all periods of interrupted earnings, whether through sickness, disability, unemployment, or old age. In addition, there would be grants for the normal incidents of life that called for unusual expenditures—birth-maternity grants, children-family allowances, and death-funeral grants.

The Labour government made several important changes in the structure of the British economy in 1945.[3] First, certain industries were nationalized. The industries were of key importance to the whole economy, but had been having difficulties in attaining efficiency in operation. Second, the Labour government instituted a most comprehensive social welfare program. From before birth—when expectant mothers were provided with medical care, special foods, and compensated vacations—until death—when grants toward funeral expenses were provided by the state—the individual Briton was insured against every hazard and insecurity possible. The British went in one respect far beyond what any free society had previously ventured; they gave every citizen free medical care. Third, the British tax system was revamped, partly to pay for these services. Changes were made in the structure of the personal income tax, with lower-income groups paying less and higher-income groups more. A special tax was levied on investment income. The most drastic change, however, occurred in the inheritance tax, with the rates pushed up to almost confiscatory levels.

It can be said that the prime desideratum of the British welfare state was a more equal distribution of income. A large part of the extra taxation necessary to finance welfare measures came from the middle- and upper-income groups. Steep progressions in tax rates began at lower income levels, and a surtax was superimposed upon the standard rate of income tax, beginning at a level of 2,000 pounds a year ($5,600 after 1949) until the Conservative government raised the lower limit to $14,000 a year in 1955. There is some indication that tax policies had some impact upon income distribution, for studies showed that the concentration of personal income, both before and after the income tax, in the hands of the top 5 percent of income recipients was reduced after the war, compared with 1938, and this tendency toward greater income equality continued during the postwar years.[4] However, it appears that this trend was arrested during the period following 1957, reflecting several factors that have occurred since that time.[5] First, the growth of employment income slowed relative to income from self-employment. Rent, interest, and dividends have shown a marked increase since 1957, and salaries of professional people have risen faster than the wages of wage earners.

THE BRITISH ECONOMY

The British economy is somewhat similar to that of the United States and West Germany. Private enterprise is dominant in terms of employment and contribution to gross national product. By international standards, and contrary to popular impressions, the public sector in the United Kingdom is about average. Both taxes and government expenditures on goods and services take a smaller share of gross national product in the United Kingdom than in France and Sweden, and about the same as in West Germany and most other European countries. For example, in 1970 total taxes, including social security contributions, accounted for 44 percent of the Swedish gross national product and 41 percent of the French gross national product. Government expenditures on goods and services in Britain account normally for around 20 percent of gross national product, a ratio similar to the government contribution in the United States, but less than government expenditures in Sweden and West Germany.

Nevertheless, public expenditures exert much influence on the British economy. The public sector directly employs nearly 25 percent of the nation's manpower, and probably about 60 percent of those with full-time higher education.[6] Public authorities own about 40 percent of the nation's capital assets, and are responsible for nearly 45 percent of the nation's annual fixed investments. About 60 percent of the nation's scientific and technological research and development is financed by government agencies. The size and structure of important private industries, such as agriculture and aircraft production, are in effect determined by the decisions of the public sector; and the purchases of the public sector provide a large and in some cases dominant part of the demand for the products of other industries. Public expenditures have effected a certain buoyancy in the British economy during the years since the end of World War II, but have also contributed to some of its shortcomings.

The British economy, then, is a mix of market-determined and government-determined resource allocation. The forces of demand and supply and the price mechanism, as determined by consumer sovereignty and producer profit motives, characterize private sector allocation. Public sector allocation, on the other hand, is accomplished through the revenue and expenditure activities of government budgeting. In addition, there is the manner in which the effective demand for economic goods is divided among the various individual and family spending units of the British economy. More specifically, this effective demand stems from the pattern of income and wealth distribution in the private sector and the pattern of political voting influence in the public sector. Both the private and the public sector have an influence on the distribution of income.

National Income

National income at factor cost is the initial or original distribution of income before alteration by income taxes and transfer

167

payments. It is the sum of wages, rent, interest, and profits, or the sum of the earnings of the factors of production. National income, though it appears on the income side and not on the product side of the national income and product account, is nonetheless a measure of product. It is a measure of product with product valued at factor cost, or in terms of the factor income earned, though not necessarily received, by the factors of production.

Table 6.1 presents national income in the United Kingdom for 1971. Incomes from employment and self-employment represent two categories of national income. The other categories are profit, rent, and interest. Wages and salaries represent approximately 70 percent of national income—a ratio similar to the relationship in the United States. Income from rent and net interest accounts for about 11 percent of national income, compared to 9 percent for the United States.

Personal Income

Personal income in the United Kingdom comes from four sources—employment; self-employment; rent, dividends and net interest; and transfer payments. Excluded from personal income are undistributed profits, which represented 12 percent of national income in 1971. In effect, ignoring undistributed profits means that a part of factor income is really not taken into consideration in studies of income distribution. In other words, factor income is reduced by 12 percent through the exclusion of undistributed profits. The rationale for their exclusion is that, assuming that they belonged to stockholders, it would be virtually impossible to allocate amounts on the basis of income groups. Since it is reasonable to assume that undistributed profits can be ignored, it is also reasonable to assume that at least a part of the corporate income tax cannot be allocated to persons, because it was borne by undistributed profits.

Table 6.2 presents personal income in the United Kingdom for 1971. In 1971 income from employment accounted for 71.1 percent of personal income; self-employment, 8.4 percent; rent, dividends, and net interest, 10.4 percent; and income transfers, 10.2 percent.[7] Some shifts have occurred in the distribution of personal income during the period from 1951 to 1971. Income from employment, the great bulk of which is wages and salaries, remained constant as a percentage of personal income—71 percent in 1951 and 71 percent in 1971.[8] Income from self-employment, on the other hand, showed a marked decline—12.1 percent for 1951 as compared to 8.4 percent for 1971. Income from property ownership remained rather constant during the period—10.7 percent in 1951 and 10.4 percent in 1971. In 1966, however, property income accounted for 12 percent of personal

TABLE 6.1

National Income in the United Kingdom for 1971

Sources of Income	Millions of Pounds
Compensation of employees	33,491
Wages and salaries	29,775
Employers' contributions to social security	1,454
Other (payments in cash and kind)	2,262
Income from self-employment	3,941
Rent and interest	3,386
Gross profit of private corporations and other enterprises	5,769
Surplus of public enterprises	1,604
Net property income from abroad	470
Less: capital consumption	-5,012
stock appreciation	- 935
Plus: residual error	490
National income	43,204

Source: Central Statistical Office, National Income and Expenditures, 1972 (London: Her Majesty's Stationery Office, 1972), p. 24.

income. The greatest relative gain was made by transfer payments, which amounted to 6 percent of personal income in 1951 compared to 10.2 percent in 1971.

It would appear that the coming of the welfare state in the United Kingdom has brought little change in the distribution of income on a functional or national income basis. There is also some carryover to personal income as well. Individuals may still receive rent for the use of their land and interest on the capital funds that they have invested in various productive projects. Some industries have been nationalized, to be sure, but their former owners have been compensated for the loss of their properties and, in some cases at least, the compensation has been such as to insure that the owners received about the same annual incomes as formerly. Outside of the nationalized industries, private enterprises are free to make profits if they are able to do so under the many economic controls that both the Labour and Conservative governments have imposed from time to time. And, of course, wages and salaries are paid and received as usual.

Income distribution is altered by taxes and transfer payments. Before proceeding to an analysis of income distribution, it is first necessary to have some knowledge of the taxes and transfers that would impinge upon the distribution. The next section is designed to encapsulate as briefly as possible the basic characteristics of British public sector taxes and expenditures, particularly transfer payments. There have been a number of changes in the British tax system in recent years, with some of these changes occurring in 1973. The most important change has been the adoption of the value-added tax.

PUBLIC FINANCE

As has been the case in preceding chapters, it is necessary to classify the taxes and benefits that have an impact upon the redistribution of income. Taxes are classified on the basis of whether or not they are direct or indirect, and benefits are classified the same way. The initial or preredistribution income refers to incomes received by households and individuals before the receipt of income transfers and other benefits and before the payment of taxes. Income redistribution or postredistributional income refers to total income of households and individuals after the receipt of all income transfers and other benefits and after the payment of direct and indirect taxes. Without some prior knowledge of British taxes and expenditures, it is impossible to assess their effects on the horizontal and vertical distribution of income. However, there is the difficulty in that when it comes time to allocate taxes and benefits, it cannot simply be assumed that all of them are additions to or subtractions from income.

Taxation in the United Kingdom

Taxation in the United Kingdom is fairly evenly balanced between direct and indirect taxes. In 1971, for example, total taxes on income and capital amounted to 8.6 billion pounds and taxes on expenditures amounted to 7.8 billion pounds.[9] The single most important British tax is the personal income tax, which accounts for approximately 40 percent of all tax revenues, exclusive of social security contributions. Indirect taxes fall heavily on tobacco, liquor, and gasoline, which supply around 50 percent of the total taxes on expenditures. The purchase tax, which was a sales tax imposed at a variable number of rates on both home and imported goods, was replaced in April 1973 by the value-added tax. Unlike in Sweden and West Germany, local government units are of no particular importance in terms of taxes. The most important local tax is the property tax.

TABLE 6.2

Personal Income in the United Kingdom for 1971

Source	Millions of Pounds
Income from employment	33,491
Wages and salaries	29,775
Income from self-employment	3,941
Rent, dividends, and net interest	4,837
Income transfers	4,781
Personal income	47,088

Source: Central Statistical Office, National Income and Expenditure, 1972 (London: Her Majesty's Stationery Office, 1972), p. 5.

The Personal Income Tax

For many years the British income tax structure included an income tax and a surtax. However, in 1973 this system was replaced by a single graduated income tax. Much revision was entailed in the changeover to a straight progressive tax. There is some differentiation between earned and investment income, with investment income of up to 2,000 pounds being subject to the same rates as earned income, and income in excess of 2,000 pounds subject to a 15 percent surcharge. The income tax is graduated by means of personal allowances and progressive tax rates. These rates, as of April 1973, ranged from 30 percent on incomes of 5,000 pounds or less to 75 percent on incomes in excess of 20,000 pounds.[10] Incomes of a husband and wife may be aggregated and treated as one income or treated as separate incomes. However, a higher personal allowance is given to couples who file jointly.

For all practical purposes, it is the income tax that was in effect prior to 1973 that must be used as a frame of reference for purposes of income distribution analysis. This income tax, which included both an income tax and a surtax, was in effect from 1909 to 1973. The income tax was charged, in principle, at a standard rate. Progressivity was obtained by providing a number of personal allowances and reliefs and by charging the first slices of income at reduced rates and incomes above a set amount (2,000 pounds in 1970) at the surtax progressive rates. All individuals whose incomes exceeded 284 pounds in the tax year 1970 were liable for the tax. There were special exemptions for elderly persons, and special reliefs for the investment income of persons with small incomes and older persons. These reliefs typically amounted to two-ninths of earned or unearned income.

The income tax was partly graduated by means of certain types of allowances. Earned income relief allowed a deduction of up to two-ninths of earned income up to a maximum amount (4,005 pounds in 1970) and one-ninth on an additional amount (5,940 pounds in 1970). Then there were personal allowances for both single persons and married couples. In 1970 the allowances were 255 and 375 pounds respectively. There were allowances for dependents, which varied with the age of the child; thus in 1970 for children under 11 years of age an allowance of 115 pounds was given, for children between 11 and 16 the allowance was 140 pounds, and for children who were 16 and over the allowance was 165 pounds as long as they were in school. In addition, there were special reliefs and allowances that were applicable to specific situations, such as blindness and dependent relatives.

There were three rates on assessable income that were progressive. In 1970 the maximum standard rate was 8 shillings 3 pence on all taxable incomes in excess of 300 pounds. Then there was the surtax, which was collected and levied separately. In 1970 it was levied on total income, earned or unearned, in excess of 2,000 pounds, after allowances for certain deductions and personal allowances, which reduced the effective rate of the surtax considerably. The surtax was imposed at rates that rose in progression from 10 to 50 percent. The income tax and surtax were part of the same scale of progression. The top marginal rate (91.25 percent in 1970) was not reached in the case of earned income until an income of 20,000 pounds (1970) was reached. The effective rate was much smaller.

The Corporate Income Tax

Corporate incomes are taxed at a rate of 40 percent on both distributed and undistributed profits. As of 1973 a number of changes were made in corporate taxation that need not be explained. In considering the general level of corporate taxation, allowances have to be made for various forms of investment incentives. The British have been liberal with measures that are designed to stimulate investment. Capital allowances are made available for capital expenditures on new machinery or equipment installed for use by manufacturing, construction, and extractive industries. The general rule is that the capital expenditure incurred may be entirely deducted from profits during the first year.

Capital Taxes

Capital taxes in the United Kingdom include the capital gains tax and death duties. The capital gains tax was modified in 1971 to exclude short-term capital gains. The tax is comprehensive and is applicable to gains on both tangible and intangible assets, subject to certain exemptions, including a basic exemption of 500 pounds. Gifts of a value up to 100 pounds are exempt from the tax. Individuals are liable to a capital gains tax of 30 percent; however, they may elect as an option to treat the gain as income subject to the personal income tax. Capital gains are treated differently for corporations and investment trusts. A number of changes were made in capital gains taxation in 1972.

Death duties were also modified in 1972. The new rates range from 25 percent on property valued from 15,000 to 20,000 pounds to 75 percent on property valued in excess of 500,000 pounds. These rates are applicable to all property, tangible or intangible. Certain allowances for deductions and expenses are permitted. Before 1969 the death duty was charged on the whole of an estate at a single rate, with the highest rate of 80 percent levied on estates of 2,000,000 pounds and over; from 1969 the tax has been levied at graduated rates on successive slices of an estate.

Excise Taxes

Excise taxes are levied on consumer goods, especially tobacco, alcohol, and gasoline. In the fiscal year 1972/73, taxes on these three commodities accounted for 25 percent of the national government's total tax revenues. The tobacco tax rate varies, with tobacco of Commonwealth origin being admitted at a preferential rate. The tax rate on alcohol varies according to the type of liquor involved, with beer and light wines carrying the lowest rates. The rates of the gasoline tax also vary depending on its use. One feature of the taxes on tobacco, alcohol, and gasoline is the large proportion they represent of the sales price. For example, the tax on cigarettes is 75 percent of the purchase price.

The Purchase Tax

The purchase tax was replaced in 1973 by the value-added tax. However, since income distribution data are for periods prior to 1973, the appropriate frame of reference must include the purchase tax. The purchase tax was an ad valorem tax that was levied at the wholesale level on a wide range of consumer goods. The rate of the tax was the same whether the goods were produced in the United Kingdom or imported from abroad. There were four sets of rates, which were based on the wholesale value of the goods. These rates ranged from 13.75 percent on most consumer goods of a nonsumptuary nature to 55 percent on certain luxury items. Certain classes of goods, such

173

as basic food, fuels, and books, were exempt from the purchase tax. The purchase tax rates were modified frequently to influence domestic demand.

Social Security Contributions

The United Kingdom has a comprehensive social welfare system. It can be divided into two categories: the medical care and social security program, which includes family allowances, and the national insurance program, which provides unemployment and sickness benefits, old-age pensions, maternity benefits, and death grants. In contrast with the income-based contributions common in other European countries, the British welfare system, like that in the United States, is based mainly on flat-rate contributions. These contributions introduce an element of regressivity into the fiscal system. However, there have been some recent modifications of flat-rate contributions in that certain contributions and benefits are now related to individual earnings.

Family allowances are financed out of general taxation; they do not depend in any way on national insurance contributions. Medical care is also separate from national insurance and is financed out of general tax revenues and from employer and employee contributions. Approximately 80 percent of the cost of health care is financed from general tax revenues, 15 percent from employee contributions, and 5 percent from employer contributions. National insurance programs are financed separately from family allowances and health care. Contributions by workers and employers account for around 70 percent of the cost of national insurance, with the remainder financed from general tax revenues. Workers are divided into three categories: employed, self-employed, and nonemployed. Contributions are paid according to the class of contributors. Separate rates are also payable for men and women. Contributions are a combination of both flat rates and earnings-related payments on the part of both workers and employers.

Government Expenditures

As was the case for the other countries used in this study, government expenditures include only those income transfers and benefits that add directly to the original incomes of households and individuals. These transfers include family allowances, old-age pensions, maternity benefits, war pensions, unemployment compensation, sickness benefits, education grants, and national health services. Then, too, there are indirect benefits, such as housing subsidies. When the

sum of these benefits is added to original incomes, then subtractions
must be made for personal income taxes, contributions to social
security, and indirect taxes on expenditures. The remainder is redistributional income. The end result is that some groups pay more in
taxes than they receive in benefits and are net losers in the process
of income redistribution, while other groups receive more in benefits
than they pay in taxes and are net gainers. So it becomes necessary
to identify who pays the taxes and who receives the benefits.

Family Allowances

Family allowances are paid to families with two or more children. They are not related to the size of family income, but are subject
to income taxation. A sum of 18 shillings ($2.16) a week is paid for
the second child, and 20 shillings a week for subsequent children.11
For example, a family with three children would receive 32 shillings
($3.84) a week. Family allowances, as mentioned previously, are
financed from general tax revenues of the British government and
have no relation to the national insurance program. The family allowance benefits most those families with low incomes who pay little or
no income tax. However, the family allowance cannot be considered
an important source of financial support to families with children.
For the average family in the United Kingdom, the family allowance
represents 6.2 percent of personal income.

National Health and National Insurance Programs

The best-known social welfare program in the United Kingdom
is medical care, which is provided under the National Health Service
as a free public service and is not a part of the regular social insurance
program. Most prescribed medicines are free. Dental services, eye-
glasses, hearing aids, and other appliances are supplied through the
National Health Service, but with some cost sharing on the part of the
patient. There is no charge for dental services to children or to
expectant or recent mothers. General practitioner care, specialist
services, hospitalization, maternity care, and treatment in the event
of industrial injuries are also provided by the National Health Service.
Expenditures on the National Health Insurance program have on the
average represented about 4 percent of British national income.

Separate and apart from the National Health Service, there
exists a comprehensive program of social security that comes under
the category of national insurance. This program provides flat-rate
sickness benefits at a rate of 5 pounds a week to men, single women,
and widows for a period of up to one year. In addition, national insurance beneficiaries can also receive benefits for dependent children.

Married women and divorced women who receive some alimony get lower benefits. Earnings-related supplements to the flat-rate benefits are payable to persons who, because of their higher earnings, have paid additional graduated contributions. The supplement is payable for up to six months in any uninterrupted period of sickness at a rate equal to one-third of a person's average weekly earnings between 9 and 30 pounds during the previous year, but the supplements cannot raise the total benefit, including allowances for dependents, above 85 percent of earnings.

Old-age pensions and unemployment benefits are similar in makeup to sickness benefits. Flat-rate unemployment benefits are payable for up to twelve months in any one period of interruption of employment. The rates of unemployment benefits are the same as sickness benefits; this has the advantage that there is nothing to be gained from claiming one benefit rather than the other. Old-age pensions are payable to persons who have reached minimum pension age—65 for men and 60 for women—and have retired from regular work. The standard weekly flat-rate pension is 5 pounds for a man or woman who qualified on his or her own insurance record. A married woman who has made no contribution is entitled to a lower pension of 3 pounds 2 shillings a week. As a corollary to regular old-age pensions, there is a graduated pension scheme that provides higher rates to higher-paid contributors. There is no set maximum amount that any contributor can receive.

There are other benefits payable under the national insurance scheme. A maternity allowance of 5 pounds a week is paid to women who give up paid employment to have a baby. The benefit is usually paid for 18 weeks, beginning with the 11th week before the expected week of confinement. In addition to the allowance, a lump-sum maternity grant of 25 pounds is paid to most mothers, either on their own or their husband's insurance. There is also a death grant of 25 pounds, which is payable on the death of an insured person or the wife, husband, or child of an insured person. There is a widows' allowance, separate from a widows' pension, which is payable at a standard rate of 7 pounds a week for 26 weeks after the husband's death. There are also supplements for dependent children. There is also a widowed mothers' allowance, which is payable when the widows' allowance ends provided there are dependent children.

Supplementary Benefits

The Ministry of Social Security Act of 1966 established a scheme to provide noncontributory benefits for people whose resources are less than minimum standard living requirements. Supplementary benefits are of two types: supplementary pensions for persons over pension age who have ceased full-time work and need to have their incomes brought up to a guaranteed weekly level; and supplementary allowances for the sick, disabled, unemployed, widows, mothers left alone with young children, and persons aged 16 or more but under pension age who have ceased full-time work and whose resources fall short of income requirements. The rationale of supplementary benefits is the provision of a minimum income standard to persons who, even after family allowances and other social welfare benefits, do not have enough income to cover essential requirements for an adequate standard of living.

Other Benefits

There are other benefits in the United Kingdom that do not take the form of income transfers but that can be regarded as at least an indirect gain to recipients. Some of these services are collective in character in the sense that they are productive of benefits that are enjoyed by the recipients only through membership in the community. National defense is an example. Economic evaluation of these services is an especially difficult problem, because they are not distributed through the machinery of the market. Other services provided by the government are, in effect, nonmonetary transfers. This would be true for such services as free medical care, housing subsidies, and free education. These benefits are available at a price lower than their real cost that would have prevailed in the absence of state action. The real disposable income of the recipients of the benefits is enhanced.

Examples of various nonmonetary transfers in the United Kingdom are school meals and school milk, milk under the national milk schemes, cod liver oil, and orange juice. Education is available free of charge for children. Medical care, for the most part, is also free. Then, too, there are grants to certain branches of the economy, such as agricultural and housing subsidies, which result in lower prices for certain goods and services. Being financed by taxation, even those who do not benefit by these goods and services contribute to their cost, which results in an indirect redistribution of income. This is the case even when services are of a general nature, as the different income groups pay widely differing amounts for them.

A Comparison of Taxes and Benefits

In order to obtain a general picture of the relationship of taxes and social welfare benefits to income distribution, it is desirable to present a table showing both taxes and benefits received. Some taxes are earmarked for the financing of specific benefits, such as old-age pensions and other payments under the national insurance program. Then there is a large segment of welfare benefits that is financed from general taxation. On the tax side, various taxes have an effect on the redistribution of income. Not only is the income tax progressive, but a large part of its revenue is repaid in the form of various benefits, such as family allowances and free medical care. Indirect taxes are also a source of general tax revenues and, as such, tend to counteract the progressivity of the income tax. These taxes presumably have a regressive effect, which, however, cannot be calculated with any degree of accuracy.

Table 6.3 presents taxes and benefits for 1971. Included on the benefits side are not only the direct monetary transfers that would redound to the advantage of certain income groups, but nonmonetary transfers as well. Included are government grants, which are designed as direct or indirect supplements to the income of certain groups in the United Kingdom. Excluded from benefits are expenditures for such purposes as national defense. On the tax side, there are the three main categories of taxes—direct taxes, indirect taxes, and social security contributions. As mentioned previously, social security taxes proper—that is, taxes levied directly on the beneficiaries of social welfare expenditures—are not adequate to cover all outlays of funds. A part of the cost, in other words, must be covered by the general revenues of the government. The aggregates of taxes and benefits do not balance in the table.

There is an obvious discrepancy between total taxes and total benefits, since many types of expenditures not related to social welfare are excluded. The purpose of the table is merely to present a comparison of taxes and benefits. From here it is necessary to find out who pays the taxes and who receives the benefits. This is the purpose of the following section, which starts off with the original distribution of income to households. To this original distribution of income many of the above benefits are added and from it the taxes to finance the benefits are subtracted.

INCOME DISTRIBUTION IN THE UNITED KINGDOM

Income as used for purposes of distribution analysis comes from four sources—income from employment, which basically consists of wages and salaries; income from self-employment, which is entrepreneurial income; rent, interest, and dividends; and various types of income transfers, such as family allowances. Excluded from income are undistributed profits and capital gains. The effect of extending the definition of personal income to include these claims on wealth is by no means certain and there are, anyway, differences of opinion

TABLE 6.3

A Comparison of Taxes and Benefits, Including Income Transfers, in the United Kingdom for 1971

Taxes	Millions of Pounds	Benefits	Millions of Pounds
Income taxes	7,953	National insurance	2,924
Personal income tax	6,509	Family allowances	362
Company income tax	1,179	Supplementary	
		benefits	634
National insurance	2,828	War pensions	125
Taxes on expenditures	8,697	Other transfers	
		and grants	736
Central government	6,610	Housing subsidies	369
Local governments	2,087	National health	
		service	2,096
Taxes on capital	683	School meals	154
Estate duties	404	Education,	
		including grants	2,539
		Other services	271
Total	20,161	Total	10,210

Source: Central Statistical Office, National Income and Expenditures, 1972 (London: Her Majesty's Stationery Office, 1972), pp. 56-59.

as to what the appropriate definition should be, for example, whether undistributed profits should be included.[12] It is probable that the shape of income distribution would be modified with their inclusion. However, the given statistical data on personal income involve defined aggregates that account for the great bulk of income on any definition.

Table 6.4 presents the distribution of personal income in the United Kingdom for 1970. Income, as defined in the table, is before taxes and includes transfer payments. The data are expressed in terms of percentage. For example, 19.7 percent of married couples with no children made between 2,000 and 4,000 pounds for the year. The table also shows that in households where both spouses work, incomes are generally higher than in households where only one person works. The table also shows that single males tend to be better off in terms of income than single females.

A starting point for an analysis of income distribution in the United Kingdom is the division of personal income into quintiles.

TABLE 6.4

Distribution of Personal Incomes in the United Kingdom
Before Income Tax by Family Circumstances
(in pounds)

	All Ranges: Thousands of Families (= 100 percent)	330-	500-	800-	1,000-	1,300-	1,500-	1,750-	2,000-	4,000 and over
						Income Groups				
Percentage of Married Couples—Wives Earning										
No children	3,090	1.3	5.3	6.0	15.2	14.4	19.6	16.2	19.7	2.2
1 child	1,122	0.7	2.6	5.3	16.1	15.7	20.9	16.8	19.7	2.1
2 children	871	0.5	2.0	3.3	12.9	14.3	21.2	18.4	24.1	3.2
3 children	341	0.7	1.9	3.0	11.0	14.7	21.0	18.8	24.3	4.5
4 or more children	181	0.9	2.4	3.0	11.3	12.9	21.4	20.6	23.4	4.1
Percentage of Married Couples—Wives Not Earning										
No children	3,174	4.2	17.5	15.1	21.5	12.0	10.8	6.3	9.4	3.0
1 child	1,453	1.9	8.9	12.5	26.7	15.4	14.2	8.0	10.1	2.2
2 children	1,605	1.4	5.4	9.4	23.9	16.5	16.6	10.3	13.7	2.6
3 children	743	1.6	5.4	8.5	21.7	15.8	18.1	11.5	14.2	3.2
4 or more children	477	2.1	6.2	7.8	21.4	16.4	18.8	12.2	12.8	2.4
Percentage of Single Males and Widowers										
No children	4,488	14.2	29.8	19.1	20.3	6.7	4.4	1.9	2.8	0.7
1 child	94	4.6	16.7	18.8	29.9	12.9	7.6	3.5	4.8	1.1
2 or more children	95	5.3	13.9	14.6	29.4	14.8	11.0	5.2	4.7	1.2
Percentage of Single Females and Widows										
No children	3,740	27.1	40.3	13.1	8.9	3.0	2.3	1.4	3.0	0.8
1 child	142	14.3	41.6	20.0	13.7	3.5	2.3	1.7	2.5	0.4
2 or more children	70	9.8	32.8	20.7	18.7	6.1	4.3	1.8	4.8	0.7

Source: Central Statistical Office, Social Trends (London: Her Majesty's Stationery Office, 1972), p. 85.

Income, as defined here, is income before taxes, but including transfer payments.[13] All transfers, with the exception of family allowances, are not taxable. There are four sources of personal income—income from employment; income from self-employment; rent, dividends, and net interest; and national insurance benefits and other income transfers. Excluded from the concept of personal income are undistributed profits, which belong in a sense to stockholders, and capital gains, both of which directly or indirectly tend to redound primarily to the advantage of the upper-income groups. Personal income, as defined for income tax purposes, excludes contributions to national insurance and all other contributions that are not liable to income taxation. Also excluded from income are other items, including nontaxable grants, accrued interest, and incomes of persons making less than a legal taxable minimum. The end result is income before taxation, which is less than personal income totals. For example, in 1959 total personal income amounted to 19.7 billion pounds, while income before taxes amounted to 16.4 billion pounds.

Table 6.5 presents the distribution of incomes before taxes by quintiles and for the top 1 percent and 5 percent for all incomes subject to the income tax and surtax. The total number of incomes includes incomes of husband and wife, which are counted as one income. A woman who is single or divorced for part of a year is counted as having a separate income of the amount received while she was single or divorced. Other single persons are also counted separately. The percentages in the table, then, are based on all persons who received income for the whole or any part of a year. This income, however, has to be above a particular amount, namely, 50 pounds. Two time periods are used in the table, 1959 and 1967.

The table is based on data of the Inland Revenue (the British equivalent of the U.S. Treasury) and is subject to certain defects.[14] The data relate only to income units and do not take into consideration the size of the units, which may range from single persons to large families. The meaning of the data can shift from year to year, making comparisons between years difficult. There can be changes in family size at different income levels without any change in the number or the income of units. For any individual year, therefore, the meaning of the data may be very different depending on whether the lowest income units are the smallest-size units or the size of units is invariant to income, and so on. Since husband and wife are counted as one unit, the distribution of personal income could be affected by changes in the age of marriage and by changes in the proportion of the total population married and of married women going out to work.

Comparisons can be made between various levels of income and shares of particular groups in terms of income ranged in order of size for 1959 and 1967. In 1959 the top 1 percent of all income units received 8.3 percent of pre-tax income and 5.2 percent of income after taxes. In 1967 the top 1 percent of income units received 7.9 percent of pre-tax income and 5.0 percent of income after taxes. The top 5 percent of all income units received 19.9 percent of pre-tax income in 1959 and 16.8 percent of after-tax income. In 1967 the top 5 percent of income units received 19.2 percent of pre-tax income and 15.5 percent of after-tax income. The burden of the income tax and surtax, as measured by the contributions of the top 1 and 5 percent of taxpayer units, also can be computed for each time period. In 1959 the top 1 percent of all income units paid 34.2 percent of total income taxes, and the top 5 percent paid 54.5 percent. In 1967 the top 1 percent paid 27.9 percent of the total income tax and surtax, and the top 5 percent paid 47.4 percent of taxes. The fall in the percentage of income taken by taxes was limited primarily to the top 1 percent.

Table 6.6 divides before- and after-tax incomes into quintiles for 1959 and 1967. The Gini coefficient of inequality is also computed for both years. The data indicate that some minor shifting occurred during the two years. These shifts were due in part to increases in the price level, which caused some inflation of money incomes, and in part to reductions in tax rates.

It is again important to call attention to the fact that Table 6.6, like Table 6.5, is based on one particular source of information, namely, Inland Revenue data, which were published annually until 1968. The table is thus subject to certain defects, as has already been mentioned. For one thing, income below exemption limits was excluded. Incomes are treated as one income unit, regardless of the fact that married couples may earn two separate incomes. Also, the definition of personal income can be criticized on the grounds that certain claims on wealth are excluded, for example, undistributed profits that are reflected in capital gains and various forms of tax avoidance incomes that fall outside income tax regulations.

Trends in Income Distribution

A comparison can be made of before- and after-tax income distribution for several time periods. The data used are based on the same source, namely, Inland Revenue tables of before- and after-tax incomes, and are subject to the defects just mentioned. Two time periods are used—from 1949 to 1957 and from 1958 to 1967. From 1949 to 1957 there was a trend toward greater equality in the distribution of income, reflecting to some degree the postwar economic policies of the Labour government.[15] After 1957 the trend toward greater income equality tended to stabilize, with shifts occurring in the rate of income taxation. But there were also other factors at

TABLE 6.5

Distribution of Income in the United Kingdom
Before and After Taxes, 1959 and 1967

Income Range (pounds)	Number of Incomes (thousands)	Income Before Taxes (millions)	Taxes (millions)	Income After Taxes (millions)
1959				
50- 250	5,760	953	1	952
250- 500	7,030	2,589	88	2,501
500- 1,000	10,490	7,479	460	7,019
1,000- 1,500	2,250	2,634	299	2,335
1,500- 2,000	445	755	136	619
2,000- 3,000	287	688	161	527
3,000- 5,000	156	588	190	398
5,000-10,000	65	430	195	235
10,000-20,000	14	181	111	70
20,000 and over	3	99	77	22
Total	26,500	16,396	1,718	14,618
Income not included		3,298		
1967				
50- 250	2,338	493	—	493
250- 500	4,956	2,258	40	2,218
500- 1,000	6,302	6,726	523	6,203
1,000- 1,500	6,741	8,251	946	7,305
1,500- 2,000	2,769	4,721	676	4,045
2,000- 3,000	1,298	3,061	490	2,571
3,000- 5,000	370	1,369	377	992
5,000-10,000	150	1,000	361	639
10,000-20,000	35	467	245	222
20,000 and over	7	233	176	57
Total	27,800	28,179	3,834	24,345
Income not included		5,386		

Source: Central Statistical Office, National Income and Expenditures, 1968 (London: Her Majesty's Stationery Office, 1968), pp. 32-33.

TABLE 6.6

Before- and After-Tax Distribution of Income in the
United Kingdom by Quintiles, 1959 and 1967

	Before Taxes	After Taxes
1959		
First quintile	5.3	6.0
Second quintile	11.4	12.3
Third quintile	18.1	20.2
Fourth quintile	23.2	21.9
Fifth quintile	42.0	39.6
Upper 5 percent	19.9	16.8
Upper 1 percent	8.3	5.2
Gini coefficient	.348	.307
1967		
First quintile	6.3	7.1
Second quintile	11.9	12.2
Third quintile	16.8	18.3
Fourth quintile	22.5	23.7
Fifth quintile	42.5	38.7
Upper 5 percent	19.2	15.5
Upper 1 percent	7.9	5.0
Gini coefficient	.332	.298

Source: Central Statistical Office, National Income and Expenditures, 1966 and 1968 (London: Her Majesty's Stationery Office, 1966 and 1968), p. 32 (1966) and p. 28 (1968).

work to slow down the trend toward greater income equality. Rent, interest, and dividends, which had increased from 1.2 billion pounds in 1949 to 1.6 billion pounds in 1957, more than doubled during the 1958 to 1967 period.[16] Income from self-employment remained fairly constant from 1949 to 1957, but increased by 50 percent from 1958 to 1967.[17] Income from employment increased from 7.3 billion pounds in 1949 to 13.0 billion pounds in 1957, and from 13.5 billion pounds in 1958 to 24.2 billion pounds in 1967. Of employment income, wages increased by 73 percent from 1949 to 1957, while salaries increased by 90 percent. However, for the period from 1958 to 1967 wages increased by 80 percent, while salaries increased by 105 percent.

Table 6.7 presents the distribution of before- and after-tax income for the upper 1 percent and 5 percent of income units for selected years. In 1949 the upper 1 percent of all income units received 11.2 percent of before-tax income and 6.4 percent of after-tax income, while the top 5 percent received 23.8 percent of before-tax income and 17.7 percent of after-tax income. In 1957 the shares of the top 1 percent and 5 percent had declined to 8.2 percent and 19.1 percent before taxes and 5.0 percent and 14.9 percent after taxes. As can be seen in the table, there has been little change in distribution from 1957 to 1967.[18] Also presented in the table is the percentage of total income tax and surtax paid by the top 1 percent and 5 percent of income units for the same years. The percentage of taxes raised from these groups has shown a decline over time.

There was some shifting of the burden of the income tax and surtax over the period from 1949 to 1967 to the middle-income groups

TABLE 6.7

Distribution of Income and Tax Payments for the
Upper 1 Percent and 5 Percent of British Income
Units for Selected Years

	Before Taxes		After Taxes		Percentage of Tax Payments	
	Top 1 Percent	Top 5 Percent	Top 1 Percent	Top 5 Percent	Top 1 Percent	Top 5 Percent
1949	11.2	23.8	6.4	17.7	46.0	69.6
1953	9.8	21.9	5.8	15.9	41.1	62.3
1957	8.2	19.1	5.0	14.9	35.3	54.2
1958	8.2	19.5	5.1	15.8	34.8	54.3
1959	8.3	19.9	5.2	16.8	34.5	54.6
1960	8.5	19.9	5.1	15.6	34.4	54.1
1961	8.1	19.2	5.5	16.0	30.0	49.9
1962	8.1	19.2	5.5	16.2	28.4	46.9
1963	7.9	19.1	5.2	15.7	28.0	47.3
1967	7.9	19.2	5.0	15.5	22.8	38.1

Sources: Central Statistical Office, National Income and Expenditures, 1960 and 1968 (London: Her Majesty's Stationery Office, 1960 and 1968), p. 32 (1960) and p. 28 (1968); R. J. Nicholson, "The Distribution of Personal Income," Lloyds Bank Review (January 1967): 14-16.

and away from the top 1 percent and 5 percent of income units. In 1949 the two highest quintiles (top 40 percent) paid 94.3 percent of the total income tax and surtax, while the remaining 60 percent of income units paid 5.7 percent of total taxes. The top 5 percent paid 69.6 percent of the income tax total, while the next 34 percent paid 24.7 percent of the tax total. In 1967 the top 40 percent of income units paid 76 percent of total taxes, while the remaining 60 percent paid 24 percent.[19] However, the top 5 percent paid 38.1 percent of the taxes, while the next 35 percent paid 37.9 percent. The lowest quintile (bottom 20 percent) share of total taxes has remained consistently at less than 1 percent over the period.

The tables on the distribution of personal income before and after taxes were discontinued in 1970 because of the increasing amount of estimation required to produce calendar year figures on a national accounts basis. However, there is nothing to indicate that any significant shifting in income distribution or tax burdens has occurred since 1967. There has been a general reduction in the rates of income taxation, as reflected in the most recent reform of the income tax. The inflation of money income has had the effect of pulling more persons into higher tax brackets, with a corresponding rise in the relative amounts of taxes taken. The impact would be primarily on the share of taxes paid by the middle-income groups. There has been little change in the relative position of property income, that is, rent, interest, and dividends, to other components of personal income, and salaries continue to increase at a faster rate than wages.[20]

Redistribution of Income Through Taxes and Benefits

It is possible to gain some idea of how the initial distribution of British income is modified by the system of transfer payments and taxation. In Table 6.8, which is based on family expenditure surveys, a range of initial incomes is presented for all households. Then household incomes are presented as averages for each income range. The initial average income received by households is then altered not only by cash transfer payments, but by direct benefits in kind, which include education and health care. These are also expressed as transfers. There are also indirect benefits, including housing subsidies. All benefits are expressed as averages. Then average taxes, both direct and indirect, are subtracted from average income for each income range. Finally, average income after all benefits have been added and all taxes have been subtracted is presented. For example, average original income in the income range 2,566 to 3,104 pounds is 2,801 pounds, and average income after benefits and taxes have been added and subtracted is 2,063 pounds.

The table also presents a breakdown of average benefits received less average taxes paid by types of households. Households are classified into several categories—retired with one or two adults, nonretired with one or two adults, and households with children. Average benefits received from all sources less average taxes paid are expressed in both monetary and percentage terms. For example, all households in the range 260 pounds and under had an average net gain of benefits over taxes of 431 pounds. This average net gain is then presented as a percentage of original income—625 percent.

Transfer Payments

Inequality in the distribution of factor income among British social classes is mitigated to some extent by the mechanism of transfer payments, the bulk of which are directed to households in the lower-income segments of the population. Low-income families with children gain, as well as persons in the nonactive population. This group has the least favored position of any social class. In looking at the table, family allowances as a source of total household income are of minimal importance, except to low-income families with four or more children. Expressed in terms of average earnings, family allowances amount to about 3.5 percent for a family with two children, 12 percent for a family with four children, and 20 percent for a family with six children.[21] However, families with four or more children comprise less than 5 percent of all British households. For the average wage earner's family, the allowances modify only slightly the fall in living standards resulting from an increase in family size.

On the other hand, national insurance retirement and widows' pensions, including supplementary pensions, are indeed of importance to low-income households. All households actually show an income gain up to 816 pounds a year, but the most significant gains are made in the three lowest income categories for both one and two adults, retired and not retired. Pensions are the main contributing factor. All direct benefits, including direct benefits in kind, vary more or less in proportion to the number of persons in the family and favor large families to a greater extent than any other main group. The relatively large direct benefits received by families with children in the lower-income ranges can be attributed in part to supplementary allowances payable to all persons who are not in full-time work and whose resources fall short of basic income requirements. When direct benefits in kind are isolated from all cash benefits, their impact is also to favor large families and families in the low-income ranges, but less than might be expected. It is also significant to note that education is the single largest direct benefit for all households with annual incomes of 1,196 pounds and over.

TABLE 6.8

Redistribution of Income Through Taxes and Benefits
in the United Kingdom in 1970
(in pounds)

Range of Original Income	Under 260	260-	315-	382-	460-
All Households					
Original income	69	289	349	419	510
Direct benefits in cash					
Family allowances	5	12	9	11	16
Pensions	291	316	304	275	215
Other cash benefits	123	64	52	88	77
Direct benefits in kind:					
Education	42	61	33	55	58
National health services	75	83	77	89	82
Welfare foods	3	6	7	4	6
Direct taxes:					
National insurance, employee					
contributions	1	2	2	5	15
Income tax and surtax	2	12	19	27	40
Indirect benefits (housing subsidies)	16	7	11	12	14
Indirect taxes	121	168	163	178	202
Implied income after all taxes and benefits	500	656	660	744	718
By Type of Household					
Net benefits received (+) less taxes paid (-)					
1 adult—retired	+331	+169	+175	+138	+69
2 adults—retired	+498	+413	+411	+318	+224
1 adult—nonretired	+316	+226	+115	+99	+52
2 adults—nonretired	+427	+431	+311	+348	+146
2 adults—1 child	+920	—	—	—	—
2 adults—2 children	+480	—	—	—	—
2 adults—3 children	—	—	—	—	—
2 adults—4 children	—	—	—	—	—
All households	+431	+367	+311	+325	+208
Net benefits received (+) less taxes paid (-) as percentage of original income					
1 adult—retired	+676	+59	+50	+33	+14
2 adults—retired	+593	+142	+116	+76	+44
1 adult—nonretired	+298	+78	+33	+23	+10
2 adults—nonretired	+309	+145	+90	+84	+29
2 adults—1 child	+657	—	—	—	—
2 adults—2 children	+686	—	—	—	—
2 adults—3 children	—	—	—	—	—
2 adults—4 children	—	—	—	—	—
All households	+625	+127	+89	+78	+41

559-	676-	816-	988-	1,196-	1,148-	1,752-	2,122-	2,566-	3,104 and Above	All Income Ranges
620	749	905	1,094	1,327	1,603	1,927	2,328	2,801	4,306	1,656
14	19	19	22	29	29	29	27	23	22	22
204	162	132	68	53	37	32	35	35	33	102
80	69	72	45	35	37	28	20	20	17	49
66	70	80	75	100	117	125	147	145	158	104
80	89	87	85	93	92	89	90	94	99	88
9	10	10	9	11	10	11	10	9	8	9
22	31	40	54	65	74	82	93	106	119	63
60	58	81	99	139	189	243	311	420	826	233
12	10	18	16	19	17	14	15	17	11	15
195	243	263	289	324	378	418	462	555	712	366
809	847	939	971	1,137	1,301	1,511	1,805	2,063	2,997	1,383
+51	-22	-186	-102	—	—	—	—	—	—	+245
+229	+211	+78	-350	—	-339	-507	-647	—	—	+264
-99	-173	-264	-236	-520	-611	-844	-822	—	-1,756	-273
+150	-23	-82	-108	-366	-488	-619	-795	-938	-1,563	-540
—	—	-70	-82	-256	-392	-525	-586	-792	-1,331	-414
—	—	+154	+133	-140	-265	-374	-447	-638	-1,113	-329
—	—	+249	—	+55	-32	-200	-219	-481	-1,236	-146
—	—	—	—	+264	+72	+31	—	—	—	+139
+189	+98	+34	-123	-190	-302	-416	-523	-738	-1,309	-273
+8	-3	-20	—	—	—	—	—	—	—	+118
+37	+29	+8	-10	—	-21	-26	-28	—	—	+50
-16	-23	-29	-32	-40	-39	-44	-35	—	-35	-26
+24	-3	-9	-22	-27	-31	-32	-34	-34	-37	-29
—	+16	-8	-10	-19	-25	-27	-25	-28	-30	-23
—	—	+17	-7	-11	-17	-19	-19	-23	-27	-17
—	—	+28	+12	+4	-2	-10	-10	-17	-26	-8
—	—	—	—	+20	+4	+2	—	—	—	+8
+30	+13	+4	-11	-14	-19	-22	-22	-26	-30	-16

Source: Central Statistical Office, Social Trends, 1972 (London: Her Majesty's Stationery Office, 1972), p. 96.

Taxes

Benefits are but one side of the income coin. On the other side of the coin are the taxes paid to finance these benefits. Determination of the pattern of income redistribution cannot, of course, be separated from the general question of the incidence of taxation. As was pointed out earlier, direct contributions to finance various benefits do not cover their cost. This means that there has to be reliance on general tax revenues of the public sector, which are fairly evenly divided between direct and indirect taxes. This creates the problem of determining which proportion of direct and indirect taxes are to be allocated to cover the expenditures on transfer payments and other types of welfare benefits.

It is necessary to remember that the data in Table 6.7 are applicable for 1970. Direct taxes include employees' contributions to national insurance and the personal income tax and surtax. The last tax is no longer in existence. Indirect taxes include the purchase tax, which is also no longer in existence, and a number of excise taxes. As the table indicates, the direct taxes, which are expressed as an average for each income range, are progressive and achieve substantial reductions of income in the higher-income ranges. On the other hand, it can be observed that benefits derived from education and national health services tend to increase somewhat as incomes increase. In total, however, direct taxes and direct benefits of the cash type—family allowances and pensions—favor households in the lower-income ranges. It can also be presumed that the direct taxes cannot be shifted. Their incidence falls directly on the households that have to pay them. When direct taxes alone are considered, there is vertical redistribution of income among different income levels.

In the matter of direct taxation, the primary effect is the reduction in income resulting from the taxes. But there is also a secondary effect that has to do with the repercussions of this upon subsequent flows of expenditures and savings. One specific point comes to mind, namely, the accumulation of wealth. It would appear that British income taxation tends to inhibit the accumulation of wealth rather than its inheritance.[22] High rates of income taxation have made it difficult for savers to accumulate enough after-tax income to build up a substantial amount of capital over their lifetimes. This is not to say, however, that fortunes cannot be made. In some cases where fortunes have been made, it has been in spite of income taxes. Inflation has been a factor, accompanied by generally favorable capital gains treatment of the sale of property. Capital gains are taxed at a considerably lower level than for other investment income, and for high incomes the rate of tax can be lower than that on earned income.

The indirect taxes are those levied directly on consumer goods and services. Excluded are those indirect taxes that fall on producers. For virtually all of the income ranges, average indirect taxes are higher than average direct taxes. When average indirect taxes are compared to average implied income after all benefits and taxes are added and subtracted, the effect on income redistribution is mildly regressive; the same holds true when average indirect taxes are compared to average total cash income for all income ranges. One explanation for the mild regressivity of indirect taxation lies in the fact that the purchase tax, which was in effect in 1971 but which has now been replaced by the value-added tax, had low rates applicable to food and basic necessities—a larger percentage of which are consumed by low-income groups—and higher rates on luxury items. But the bulk of indirect taxes falls on other items—tobacco, alcohol, and gasoline—and would tend to be regressive. So in terms of their impact on income redistribution, indirect taxes would achieve a minor offset to direct taxes.

Only a small percentage of taxes are directly earmarked for benefits. Referring to Table 6.3, those taxes (national insurance contributions) that directly go to finance a specific benefit (national insurance) amounted to 2.8 billion pounds, while all benefits amounted to 10.2 billion pounds. So individuals in the aggregate pay out less in social security taxes than they receive back in related benefits. The actual pattern is one of dependence on both direct and indirect taxes separate from social security contributions, with some diffusion of the real costs of all benefits throughout the economy via the mechanism of prices. It is difficult to estimate the proportion of direct and indirect taxes taken from general tax revenues to cover the segment of benefits not covered by national insurance contributions.

Redistribution in Terms of Inequality

Various estimates have been made of the overall impact of taxes and benefits on the redistribution of British household incomes.[23] One such estimate, made by J. L. Nicholson, was based on family expenditure data very similar to the data upon which Table 6.8 is based.[24] Although the data were for 1959, the results still possess some current relevance. The Gini coefficient was used to measure the degree of income inequality before and after taxes and benefits for all types of households and for a weighted composite of all households. The Gini coefficient was 32.1 percent for all households before taxes and benefits were taken into consideration and 25.1 percent after taxes and benefits.* Income inequality was reduced by 7 points. However, it is important to point out that capital gains from wealth ownership were excluded from the calculations upon which the estimates were based. Given that the distribution of personal wealth in the United Kingdom is much more skewed than that of personal income, one would expect inequality to be greater when capital gains are included.

The effects of both taxes and benefits on the reduction of 7 points varied widely. Direct benefits, including cash transfer payments and nonmonetary benefits, had by far the greatest impact on reducing income inequality. A total reduction of 6.2 points in the Gini coefficient was accomplished through direct benefits. Next in terms of impact came the income tax and surtax, which accounted for a reduction of 2.8 points.[25] Indirect benefits, which include food and housing subsidies, achieved a very minor reduction in income inequality. On the other hand, national insurance contributions and indirect taxes served as an offset to direct benefits and taxes in that each increased income inequality. In particular, indirect taxes increased the Gini coefficient of inequality by 1.6 points.[26] The regressiveness of these taxes, however, varied widely by types of families. They were least regressive on families with children, where food is the most important item of consumption. Finally, national insurance contributions increased the Gini coefficient by .9 points.

In a broad sense, redistribution of income may be horizontal or vertical. The term "horizontal" refers to the redistribution of income among members of the same income class. Welfare benefits that accrue to persons on some basis other than income status may bring about a horizontal redistribution. This is the case, for example, with family allowances, for they tend to redistribute income from small to large families, irrespective of the income condition of the latter. Income taxes also can have a horizontal impact on families of different sizes in that reductions in taxes occur as the size of the family increases. The term "vertical" refers to the distribution of money income among different income groups, that is, from the upper

---

*The Gini coefficient as used here was computed as follows:
$$G = \frac{\text{mean difference}}{2 \text{ X mean income}}$$
where the mean difference is given by the average of the absolute values of the differences between every possible pair of incomes in the series, but without pairing any given income with itself.

However, the Gini coefficient as it has been used elsewhere in the book is based on the Lorenz curve, where G measures the ratio of the area between the diagonal and the income distribution line to the area under the diagonal.

to the lower ranges, and the usual mechanism for this is the progressive income tax.

Based on the data in Table 6.8, it can be said that direct benefits, particularly those of the cash type, add much more proportionately to low incomes than to high incomes and so are very progressive. Direct benefits have a much larger effect on inequality than income taxation, although the income tax and surtax also achieve vertical redistribution through their progressiveness. The horizontal effect of direct benefits also appears to be somewhat progressive. For example, at the average income of 676 pounds, adult households without children pay out more taxes than they receive in benefits, while on balance families with children gain more in benefits than they pay out in taxes. The inclusion of the horizontal effects makes the incidence of indirect taxes and indirect benefits combined appear less regressive. At the higher levels of income, indirect taxes are larger but absorb a smaller proportion of income. Indirect taxes as a whole are therefore regressive, but have less redistributive effect than any other main type of tax or benefit. They show little variation among families of different sizes, and so favor the smaller families, which, at the same income level, have higher incomes per head.

THE DISTRIBUTION OF WEALTH IN THE UNITED KINGDOM

Inequality in the distribution of wealth is perhaps more closely identified with the United Kingdom than with any other major industrial country, because, after all, the Industrial Revolution really developed in this country. A concomitant of the Industrial Revolution was the concentration of property in the hands of a few persons. Vast fortunes were made, particularly during the development of the British Empire, with its markets and resources. These fortunes, for the most part, were not touched by taxation, but were allowed to accumulate and be passed down from generation to generation. Inequality in the distribution of wealth was also connected with inequality in the distribution of income, since it meant that income from property was concentrated in relatively fewer hands.

Studies of the distribution of wealth are not often made. One of the first studies of the distribution of wealth in the United Kingdom covered the years 1912 and 1924.[27] In 1912, 43 percent of all wealth was owned by 0.2 percent of all wealth-owners, while well over half of the wealth of the country was owned by only 0.8 percent of wealth-owners.[28] During the intervening twelve-year period, World War I occurred, causing some dislocations in the British economy. Also, the tax structure was revised considerably in 1914, and in subsequent years during the war, in that a surtax was imposed on incomes exceeding a particular level—3,000 pounds in 1914 and 2,000 pounds in 1918. Minor shifts occurred in the distribution of wealth. In 1924 two-thirds of the wealth was owned by 1.6 percent of all wealth-owners, compared to 0.9 percent in 1912.[29] Some 93 to 94 percent of all of the wealth was owned by 13.3 percent of the owners in 1912 and by 23.0 percent of the owners in 1924.

Considerable shifting has occurred in the distribution of wealth since 1924. The most current data indicate that in 1971 the top 1 percent of all wealth-owners in the United Kingdom owned around 21 percent of all wealth, while the top 5 percent owned 41 percent of the wealth.[30] On the basis of individual net wealth, 0.3 percent of all wealth-owners with assets covered by estate duties had property valued in excess of 100,000 pounds.[31] However, this 0.3 percent of wealth-owners owned around 10 percent of wealth and had average property valued at around 400,000 pounds. Based on estate duty returns, evidence indicates a greater concentration of individual wealth. The top 1 percent owned about one-third of total wealth in 1971, while the top 5 percent owned more than 50 percent.[32]

The distribution of wealth in the United Kingdom is presented in Table 6.9. Two time periods are used, 1961 and 1970. Wealth is presented on the basis of three categories. The first category is the distribution of wealth by type. The second category presents wealth on the basis of distribution by groups of owners. The third category presents wealth on the basis of estate duty payments. In its annual reports the Inland Revenue provides data on the value of estates of deceased persons. The data are subject to fairly wide margins of error, but can be considered reliable for interpreting relative changes over time. Also, it is necessary to point out the Small Payments Act of 1965 increased the number of persons in the British population who are treated as having no wealth.

The table indicates that there has been a trend toward greater equality in the distribution of wealth during the period from 1961 to 1970. The Gini coefficient of concentration can be used in two ways to measure changes in wealth distribution. One way involves the exclusion of wealth-holders not covered by wealth estimates based on estate duty statistics, and thus understates the concentration of wealth. Using this approach, the Gini coefficient of wealth distribution declined from .72 in 1961 to .65 in 1970.[33] The second approach assumes that all those with wealth of the kind not covered by the estimates have no wealth at all. This tends to overstate the actual distribution of wealth in the United Kingdom, for it excludes small amounts of wealth owned by a large segment of the population. Based on the second approach, the Gini coefficient of concentration shows a decline from .87 in 1961 to .85 in 1970.[34]

TABLE 6.9

Wealth Distribution of Individuals in the United Kingdom, 1961 and 1970

	1961	1970
Distribution of Wealth by Type[a]		
Company shares and debentures	12.7	18.9
Securities, mortgages, and building society shares	10.5	15.9
Life insurance policies	6.5	16.0
Cash at the bank	7.4	9.7
Land and buildings	12.5	32.9
Other assets	9.3	14.8
Total gross wealth	58.9	108.2
Distribution of Wealth by Groups of Owners[b]		
Most wealthy 1 percent	28.4	20.7
Most wealthy 2 percent	37.1	28.0
Most wealthy 5 percent	50.6	40.9
Most wealthy 10 percent	62.5	51.9
Most wealthy 50 percent	92.5	90.2
Net wealth (billions of pounds)	54.9	96.8
Distribution of Owners of New Wealth[c]		
0 and under 1,000 pounds	49.1	23.0
1,000 and under 3,000 pounds	32.6	31.7
3,000 and under 5,000 pounds	7.8	16.2
5,000 and under 10,000 pounds	5.7	18.8
10,000 and under 25,000 pounds	3.3	7.3
25,000 and under 100,000 pounds	1.4	2.6
100,000 and over	0.1	0.3

[a]Billions of pounds.
[b]Percentage of wealth owned by.
[c]Percentage of owners with assets covered by estate duty statistics.

Source: Central Statistical Office, Social Trends (London: Her Majesty's Stationery Office, 1972), p. 86; Table 35.

It is to be emphasized that Table 6.9 is based on Inland Revenue estate duty statistics only. Using different approaches, other studies indicate greater inequality in the distribution of wealth.[35] One approach is based on investment income, which is based on the ownership of wealth.[36] Income is related backward to the wealth from which it is derived and is expressed in terms of family units aggregated for income tax purposes. Investment income also depends on the type of asset held, with cash held by those with low wealth, and stocks and bonds held by those with great wealth. Using this approach, results indicated that in 1959/60 the top 5 percent of investment income recipients owned 72 percent of personal wealth and the share of the top 10 percent amounted to around 91 percent.[37]

Trends in Distribution of Wealth

Studies also indicate that the long-run trend is toward a lessening of the concentration of wealth in the hands of a very few persons. One such study, based on estate duty returns, showed that the share of wealth held by the top 1 percent of wealth-holders declined from 69 percent in the period from 1911 to 1913 to 42 percent in 1960, while the share of the top 5 percent declined from 87 percent to 75 percent.[38] The shift, however, was not so much toward greater equality in the distribution of wealth among all elements of the population, but toward distribution from the very rich to the rich. For example, the top 1 percent owned 69 percent of the wealth in 1911-1913, while the share of the next 4 percent amounted to 18 percent (87-69). In 1960, however, the share of wealth held by the top 1 percent had declined to 42 percent, while the share of the next 4 percent had increased to 33 percent (75-42).[39] Moreover, the proportion of wealth held by the top 10 percent of wealth-holders declined from 92 percent in 1911-1913 to 83 percent in 1960. The share of the 9 percent below the top 1 percent increased from 23 percent in 1911-1913 to 41 percent in 1960. This means that 18 percent of the 27 percent lost by the top 1 percent during the two time periods went to the next 9 percent, and 9 percent went to the bottom 90 percent.

The Effect of Wealth on Income Distribution

Inequality in the distribution of wealth is directly linked to inequality in the distribution of income, since property is concentrated in relatively few hands. In 1970 company shares and debentures, and securities, mortgages, building society shares and deposits amounted to 34.8 billion pounds. In the same year dividends from preferred and common stock amounted to 1.8 billion pounds, interest on debentures amounted to 555 million pounds, and income from securities, mortgages, building society shares and deposits amounted to 1.3 billion pounds.[40] On an a priori basis, it is logical to assume that the great bulk of this income of 3.6 billion pounds would go to those family units and individuals that own the bulk of this type of wealth. These figures exclude the important element of capital gains that would also be attached to the ownership of securities.

Wealth distribution takes the form of other assets that also have some effect on income distribution. The largest single wealth item, land and buildings, was valued at 32.9 billion pounds in 1970. Rent from this source amounted to 800 million pounds in 1970. Not included in this total is imputed rent from owner-occupied homes. Rental income, imputed or otherwise, would not necessarily redound solely to the advantage of upper-income groups, for there are also many small wealth-holders who would receive this form of income. Cash and bank deposits tend to be held more by those with low wealth, and yield no money return, although a benefit is presumably derived from the ability to use these assets as transactions. The ownership of government securities is another type of wealth. In 1970 interest from this source amounted to 1.4 billion pounds, approximately half of which can be counted as a source of personal income.

In total, it can be expected that income from all forms of wealth would go primarily to the upper-income groups. This expectation is confirmed by British studies on wealth distribution. One such study indicated that in 1959 the top 1 percent of all income earners received 60 percent of total income from wealth, while the top 10 percent of income earners received 99 percent of total income from wealth.[41] The data involved before-tax income received by various income units. The distribution of income from wealth was more concentrated in the hands of a few than the actual distribution of wealth itself. The data, however, tended to understate income from certain types of assets, such as houses, that would tend to be broad-based in terms of their distribution.

Other Observations on Distribution of Wealth

Inequality in the distribution of wealth appears to be somewhat greater in the United Kingdom than in the United States, although a pattern of similar decline in inequality is observable in the two countries. For example, in 1954 the top 1 percent of wealth-holders in the United Kingdom owned 43 percent of the wealth. In 1953 fairly comparable data for the United States indicated that the top 1 percent of wealth-holders owned 24 percent of all wealth.[42] Although these statistics are out of date, they may well still be valid, even though there has been a downward trend in the concentration of wealth in the United Kingdom, particularly during the last decade.

Finally, it is necessary to make some comments on the impact of British taxes on the accumulation of wealth. Probably the one single tax that is identified with the welfare state is the progressive income tax. This tax, although it has brought about greater equality in the distribution of income, really has far less impact upon the distribution of wealth. Unlike in Sweden, in Britain there is no tax on wealth itself, but only on the income from wealth or on the transfer of wealth. The main tax that is of direct relevance to wealth is the estate tax. This tax has been altered frequently; the current rates, which are progressive, reach a maximum of 75 percent on estates of 500,000 pounds and over. This rate, however, is the nominal rate rather than the effective rate. In actuality, the effective rate, all the way down the rate schedule, is far less than the nominal rate. The lower effective rate is attributable in part to various types of avoidances written into the tax laws.

In summary it can be said that the long-term trend in the distribution of wealth in the United Kingdom has been toward a decline in the degree of inequality. This decline is particularly pronounced for the top 1 percent of all wealth-holders. It would appear, however, that the shifts in wealth distribution have been really to the wealth-holders directly below the top 1 percent. In the short run, as Table 6.9 indicates, there have been more pronounced shifts in wealth distribution. To some extent these shifts over time may be attributable to estate duties. The income tax may also have had some impact on the accumulation of wealth, by reducing the level of savings. One counterbalancing factor over time has been the generally favorable tax treatment of capital gains. The nominal rate of tax is lower than that on other investment income. The wealth of the rich has been concentrated in those assets, such as stocks and land, that are most likely to yield capital gains.

SUMMARY

In spite of certain conceptions based on the welfare state as it has developed in the United Kingdom, income distribution follows a pattern similar to that which exists in the United States, West Germany, and other countries that have market-oriented economies. The top 20 percent of income earners receives around 42 percent of income before taxes. The income tax, as is also the case in Sweden, does achieve some alteration in the distribution of income. Over a long period of time there has been a trend toward greater equality in the distribution of both income and wealth.

But despite this long-term trend toward more equality in the distribution of wealth, there is little doubt that the present distribution is highly concentrated. The Gini coefficient of wealth distribution, which is based on estate duties, was .65 in 1970, which is about twice that for the distribution of income. Reliance on estate duty data, however, provides an incomplete picture of wealth distribution. For one thing, the exemption level has been changed frequently, with the result that many estates are not subject to the duty. In addition, there are various ways in which the estate duty is circumvented. For example, property to which title can pass by delivery, cash, personal possessions, and household goods are not subject to the duty. The end result is that there is no clear-cut picture of the actual extent of concentration of wealth in the United Kingdom.

NOTES

1. James Wedgwood, The Economics of Inheritance (London: George Routledge and Sons, Ltd., 1929), p. 42.
2. Sir William Beveridge, Social Insurance and Allied Services (London: His Majesty's Stationery Office, Cmd. 6406, 1942).
3. Sir Roy Harrod, The British Economy (New York: McGraw-Hill Book Company, 1963), pp. 27-28.
4. See F. W. Paish, "The Real Incidence of Personal Income Taxation," Lloyds Bank Review (January 1957); and H. F. Lydall, "The Long-Term Trend in the Size Distribution of Income," Journal of the Royal Statistical Society, Series A, 122 (1959): 1.
5. R. J. Nicholson, "The Distribution of Personal Income," Lloyds Bank Review (January 1967); also John A. Brittain, "Some Neglected Features of Britain's Income Levelling," American Economic Review (May, 1960).
6. Sir Richard Clarke, "The Management of the Public Sector of the National Economy" (London: University of London, The Athlone Press, 1964), pp. 6-7.
7. Central Statistical Office, Social Trends (London: Her Majesty's Stationery Office, 1972), p. 83.
8. Ibid., p. 83.
9. Central Statistical Office, National Income and Expenditures, 1972 (London: Her Majesty's Stationery Office, 1972), p. 27.
10. Central Office of Information, The New British System of Taxation (London: Her Majesty's Stationery Office, 1973). All tax data are derived from this publication.
11. Central Office of Information, Social Security in Britain (London: Her Majesty's Stationery Office, 1971). All social security data are derived from this publication.

12. Alan Peacock and Robin Shannon, "The Welfare State and the Redistribution of Income," Westminster Bank Review (August 1968).

13. Central Statistical Office, National Income and Expenditures, 1967 (London: Her Majesty's Stationery Office, 1967), p. 26.

14. Ibid., p. 26.

15. R. J. Nicholson, op. cit., pp. 11-15.

16. Central Statistical Office, National Income and Expenditures, 1972 (London: Her Majesty's Stationery Office, 1972), pp. 4 and 5.

17. Ibid., p. 5.

18. Central Statistical Office, National Income and Expenditures, 1968 and 1969 (London: Her Majesty's Stationery Office, 1968 and 1969), pp. 34 and 35 (1968) and pp. 27 and 28 (1969).

19. R. J. Nicholson, op. cit., p. 18, National Income and Expenditures, 1969, p. 28.

20. National Income and Expenditures, 1972, pp. 4 and 5.

21. Martin Schnitzer, "Guaranteed Minimum Income Programs Used by Governments of Selected Countries," Joint Economic Committee, 90th Congress, 2nd Session (Washington: Government Printing Office, 1968), p. 36.

22. James Meade, Efficiency, Equality and the Ownership of Property (London: George Allen and Unwin, 1964), Table 1.

23. Alan Prest and Thomas Stark, "Some Aspects of Income Distribution in the United Kingdom," Manchester School of Economic and Social Studies 55, no. 3 (September 1967).

24. J. L. Nicholson, Redistribution of Income in the United Kingdom (London: Bowes and Bowes, 1964).

25. Ibid., p. 27.

26. Ibid., p. 46.

27. Wedgwood, op. cit., p. 47.

28. Ibid., p. 47.

29. Ibid., p. 47.

30. Social Trends, Table 35, p. 86.

31. Ibid., p. 86.

32. A. B. Atkinson, The Distribution of Wealth in Great Britain, University of Essex, forthcoming monograph.

33. Social Trends, p. 190.

34. Ibid., p. 190.

35. H. F. Lydall and D. G. Tipping, "The Distribution of Personal Wealth in Britain," Bulletin of the Oxford University Institute of Economics and Statistics (February 1961); A. B. Atkinson, Unequal Shares (London: The Penguin Press, 1972).

36. Cited in Atkinson, op. cit., p. 15.

37. Ibid., p. 15.

38. J. R. Revell, The Wealth of the Nation (Cambridge: Cambridge University Press, 1967), Table 5.

39. Ibid.

40. National Income and Expenditures, 1972, pp. 4 and 5.

41. Meade, op. cit., Table 1.

42. H. F. Lydall and J. B. Lansing, "A Comparison of the Distribution of Personal Income and Wealth in the United States and Great Britain," American Economic Review (March 1959), Chart 1.

7

INCOME DISTRIBUTION
IN JAPAN

The final country to be considered in this study of income distribution in selected countries is Japan. Its inclusion is important for several reasons. First, Japan has the fastest growth rate of all major industrial countries. In a relatively short period of time it has overtaken such industrial countries as France, the United Kingdom, and West Germany to currently rank third in the world in terms of the size of gross national product. It is envisioned by some that Japan will eventually overtake the Soviet Union and the United States and become the most important industrial country.[1] Second, in terms of its position on the capitalist-socialist spectrum, it has perhaps the most capitalistic, or least mixed, economy of all major countries. This statement is based on the extent to which the government contributes to the economy as a purchaser of goods and services, and the extent to which it diverts income flows from the private to the public sector through taxation and rechannels income through transfers.

In 1970 government expenditures on goods and services amounted to only 8.2 percent of Japanese gross national product—the lowest percentage for all Organization for Economic Cooperation and Development countries.[2] In Sweden government expenditures on goods and services amounted to 21.2 percent of gross national product, and in the United Kingdom, the United States, and West Germany, the percentages were 17.9, 20.8, and 15.6 respectively.[3] Taxes and transfer payments, as mentioned repeatedly, are the major means for effecting changes in the distribution of income. Through them a government can use its power to alter the distribution of money income that results from the play of market forces. Both taxes and transfer payments are lower in Japan when compared to such factors as personal income and gross national product than they are in countries with mixed economic systems. In 1970 receipts from taxation and social security contributions amounted to 21 percent of gross national product, compared to 43 percent in Sweden and 30 percent in the United States.[4] Social security contributions amounted to 5 percent of national income in Japan, compared to 19 percent in France. On the other side of the coin, transfer payments amounted to about 6 percent of personal income, compared to 20 percent in France and 14 percent in Sweden.[5]

A major explanation for the fact that government social welfare payments are lower in Japan than in other industrial countries lies in the role of the industrial enterprise as a social force in modern Japan. It is considered to be a social unit from which the nation expects more than mere production of goods and services. It provides employees with the security of a lifetime commitment to employment, and it provides family allowances, housing and travel allowances, substantial retirement allowances, medical benefits, and many noncash benefits as well. The industrial enterprise can be regarded as an industrial family. The employee, rather than being hired, is adopted as a member of the family, and his participation in it is based on grounds larger than his actual contribution in terms of skill. The wage system is not simply compensation for work but is rather a kind of "life income" determined by the employee's age and family changes. The basic wage often comprises only 50 percent of annual income; the remainder is paid in various allowances and benefits.

This is not to say, however, that the government is of no importance in Japan. A combination of free enterprise and government control in Japan dates back to the Meiji Restoration. Government and business have been closely associated in working out economic policy. This cooperation is facilitated in part by economic planning that sets goals of long-range economic growth per annum over a base period. There is no element of coercion or centralized government control, but rather an arrangement based on induced cooperation on the part of business enterprises through the use of monetary and fiscal controls, and through planned expenditures on the part of the government.

THE JAPANESE ECONOMY

As mentioned above, the Japanese economic system is essentially capitalistic. With the exception of certain public services and monopolies that are operated by the Japanese government, private enterprise is dominant in the economy. This fact is exemplified in Table 7.1, which presents the Japanese gross national product for 1972. The gross national product can be divided into three basic categories —consumption expenditures, both private and public; investment

TABLE 7.1

Japanese Gross National Product for 1972

Components	Millions of Yen*
Private consumption expenditures	47,103.9
General government expenditures	8,132.4
Gross domestic capital formation	33,107.6
Gross fixed investment	31,557.5
Private	22,427.6
Government	9,129.8
Increase in stock	1,550.1
Private	1,556.9
Government	-6.8
Surplus of the nation on current account	2,151.9
Exports	10,388.5
Imports	8,236.6
Gross national product	90,495.8

*The exchange rate as of September 1973 is about 333 yen to $1.00.

Source: Ministry of Foreign Affairs, Economic News from Japan (Tokyo, March 1973), p. 6.

expenditures, private and public; and surplus from foreign trade, or exports less imports. Out of total consumption expenditures on goods and services of 55 trillion yen, private consumption expenditures consisted of 47 trillion yen and public consumption expenditures amounted to 8 trillion yen, a ratio of 85 percent to 15 percent. Gross domestic capital formation amounted to 33 trillion yen, with the private sector contributing 72 percent of the amount and the government sector contributing the remaining 28 percent. It is also safe to assume that the great bulk of income from foreign trade accrues to the private sector of the economy.

The role of the Japanese government in the economy is more indirect than direct. There has long been a tradition in Japan of the government promoting business interests by the means of special financial privileges, subsidies, and low interest rates. Selective or discriminatory treatment of various industries has been an integral part of postwar Japanese economic policy. The government has tried to favor certain industries, certain types of economic activity, or certain types of firms, through such measures as an import licensing system, control and allocation of investment funds, and special tax policies to promote investment and corporate savings. Examples of tax policies include accelerated depreciation provisions, to stimulate the modernization of industrial facilities and the advancement of new technology, and tax-free reserves, which are deductible from the Japanese corporate income tax and are used to increase the total supply of national savings.

Fiscal policy has played an important role in the postwar development of the Japanese economy. Changes in the level of taxation, in expenditures in the government general accounts budget, and in the government financial loan and investment program are the three devices that have been used to affect the level of aggregate demand. Maintenance of a high rate of economic growth, as opposed to income redistribution and the provision of socially desirable goods and services, has been the dominant objective of fiscal policy. However, the emphasis on economic growth can also be recognized as an acceptance of responsibility on the part of the government to provide a sustained rate of economic growth, which has redounded to the advantage of the Japanese people in the form of a continued increase in the per capita output of real goods and services. However, economic growth has not been an unmixed blessing, as witnessed by the problem of pollution and a generally low investment in social capital. The Japanese are now beginning to shift priorities.

National Income

The initial distribution of income at factor cost always begins with national income. The method of calculating national income consists in adding up all of the wages, profits, rents, and interest—in short, "factor incomes"—received by the factors of production in a given period. The main significance of the national income concept thus formulated lies in revealing the distribution side of national economic activity or the manner in which the total product is allocated to the factors of production relative to the productive services rendered. Table 7.2 presents the Japanese national income at factor cost for 1971.

Personal Income

From the standpoint of examining the distribution of individuals and households, the appropriate statistical concept to use is personal income. Personal income is derived from national income by

TABLE 7.2

Distribution of National Income
at Factor Cost in Japan, 1971

Components	Billions of Yen
Compensation of employees	36,543
Wages and salaries	34,625
Employer contributions to social security	1,918
Income from unincorporated enterprises	11,448
Rent	2,994
Interest	3,987
Corporate profits	8,230
Government income from property and	
entrepreneurship	681
National income	63,202

Source: Ministry of Foreign Affairs, Statistical Survey of
Japan's Economy, 1972 (Tokyo, 1972), p. 73.

subtracting from the latter such items failing to reach individuals
as undistributed corporate profits and corporate income taxes and
social security contributions, and by adding thereto business and
government transfer payments and government bond interest. Japanese
personal income for 1971 is presented in Table 7.3. Personal income
is divided into four major sources of income—wages and salaries,
income of unincorporated enterprises, property income, and transfer
payments. The most significant aspect of the table is the low ratio
of government transfer payments to personal income. Government
transfer payments accounted for less than 6 percent of personal income.

In connection with personal income, it is also necessary to
make reference to the high rate of personal saving in Japan. Personal savings have averaged around 18 percent of disposable income
(personal income less taxes) over the period from 1950 to 1971.[6] In
1971 personal savings in Japan amounted to 20.3 percent of disposable
income—a rate more than twice that for the United States.[7] The high
rate can be attributed to several factors—the frugality of the Japanese,
a substantial increase in disposable income during the postwar period,
and tax policies, such as the tax exemption of interest income on
small accounts. The average propensity to save out of disposable
income is considerably higher than zero even for low-income families.

There may be, however, higher marginal propensity to save out of property income than out of wages and salaries. To the extent that higher-income families receive a higher proportion of their income from property holding, favorable treatment of savings makes income distribution more unequal.

PUBLIC FINANCE

One of the factors complicating the whole subject of public finance in Japan is the role that the industrial enterprise plays in the life of the average Japanese worker. It can be said that the enterprise has usurped many of the functions of the welfare state. A number of functions that are normally provided, at least in part, by the public sector, are provided by the Japanese enterprise. Such things as free medical care, low-cost housing, and subsidized meals, all of which would count in the income redistribution process, emanate from industrial enterprises. This means that social welfare expenditures are low in comparison with other countries.

Japanese government expenditures are carried in the national budget, which consists of general accounts, special accounts, and government agency accounts. General accounts are incorporated into a general accounts budget and include direct expenditures for

TABLE 7.3

Distribution of Personal Income In Japan

Components	Billions of Yen
Wages and salaries	34,625
Income of unincorporated enterprises	11,448
Property income	7,849
Rent	2,994
Interest	3,987
Dividends	868
Transfer payments	3,711
Government	3,600
Business	111
Personal income	57,633

Source: Ministry of Foreign Affairs, Statistical Survey of Japan's Economy, 1972 (Tokyo, 1972), p. 75.

education, science and technology, social security, allocations to local governments, and national defense. Main revenue sources are taxes, monopoly profits, and bond revenues. The general accounts budget is important from the standpoint of an analysis of income distribution, for it contains both current expenditures on goods and services and transfer payments as well as the sources of revenue to finance these expenditures. Special accounts are used where the government either undertakes specific projects or finances a specific expenditure with a specific revenue. Principal among the special accounts are those for national hospitals, harbor improvement, and export insurance. Government agency accounts are subject to the approval of the Japanese Diet.

Taxation in Japan

The two most important taxes in the Japanese tax system are the personal and corporate income taxes. In 1972 these taxes accounted for 70 percent of national government revenue obtained from tax sources.[8] Local government units in Japan rely on a system of grants from the national government, as well as a number of taxes, to support their expenditures. Half of the revenues of local government entities are provided by grants and subsidies from the national treasury. However, Japan has had a long tradition of local autonomy, and the importance of local finance in relation to national finance is greater in Japan than it is in the United Kingdom and West Germany. The most important local tax is a business enterprise tax that is levied on earned income.

A peculiar characteristic of the Japanese tax system is an enormous number of special tax provisions under which taxes are reduced selectively to accomplish specific national policy objectives. Examples of these provisions are as follows:

1. To stimulate savings, provisions of the personal income tax provide for tax exemption of interest income from small deposits, separate low taxation of interest income, favorable tax treatment of dividend income, exemption of capital gains on securities, and deduction of life insurance premiums.

2. Considerable use has been made of accelerated depreciation provisions to stimulate investment. These provisions are selective in their application and apply only to industries designated as contributing to exports or to the modernization of the economy.

3. There are provisions to promote the introduction of new products and technology. These include exemptions from personal or corporate income taxation of income from the sale of new products approved by the Ministry of Finance, duty-free importation of certain

types of machinery and equipment, and favorable tax treatment of certain royalties and patents.

The Personal Income Tax

One problem with the Japanese personal income tax is its frequency of change. The national government has the authority to alter the rates and base annually and usually does. The most current rates, those for 1972, are used here.[9] The income tax is progressive and begins with a rate of 10 percent on incomes of 400,000 yen or less and goes up to 75 percent on incomes of 80 million yen and over. The bracket method of progression is used, with the income tax increasing by brackets. The effective rate of the income tax is far less than the marginal rate for each income bracket. For example, the effective tax on an income of 80 million yen is 12.2 million yen, while the marginal tax rate is 75 percent.

There are a number of deductions and allowances that reduce the effective rate of income taxation. Then, too, there is a special treatment of capital gains, interest, dividends, and real estate income. With respect to allowances, there is a basic allowance of 200,000 yen that a taxpayer may deduct from total income. Then there are allowances for dependents, which are based on the consanguinity of the dependent to the taxpayer, and an allowance for the spouse of a taxpayer that amounts to 200,000 yen. Deductions are permitted for life insurance premiums and for contributions. The latter deduction is limited to 3 percent of total income. There is a reduction for medical expenses that amounts to total expenses less 5 percent of income, or an optional 100,000 yen with a ceiling of 1 million yen.

Income from dividends, interest, capital gains, and royalties is segregated from ordinary income and taxed at preferential rates. For example, long-term capital gains are taxed at a flat rate of 15 percent. Capital losses may be used as offset in computing ordinary income or capital gains. Special deductions up to a maximum of 12 million yen are permitted in computing taxable capital gains. Short-term capital gains are treated as ordinary income. Income from dividends is also treated differently from ordinary income, and is also subject to a flat-rate tax of 15 percent. Interest on government bonds and bank deposits is exempt from income taxation provided that the value of the bonds or deposit is not in excess of 1 million yen. Interest on company bonds and debentures is subject to a withholding tax of 15 percent. There is no double taxation of either dividends or interest; the flat-rate tax is withheld at the source. The tax on dividends of 600,000 yen would be 90,000 yen, which may be used as a credit in computing the regular income tax.

The Corporate Income Tax

The corporate tax is the single most important source of tax revenue to the national government. In 1972 it accounted for 35 percent of national tax revenues. The corporate income tax rate on ordinary income that is not distributed as dividends is 28 percent on incomes of up to 3 million yen and 36.5 percent on incomes of over 3 million yen. Rates are reduced on ordinary income that has been redistributed in the form of dividends to 22 percent on incomes of under 3 million yen and 26 percent on incomes over 3 million yen. The income base for tax purposes is reduced considerably by favorable tax provisions in the tax system that have been instituted by the government to facilitate economic policy objectives. An example would be the deduction of expenses involved in developing overseas markets. Another example is accelerated depreciation for certain export industries. A third provision, which is of some relevance to the subject of income distribution, is the very favorable treatment of expense accounts, which has enabled many Japanese, executives and otherwise, to live quite well.

Annual changes in the tax laws constitute an important part of the national government's budgetary policy and are called the "tax-cut" policy in Japanese. Because of the high rate of economic growth, the government has reduced both the rates of the personal and corporate income taxes almost every year since 1950. Since the income elasticity of both taxes is greater than one, if tax rates had not been cut, tax revenues would have increased at a much faster rate than national income. The largest proportion of total tax reduction has been represented by reductions in personal income taxes. During the period from 1950 to 1971 the basic exemption has been raised from 25,000 to 200,000 yen and the exemption for dependents has been raised from 12,000 yen to 200,000 yen for the spouse, and from 10,000 yen to 140,000 yen for each child. The increase in the basic exemption has been somewhat greater than the increase in per capita national income. Tax rates at higher-income levels have also been reduced; for example, the marginal rate at 300,000 yen, which was 55 percent in 1950, was 10 percent in 1971.

On the other hand, the proportion of corporate income taxes to total tax revenues has risen during the same period. There have been fewer changes in the corporate income tax laws. The corporate income tax has been affected much more by selective tax reductions than by across-the-board changes in rates. One end result is a very high level of corporate savings, which, in turn, has led to a high rate of capital formation. In connection with savings, Japanese corporations can hold down the ratio of dividends to corporate profits because new shares are issued at face value; the shareholders are given the difference between the market and face values as capital gains, so that dividends represent only a small part of their earnings.

Inheritance and Gift Taxes

Inheritance and gift taxes are used as a supplement to the personal income tax. The inheritance tax is levied on the increase in net assets of an individual resulting from an inheritance or bequest. The rate of the inheritance tax is progressive and ranges from 10 percent on inheritances of 600,000 yen or less to 70 percent on inheritances in excess of 150 million yen. There is a basic estate allowance that amounts to 4,000,000 yen plus 800,000 yen multiplied by the number of statutory heirs. There is also a surtax of 20 percent of the prorated share when a legatee is not related by blood to the decedent. The gift tax is levied annually on gifts received by taxpayers. Its rates are also progressive and range from 10 percent on gifts of 300,000 yen or less to 70 percent on gifts of 30 million yen and above. There is a basic allowance for the gift tax that amounts to 400,000 yen a year. In addition, there are other allowances that reduce the effective rate of the gift tax. The inheritance and gift taxes combined account for less than 2 percent of national government tax revenues.

Indirect Taxes

Indirect taxes account for approximately 45 percent of total government tax revenues, and are levied on a wide variety of goods and services. The liquor tax is the most important indirect tax. In 1971 it accounted for 9.3 percent of national tax revenues. The tax rates on liquor are substantially higher than those on other commodities subject to consumption taxes, and the tax base is the quantity of liquor shipped from the manufacturer. The tax is a flat-rate levy based on the kind, class, and percentage of alcohol. Another important indirect tax is a levy on the consumption of tobacco. This, too, is a flat-rate levy based on the kind and price of tobacco. The burden of the tobacco tax is high—the amount of the tax averaging 50 percent of the purchase price of a package of cigarettes. The gasoline tax, which is also an important source of revenue, amounts to 55 percent of the purchase price of a liter of gas. There is also a commodity tax, which is levied on such items as automobiles, television sets, cameras, records, cosmetics, and other consumer goods. The base of the tax is either the retailer's sales price or the manufacturer's sales price, depending on the commodity. The rate of the commodity tax varies considerably by product. It is highest on cars, averaging 25 percent for a large car and 9 percent on a small car, and lowest on perfume and matches.

Other Taxes

Local governmental units in Japan can be divided into two categories—prefectures and municipalities. Prefectures generally correspond to large metropolitan areas—Tokyo, Osaka—while municipalities cover smaller cities and towns. Each local unit levies a tax on both personal and corporate income. The taxes on personal income at the prefectural level are divided into two types—a per capita tax on inhabitants and an income tax. The per capita tax rate is 100 yen per person. The prefectural income tax is 2 percent on incomes of 1.5 million yen or less, and 4 percent on incomes in excess of 1.5 million yen. Allowances and deductions somewhat similar to those permissible under the national income tax laws are available. Neither tax, however, can be used as an offset against the other. Municipalities levy only an income tax, which is levied at rates ranging from 2 percent of incomes of 150,000 yen or less to 14 percent on incomes in excess of 50 million yen. There are also allowances and deductions similar to those permitted under the national income tax laws. The municipal tax cannot be used as an offset against the national tax. The total of national, prefectural, and municipal income taxes cannot exceed 80 percent of taxable income.

Social Security Contributions

In preceding chapters social security contributions have been kept separate from the basic direct and indirect taxes. According to some definitions, however, direct taxes on households include not only the personal income tax, death duty, and other direct taxes on individuals, but also contributions to social security funds by employees and employers. There are problems in classifying social security contributions as direct taxes. Theoretically, it is feasible to view the social security tax levied against the employer as a direct tax on income if the amount of such taxes is treated as income in the national income accounts. In national income accounting such taxes are considered as part of the wages and salaries component of the factor cost of the national output, hence they are looked upon as income earned in the production process. In fact, it is more in keeping with reality to view such taxes as an indirect levy against the employer that may be shifted. Then, too, in the budgets of most national governments, social security contributions are segregated from regular tax revenues.

Social security contributions account for approximately 15 percent of total public sector tax revenues and are designed to provide coverage for old age, sickness, unemployment, and work injuries.

Old-age pensions are financed by a tax on insured persons of 2.75 percent on incomes of up to 60,000 yen a month, and a tax of 2.75 percent of payrolls on the employer. There is also a dual system for special classes of workers—seamen, teachers, and public servants. Sickness and maternity benefits are financed out of a tax of 3.25 percent on insured persons on incomes of up to 52,000 yen a month, and a 3.25 percent payroll tax on employers. Work-injury compensation is financed out of a tax on the employer that ranges from 2 to 8 percent of his payroll, based on three-year accident rates. Finally, unemployment compensation is financed out of a tax of 0.7 percent of earnings of insured persons, and a tax of 0.7 percent on the employer. These contributions cover two-thirds of social security expenditures; the remaining one-third is covered by general tax revenues of the national government, with local governments making a minor contribution.

The Burden of Japanese Taxes

The two most important Japanese taxes are the corporate and personal income taxes, in that order. An analysis of the burden of the corporate income tax tends to be obfuscated because of the wide variety of special features built into the Japanese tax system. These privileges work somewhat to the advantage of the export-oriented industries and to the disadvantage of domestic industries. One end result is the high rate of corporate savings, which have generally been in excess of corporate income taxes. These savings are channeled into investment, which, in turn, would have an effect upon income distribution for the reason that capital accumulation and the income inequality that goes with it implies a systematic differentiation between capitalists and workers. The volume of savings would have some impact on both dividends and capital gains, both of which would affect income distribution. Dividend policies, however, have been conservative, reflecting the fact that Japanese corporations can hold down the ratio of dividends to corporate profits through issuing stock at face value. During the period from 1963 to 1971 dividends declined from 18 percent of property income to 11 percent.[10]

In 1971 the corporate income tax amounted to 5.8 percent of national income, while corporate savings were in excess of corporate taxes, amounting to 6.1 percent of national income.[11] It can be said that 5.8 percent of national income was diverted from the private to the public sector through corporate income taxation. The burden of this flow more than likely did not rest upon the corporations, but upon Japanese consumers and wage earners. Given the more favorable tax treatment of export industries the Japanese consumer would generally be expected to carry the burden of taxes on domestic industries in the form of higher prices and fewer consumer goods. Wide variations exist, however, in the effects on different corporations. Moreover, the impact of the tax is inextricably mingled with the many dynamic changes that are constantly taking place in the Japanese economy.

The relationship of personal income to personal income taxes and social security contributions is important because of the way in which it indicates the tax burden assumed by Japanese citizens. In 1971 Japanese income taxes, national and local, amounted to 5.6 percent of Japanese personal income, while employee social security contributions amounted to 2.7 percent. In the same year income taxes amounted to 13.8 percent of personal income in the United Kingdom, while social security contributions amounted to 6.0 percent.[12] Thus we can say that in the United Kingdom the government is more deeply involved in the nation's economic affairs simply because of the larger proportion of personal income that flows out into the public sector. The proportion of personal income that is channeled into the government sector for public purposes was 19.8 percent in the United Kingdom and 8.3 percent in Japan. Comparable studies are much higher for Sweden, with personal income taxes and social security contributions amounting to 35.2 percent of personal income in 1971.

Government Expenditures

In 1972 total national and local government current expenditures on goods and services amounted to less than 10 percent of the Japanese gross national product. However, fixed capital expenditures by the national government amounted to 10 percent of gross national product and one-third of domestic investment expenditures—a high ratio in comparison to other capitalist countries.[13] National government expenditures on goods and services are contained in the general accounts budget and consist of several categories—income transfers to local governments, expenditures on education, aid to industry, social welfare expenditures involving transfer payments, and expenditures on national defense. The last expenditure is a relatively minor item in the Japanese budget. Local governments are primarily concerned with direct expenditures on public works, education, police protection, and the promotion of industrial development. Direct income transfers to people are of no particular importance at the local level.

There is a wide disparity between national wealth and social welfare. It is now openly acknowledged that Japan is a backward society by most measures of public well-being, from social security coverage to public park space. A recent government analysis revealed that the country lags a decade behind the United States and Western Europe in housing, sanitation, and other basic essentials. In a nation that ranks among the top economic powers, only 15 percent of the homes are connected to sewers. Because production has been expanded to satisfy domestic consumption as well as the world export market, the evil influences of a high-density economy and society have been intensified, as represented by the aggravation of environmental pollution. With the emphasis on achieving economic growth, other social needs have also been neglected. Japan devotes less than 6 percent of its national income to social security, compared with 15 to 20 percent in most West European nations. Though most workers retire at 55, they must wait until 60 to qualify for social security pensions. The social security pensions themselves are considered low by Western standards.

Social Security Expenditures

Social security expenditures of the income transfer type amounted to 16 percent of the general accounts budget for 1972 and are of four types—old-age pensions, sickness and maternity benefits, work-injury compensation, and unemployment benefits. The family allowance, which is one of the most important social welfare measures used by other industrial countries, is not used in Japan. Old-age pensions account for the largest percentage of social security, and provide as of 1973 a maximum benefit range of from 3,000 to 5,000 yen a month. Medical care to the aged is free. The old-age pension is paid monthly at a rate based on the years of coverage multiplied by a sum of 275 yen plus 1 percent of lifetime average monthly earnings. There are also supplements for dependents. Although the cost of old-age pensions is supported by a tax on both employees and employers, the bulk of the cost is covered by general tax revenues of the Japanese government.

National health programs cover some 40 percent of the population, with the remaining 60 percent having recourse to private schemes that vary widely with respect to coverage. Very large firms have health programs as good as, or better than, those provided by the government, but the majority of programs sponsored by firms is below government standards. Benefits under health insurance are generally low by Western standards, with patients carrying some of the cost. There is a lump-sum maternity grant of 5,000 yen. Work-injury benefits do not cover all of the labor force, and are limited in what they provide. Permanent disability pensions of up to 60 percent of earnings are payable, plus medical benefits and certain supplements for dependents. A widows' pension of 30 percent of earnings is also payable. Unemployment compensation of up to 60 percent of average weekly earnings is payable for a period of up to a maximum of 270 days. There are supplements available to dependents. Maximum unemployment compensation is 860 yen a day.

These programs are mostly of the income maintenance type, meaning that something has to happen before they are payable. They maintain rather than supplement income. There are other types of transfers, such as subsidies to farmers and education grants, that tend to supplement incomes. Then, too, it is necessary to mention the paternalism of many Japanese companies. Numerous benefits are received by Japanese workers that certainly are in the nature of business transfer payments. For example, many companies have private old-age pension plans that are separate from the national pension program. Subsidized housing, free medical care, family allowances, and income in kind are also provided by private companies. To some extent Japanese business firms are providing benefits that would normally be provided by the public sector in other countries.

Government expenditures on goods and services and transfer payments cannot be linked together in comparing Japanese public expenditures as a percent of an appropriate national income aggregate. These two expenditure categories reflect performances of distinctly different economic functions, and they should be compared to different national income aggregates. The economic significance of the Japanese public sector as a supplier of social goods can be determined by computing government expenditures for goods and services as a percentage of gross national product. This will show what proportion of total output is being absorbed by public bodies and presumably being utilized for the satisfaction of social rather than private wants. The degree to which the government has become an instrument for the redistribution of income can be measured by computing transfer expenditures as a percent of national income. National income is a measure of income earned by resource owners by supplying the services of economic resources to the productive process. If transfers are computed as a percentage of this total, it will show the proportion of earned income that has been redistributed by action of the public sector.

Some International Comparisons

General comparisons can be made between Japan and some of the other countries used in this study. Government expenditures on goods and services is currently much smaller in Japan than in the other countries. Excluding East Germany for obvious reasons, some of the comparisons are as follows: In 1968/69 expenditures on goods and services, excluding defense expenditures, amounted to 7.4 percent of gross national product in Japan, compared to 17.4 percent in Sweden, 12.0 percent in the United States, 12.7 percent in the United Kingdom, and 12.4 percent in West Germany.[14] When defense expenditures are taken into consideration, the discrepancy between Japan and the other countries is much greater. On the other hand, public sector investment is higher than in the United States and West Germany and at least as high as in Sweden and the United Kingdom. On this basis, the Japanese public sector accounted for 8.1 percent of the gross national product in 1971. However, a very large percentage of public sector investment was devoted to expenditures linked to the development of the business sector, while less than one-fourth of investment was spent in fields such as health, welfare, and education. This spending compared unfavorably with those of the other countries.

By any measure of comparison, income transfers in Japan are lower than in the other countries used in this study. In 1970, for example, transfer payments amounted to 5.3 percent of national income, compared to 12 percent for Sweden and 16 percent for West Germany.[15] Using another method of comparison, transfer payments to the private sector amounted to 4 percent of Japanese gross national product in 1968/69, compared to 13.5 percent for West Germany, 11.8 percent for Sweden, 8.6 percent for the United Kingdom, and 6.2 percent for the United States.[16] When transfer payments are expressed as a percentage of personal income, the results are the same—Japanese transfer payments are lower than in the other countries. In 1970 Japanese transfer payments amounted to 5.5 percent of personal income, compared to 7.5 percent for the United States, 16 percent for West Germany, 13.5 percent for Sweden, and 10.1 percent for the United Kingdom.[17] Transfer payments accounted for 19 percent of French personal income for the same year. The significance of the comparisons is apparent. Transfer payments are a method by which governments redistribute income from one group of individuals to another. This being the case, it can be said that transfer payments are of far less importance in the income redistribution process in Japan in comparison to Sweden or West Germany.

INCOME DISTRIBUTION IN JAPAN

A starting point for an analysis of income distribution in Japan is the division of national income at factor costs for 1971. These factor costs consist of necessary payments that have to be made in either money or kind in order to secure the services of the factors of production. Payments in 1971 were as follows: compensation of employees, 36.5 trillion yen; incomes of unincorporated enterprises, 11.4 trillion yen; corporate profits, 8.2 trillion yen; rent, 3.0 trillion yen; and interest, 3.9 trillion yen.[18] Also included is general government income from property and entrepreneurship of 681 billion yen.

TABLE 7.4

Distribution of Japanese Income at Factor Cost, 1960-71
(billions of yen)

	1960	1963	1965	1967	1969	1971
Compensation of employees	6,434	10,682	14,297	18,962	25,803	36,543
Income of unincorporated enterprises	3,393	4,900	5,981	7,949	10,255	11,448
Rent	491	778	1,176	1,614	2,173	2,994
Interest	548	961	1,357	1,906	2,716	3,987
Corporate profits	1,818	2,352	2,667	4,217	6,508	8,230
Government income from business	204	330	208	332	539	681
Property income (rent, interest, dividends)	1,253	2,129	2,979	4,028	5,563	7,849

Source: Bureau of Statistics, Japan Statistical Yearbook, 1972
(Tokyo: Office of the Prime Minister, 1972), p. 501.

Compensation of employees, including social security contributions, accounted for 58 percent of national income, a low percentage in comparison to other countries used in this study. Income from property, which amounted to 7.8 billion yen in the form of rent, interest, and dividends, accounted for 12.5 percent of national income. Interest and rent accounted for 90 percent of property income.

In Table 7.4 the distribution of national income at factor cost is presented over a period from 1960 to 1971. Some shifts in the relative shares of the factors of production have occurred over the twelve-year period. Using 1960 as a base period of 100 percent, the most significant shifts are in the form of interest and rent. Interest income in particular increased by 620 percent over the twelve-year period, compared to an increase of 410 percent in national income. Rental income also increased at a faster rate than national income over the period, 500 percent compared to 410 percent. Interest income represented 4.1 percent of national income in 1960 and 5.3 percent in 1971, while income from rent amounted to 3.7 percent of national income in 1960 and 4.6 percent in 1971. Property income (interest, dividends, and rent) amounted to 9.5 percent of national income in 1960 and 12.4 percent in 1971. A sharp decline in the position of income of unincorporated enterprises occurred relative to the other distributive shares. The decline was from 26.8 percent of national income in 1960 to 18.1 in 1971. Compensation of employees increased from 49.9 percent of national income in 1960 to 57.9 percent in 1971, while corporate profits decreased from 14.2 percent in 1960 to 13.0 percent in 1971.

Shifts have also occurred over the same time period in the distribution of national income by industrial origin. In particular, there has been a decrease in the importance of agriculture as a source of national income, and an increase in the relative importance of the finance and service industries. Agriculture contributed 15 percent of national income in 1960, but only 6 percent in 1971, while finance and insurance contributed 9.1 percent of national income in 1960 and 11.2 percent in 1971.[19] The service industry contributed 10.5 percent of national income in 1960 and 12.8 percent in 1971. The contribution of manufacturing to national income has remained constant at around 30 percent, while wholesale and retail trade showed an overall minor increase from 15.5 percent in 1960 to 17.9 percent in 1971. The significance of these shifts is reflected in the fact that average monthly earnings are higher and have increased more rapidly in those industries that have made the greatest gains in terms of contributions to national income. In other words, there has been a shift of the Japanese labor force into the faster-growing and higher-paying industries.

Japanese personal income includes all of national income at factor cost, with the exception of corporate savings and income taxes on corporations. Also excluded are social security taxes levied against employers. Realism demands that personal income be computed on the basis of money income actually received by persons, and thus it is neither reasonable nor desirable to include in this total employer contributions to social security, even though these outlays eventually appear as one form of personal income received. On the other hand, there are certain additions to personal income that are not included in national income—transfer payments from business and government and interest on the public debt. Personal income, then, can be divided into the following categories: compensation of employees, which consists of wages and salaries; income from property and entrepreneurship, which includes dividends, interest, and rent, and income of unincorporated enterprises; and business and government transfer payments. This division of personal income for 1971 can be presented in percentages as follows:

219

Wages and salaries	60.0
Self-employment	20.0
Rent, dividends, and interest	13.5
Transfer payments	6.5
Total	100.0

The Effect of Socioeconomic Factors
upon the Distribution of Wages and Salaries

Wage and salary payments in Japan are influenced by a number of socioeconomic factors. One such factor is sex. Reflecting in part the fact that Japan has long been a bulwark of male chauvinism, females on the average are paid about one-half as much as males. Average monthly earnings in manufacturing for males in 1970 amounted to 69,500 yen (approximately $208), while average monthly earnings for females amounted to 33,400 yen (approximately $102).[20] The average monthly payment for males in wholesaling and retailing was 62,300 yen, in comparison with an average monthly payment of 34,500 yen for females. The average monthly cash payment for all males in industry was 68,400 yen (approximately $204), while the average monthly cash payment for all females was 35,200 yen (approximately $105).[21]

Average monthly earnings also show considerable variation on the basis of age, particularly for men. In 1970 average monthly earnings for males employed in industry ranged from 29,300 yen for workers 18 and under to 87,200 yen for workers in the 40 to 49 age category.[22] Earnings were highest in the age categories from 35 to 59 and lowest for workers under 24 and 60 and over. On the other hand, age had far less impact on the earnings of females. The average payment in all industrial categories for females 18 to 19 was 30,800 yen, while the average monthly cash payment for females 40 to 49 was 38,600 yen. The spread between the highest and lowest average monthly payment based on age was 58,000 yen for males and 12,000 yen for females.

Other factors that have an impact on earnings are education, the type of industry, and the size of an enterprise.[23] In 1970 average monthly industrial earnings of male Japanese with the equivalent of a high school education were 67,400 yen, compared to 32,900 yen for females with the same education. The benefits of education increase as the years of education increase proportionately more for men than women. Males with the equivalent of a junior college education received an average industrial wage of 91,300 yen, compared to 37,300 yen for females. As would be expected, there are variations in earnings based on the type of industry. Average monthly earnings of all industrial workers in 1970 were 58,400 yen. The lowest average monthly payment was 35,900 yen, for workers in the apparel industry, while the highest average monthly payment was 81,900 yen, for workers in the iron and steel industry. Average monthly earnings are also related to the size of the enterprise. In 1970 the average monthly earning for industrial workers in enterprises with 1,000 or more employees was 71,000 yen, compared to average earnings of 54,000 yen for workers in enterprises employing between 10 and 100 workers.

In addition to regular monthly earnings, bonuses and other cash payments add the equivalent of about three months' income.[24] In 1970 annual special earnings of the average Japanese worker amounted to 171,100 yen (approximately $520), compared to the average monthly payment of 58,100 yen. Again there are sharp differences between male and female workers. The average male worker received annual special earnings of 206,400 yen, compared to 90,100 yen for women. Bonuses and other special earnings varied widely on an industry-by-industry basis, with the highest payment, 301,500 yen, recorded for the electricity, gas, and water industry and the lowest payment, 71,900 yen, recorded for the apparel industry. When bonuses and regular monthly payments are added together, a considerable differentiation in incomes exists in industry. The average yearly income in the apparel industry was 510,000 yen (approximately $1,530), compared to an average yearly income in the iron and steel industry of 1,010,000 yen (approximately $3,030).

Distribution of Japanese Income on a Before-Tax Basis

There are several problems associated with an analysis of Japanese income distribution. First, annual changes are usually made in the rate and base of the personal income tax. The minimum taxable income also changes from year to year. Second, incomes are treated differently based on the source. Income from property is generally treated more favorably than income from employment. Dividends and interest are in general subject to a tax of 15 percent. In special cases the rate of the tax is less. Interest paid on loans for the purchase of stock can be credited against the amount of assessed income tax. Long-term capital gains are also taxed at a rate of 15 percent. However, capital gains derived from the sale of securities by individuals is exempt from taxation. A transactions tax on the sale of securities is levied instead. There are also various deductions and exemptions that reduce the base of capital gains taxation. All of these tax features tend to relax the progressiveness of the personal income tax. One result has been an increase in the importance of indirect taxes in relation to the total of national taxes.

The high rate of capital formation, with its concomitant effect upon the distribution of income, is also a factor that has to be taken into consideration. Aside from the growth-inducing effect of capital accumulation, there is the multiplier effect on aggregate money income. Finally, there is the institutional arrangement of a large part of the Japanese labor force, which also may have some impact on income distribution. Reference has already been made to the fact that many Japanese form a lifetime attachment to business firms. The system of guaranteed lifetime employment carries with it certain benefits that are difficult to impute to incomes.

Japanese taxpayers can be divided into two categories: wage and salary earners whose incomes are usually subject to a withholding tax and self-employed persons who have to file a tax return at the end of the year. In 1971 there were approximately 22 million wage and salary earners who earned around 16 trillion yen and around 4.4 million self-employed persons who earned 10.1 trillion yen. Given the year by year change in Japanese income taxation, there is a continuous shifting in the number of Japanese taxpayers.

Table 7.5 combines the separate categories of taxpayers into a whole for the purpose of gaining a clearer picture of income distribution in Japan. The year 1972 is used rather than 1971. The reason is simply that a more current breakdown of incomes can be obtained for the later year. In 1972 there were some 27 million taxpayers who received a before-tax income of 25.5 trillion yen a year. The table also presents the percentage of taxpayers in each income class relative to the total number of taxpayers, as well as the percentage of income each income class receives.

Some general observations about Table 7.5 are in order. First, the before-tax income of 25.5 trillion yen is less than half of personal income for 1972. Thus, a considerable part of personal income is not reflected in the before-tax total. Second, expense accounts, which would constitute a form of income for many Japanese, are not reflected in the total. Third, the data are not broken down into family units or other categories that could alter the distribution of income. Fourth, there is income which is left out at both ends of the income spectrum. Many low-income families have insufficient income to declare, and high-income earners have incomes in various forms which are not included in the tax total. Finally, although comparisons between Japan and other countries are difficult because of the different data used, it would appear that there is greater income equality in Japan than in the United States and West Germany. The rich and super-rich syndrome that is prevalent in the latter countries is far less apparent in Japan.

It is possible to get a general idea of the distribution of pre-tax income in Japan by dividing the data in Table 7.5 into quintiles.

222

TABLE 7.5

Distribution of Income of Japanese Taxpayers
by Income Classes, 1972

Income Classes[1]	Taxpayers[2]		Income[3]	
	Numbers	Per-centage	Amount	Per-centage
0 and under 400	1,482.9	5.5	387,881	1.5
400 and under 500	1,384.8	5.4	535,871	2.1
500 and under 700	3,975.6	14.7	1,950,167	7.9
700 and under 1,000	6,328.8	23.2	4,206,907	16.4
1,000 and under 1,500	7,391.0	27.1	7,125,084	27.8
1,500 and under 2,000	3,559.2	13.0	4,679,660	18.3
2,000 and under 3,000	2,068.7	7.7	3,728,602	14.4
3,000 and under 5,000	731.8	2.7	2,017,117	8.0
5,000 and under 10,000	161.7	0.6	771,608	3.1
10,000 and under 20,000	9.7	0.0	86,745	.3
20,000 and over	.6	0.0	10,927	.0
Total	27,093.8	100.0	25,500,574	100.0

[1]Thousand yen (000 omitted)
[2](00) omitted
[3]Million yen (000,000 omitted)

Source: Unpublished data provided by the Tax Administrative Agency of the Finance Ministry of Japan.

In 1972 the bottom 20 percent of Japanese taxpayers received 8.4 percent of before-tax income, while the upper one-fifth of taxpayers received 38.2 percent of before-tax income. The top 5 percent of all Japanese taxpayers received 12.9 percent of income, while the top 1 percent received 4.6 percent. A summary of the distribution is presented in Table 7.6.

The Effect of Taxes and Transfer Payments on Income Distribution

The personal income tax on ordinary income in Japan is progressive, reaching the highest rate of 75 percent on incomes of 80 million yen (approximately $240,000) or more. Income from sources other than ordinary income is treated differently, for great emphasis has been placed upon the promotion of capital formation and economic growth as policy objectives of the tax system. Dividends, interest, and capital gains are subject to lower tax rates than ordinary income. On the other hand, Japanese "tax-cut" policy has mainly stressed the reduction of the personal income tax. In recent tax reforms, reductions of tax rates have been both small in size and have been limited to the low-income brackets.

The income redistribution effect of the personal income tax would appear to be minor except at the highest levels of income. Even at these levels, the effective rate of the tax would be affected by the sources of income. Given the fact that higher-income taxpayers would be more likely to receive a larger part of their income in the form of dividends and interest, both of which are subject to favorable tax treatment, the effective tax rate is lower than it would be on or-dinary income. Aside from this point, the ratio of income taxation to personal income is very low. In 1969 the personal income tax accounted for 4 percent of personal income; in 1971 it accounted for 4.3 percent of personal income. When all direct taxes, including local income taxes, death duties, and employee contributions to social security funds, are taken into consideration, the burden is around 10 percent of personal income.

An idea of the redistributional effect of the Japanese personal income tax can be gained from Table 7.7. This table is based on

TABLE 7.6

Distribution of Income of Japanese
Taxpayers by Quintiles, 1972

Quintiles	Percent
Lowest quintile	8.4
Second quintile	13.4
Third quintile	17.8
Fourth quintile	22.2
Fifth quintile	38.2
Upper 5 percent	12.9
Upper 1 percent	4.6

Source: Computations based on Table 7.5 and made by the author.

224

TABLE 7.7

Before-Tax Distribution and Tax Payments
For Self-Employed Taxpayers in Japan, 1971

Income Classes (thousands)	Taxpayers (thousands)	Income[1] (100 million yen)	Income Taxes[2] (100 million yen)
0 and under 400	259	73.7	.2
400 and under 500	205	95.7	.3
500 and under 700	542	388.6	1.0
700 and under 1,000	959	830.4	24.8
1,000 and under 1,500	953	1,189.0	46.6
1,500 and under 2,000	473	821.6	40.1
2,000 and under 3,000	423	1,025.1	62.2
3,000 and under 5,000	310	1,180.8	87.5
5,000 and under 10,000	200	1,373.3	123.6
10,000 and under 20,000	80	1,086.2	142.9
20,000 and over	46	2,102.5	270.1
Total[3]	4,450	10,116.9	800.3

[1]Example: 737,000,000,000
[2]Example: 2,000,000,000
[3]Rounding understates the total income and total taxes. The actual amounts were 10 trillion, 131 billion yen and 810 billion yen.

Source: Unpublished data provided by the Tax Administrative Agency of the Ministry of Finance.

income returns for all self-employed persons in Japan for the tax year 1971, and presents the number of self-employed persons for each income bracket, the total income for each bracket of taxpayers, and the actual amount of taxes paid. Excluded from the table are wage and salary earners. The effective rate of income taxation is low regardless of the income category. The total of 4,452,946 taxpayers had a before-tax gross income of 10.1 trillion yen. Total deductions amounted to 2.5 trillion yen, leaving a total taxable income of 7.6 trillion yen. The total amount of income tax paid was 811 billion yen, which amounted to an effective rate of 8 percent of before-tax gross income and 11 percent of adjusted gross income. There were 45,731 taxpayers in the highest income category of 20 million yen (approximately $65,000) and over. Total gross income amounted to 2.1 trillion yen, adjusted gross income amounted to 1.9 trillion yen, and the amount of income tax amounted to 270 billion yen. The effective income tax rate on gross income was 13 percent, and on adjusted gross 14 percent.

The effective rate of the Japanese income tax for each income class can be computed by comparing taxes paid to gross income before deductions. The rate ranges from roughly 3 percent of total income in the income class 0 to 400,000 yen to roughly 13 percent of total income in the income class 20 million yen and over. The effective rate is mildly progressive throughout the remainder of the income classes. It is readily apparent that the personal income tax does not have much of a redistributional impact on incomes of the self-employed.

A comparison of income and income taxes can also be made for wage and salary earners in Japan. These taxpayers are divided into two categories—those whose taxes are directly withheld from their income and those whose taxes are paid at the end of the tax year. The difficulty in combining the two categories precludes the use of a table, but a general idea of the redistribution effect of the Japanese personal income tax can be obtained. In 1971 there were 22.1 million wage and salary taxpayers, 15.5 million of which were subject to withholding taxes.[25] Total gross income amounted to 16 trillion yen and income taxes withheld amounted to 1.3 trillion yen, for an effective tax rate of around 8 percent. The effective rate of income taxation was much more progressive for wage and salary earners than for the self-employed, basically for the reason that the self-employed are able to claim more exemptions and deductions. The effective tax rate for all wage and salary taxpayers in the lowest income category (0 to 40,000 yen) was 0.6 percent while the effective tax rate for wage and salary taxpayers in the highest income category (20 million yen and over) was 41 percent.

Japanese indirect taxes are generally regressive: that is, lower-income families pay more indirect taxes in proportion to income than higher-income families. A large proportion of indirect tax revenue comes from taxes on liquor, tobacco, sugar, electricity and gas, and admissions. These taxes are undoubtedly regressive. According to Ministry of Finance estimates, on the assumption that these taxes are shifted to consumers, the average ratio of indirect taxes to family income is 5.2 percent for families subject to the national income tax, whereas it is 8.4 percent for lower-income families paying no income tax.[26] In 1969 approximately 34 percent of all income earners paid no income tax, while 86 percent of income earners in agriculture paid no income tax. Also, a substantial part of some indirect taxes, such as the local and national automobile tax, the amusement tax, and the liquor tax, is very likely shifted to consumers through price increases. However, food and basic services are exempt from sales and excise taxes. Thus to some extent the regressivity of indirect taxes is negated by the exemption of food.

Transfer payments are the reverse side of the process of income redistribution. As has been previously emphasized, the level of government transfer payments in Japan is low, reflecting in part the traditional paternalism of Japanese companies. Medical care to the aged was made free in January 1973. Old-age and invalidity pensions were also increased from 2,300 to 3,300 yen and from 3,400 to 5,000 yen a month respectively, but the new levels can be compared to average monthly earnings of workers, which as of the middle of 1973, were around 100,000 yen a month. Expressed in dollars, the comparison is of around $15 a month for invalidity pensions to $300 average monthly earnings. Transfer payments have also shown a relatively low elasticity in comparison with changes in the gross national product. In the period from 1968 to 1969, for example, the elasticity of transfer payments in relation to gross national product was 0.97 for Japan, compared to 1.69 for Sweden, 1.17 for West Germany, 1.62 for the United Kingdom, and 1.61 for the United States.27

Trends in Japanese Income Distribution

A general comparison can be made of income distribution in Japan for three time periods, 1939, 1955, and 1969. Prewar Japanese capitalism was characterized by the concentration of economic power in the hands of such Zaibatsu combines as Mitsui, Mitsubishi, Sumitomo, and Yasuda. These combines were vast industrial empires under the control and management of a few family dynasties. There was a very high concentration of income and wealth in the hands of a few families. After World War II, land reforms, the dissolution of the Zaibatsu regime, the diffusion of labor unions, and other reform measures resulted in a more equitable distribution of income than in prewar years. The land reform, in particular, led to a rise in the living standards of the peasants. Then, too, changes were made in the Japanese system of taxation. The Shoup Mission promoted a much greater reliance on direct taxation than had existed before the war. All income, including capital gains, was made taxable for individual income tax purposes.

Table 7.8 compares the distribution of before-tax income in Japan for 1939 and 1955. A later comparison will incorporate the year 1969. As can be seen from the table, significant shifts in income distribution occurred from 1939 to 1955. In 1939 the top 5 percent of all Japanese income earners received around 37 percent of before-tax income; in 1955 the top 5 percent received 17.7 percent of before-tax income. In 1939 the top 1 percent of income earners

TABLE 7.8

Before-Tax Distribution of Income in Japan by Quintiles and for the Upper 5 Percent and 1 Percent, 1939 and 1955

Quintiles	1939	1955
Lowest quintile	6.3	6.6
Second quintile	8.0	11.1
Third quintile	10.2	15.3
Fourth quintile	20.4	23.1
Highest quintile	55.1	43.9
Upper 5 percent	36.8	17.7
Upper 1 percent	20.2	5.8
Gini coefficient	.44	.346

Source: Computations based on tables 1-4 of the Annual Report of the Ministry of Finance for 1963. The data are based on taxpayers subject to tax returns in both years as gathered by the Tax Bureau.

received 20 percent of income; in 1955 the top 1 percent received 6 percent of income. The highest quintile (upper 20 percent) of income earners received 55 percent of income in 1939 and 44 percent in 1955, while the lowest quintile (bottom 20 percent) of income earners received around 6 percent of income in 1939 and 6.6 percent of income in 1955. The data for 1939 are compiled for a far smaller number of taxpayers, 1.5 million, in comparison to a total of 8.2 million taxpayers for 1955. Before-tax income amounted to 4.6 trillion yen in 1939 and 1.7 trillion yen in 1955. The data for 1939 have been adjusted so that comparisons between the prewar and postwar statistics can be made in terms of the price level of 1955.

It is necessary to emphasize the fact that Table 7.8, as well as some of the preceding tables, is based on Japanese income tax returns. What this means is simply that a considerable amount of money is left out of the calculations. This holds true at both ends of the income spectrum. Millions of Japanese in 1939, 1955, or whatever year was used did not have the minimum income required to file a tax return. On the other hand, at the opposite end of the income spectrum, there is income that is not listed in the returns. The total amount of income listed on the tax returns for Japanese taxpayers is far less than actual personal income. This complicates any analysis of income distribution.

Based strictly on tax returns, there is some movement toward greater equality in the distribution of Japanese income. In 1939 the average before-tax income of the bottom 20 percent of Japanese taxpayers was approximately $321, while the average before-tax income of the highest 20 percent of taxpayers was approximately $2,700 —a ratio of 8.8 to 1.[28] The total amount of income for all taxpayers, however, was 456 billion yen, compared to a total personal income for 1939 of 3.2 trillion yen. In 1955 the average before-tax income of the bottom 20 percent of taxpayers was approximately $205, while the average before-tax income of the highest 20 percent of taxpayers was approximately $1,370—a ratio of 6.6 to 1. The estimates for 1955 are lower than the 1939 estimates for the reason that a much larger number of taxpayers (8.2 million compared to 1.4 million) was included.

The tax returns for 1969 also show some change toward more equality in the distribution of income. The top 20 percent of taxpayers received 41 percent of before-tax income in 1969, compared to 44 percent in 1955 and 55 percent in 1939, while the bottom 20 percent of taxpayers received 7.3 percent of before-tax income in 1969, compared to 6.6 percent in 1955 and 6.3 percent in 1939. The number of taxpayers increased from 1.5 million in 1939 to 26 million in 1969, while the amount of income included in the before-tax calculations in 1939 was about 15 percent of total personal income; however, in 1969 about 65 percent of personal income was included in the before-tax total. The base of the income tax in terms of the total number of taxpayers and the amount of money included has been expanded greatly.

THE DISTRIBUTION OF WEALTH IN JAPAN

There is some difficulty in measuring the distribution of wealth in Japan. In particular, reference is made to the role of banks in the capital market. The largest borrowers of funds in Japan are the corporate business concerns, which dominate investment activities in the country. In Japan most of savings flow from individuals to corporate enterprises through the channel of various financial institutions. The use of direct financing through the securities market is small. Instead, banks have played the principal role in supplying the funds necessary for the rapid expansion of the economy. The government itself is engaged in substantial financial activities through the ownership of a number of specialized credit institutions. Funds to support these institutions are obtained from a special counterpart fund in the budget and from individual savings in the form of postal savings, postal annuities, and postal life insurance. What all of this

TABLE 7.9

Shareownership in All Listed Japanese
Companies for 1970
(millions of shares)

Number of companies	1,584
Total shares	119,142
Shareowners by type	
Government	290
Financial institutions	38,524
Securities companies	1,412
Other domestic companies	27,515
Foreign companies	3,617
Individuals and others	47,570
Foreigners	213
Shareowners by size	
Below 500 shares	544
500-999	1,240
1,000-4,999	20,101
5,000-9,999	10,134
10,000 and over	87,122

Source: Bureau of Statistics, Monthly Statistics of Japan (Tokyo: Office of the Prime Minister, September 1972), p. 42.

means is that the composition and ownership of wealth in Japan tends to be concentrated in the hands of various financial institutions. For example, 70 percent of industrial bonds are owned by commercial banks.

Table 7.9 presents the division of stock ownership in Japanese companies based on shareowners by type and shareholders by size for 1970. The average dividend ratio of all companies listed on the Tokyo Stock Exchange for 1970 was 12.9 percent—a low ratio in comparison to American firms listed on the New York Stock Exchange. The average yield for all dividend-paying companies listed on the Tokyo Exchange was 3.86. Individuals and financial institutions owned 63 percent of the total number of shares.

The distribution of various forms of wealth can also be presented on the basis of ownership by quintiles. In Table 7.10 wealth is divided into seven categories—currency, time deposits, insurance, stocks, bonds, trust funds, and miscellaneous. Excluded from the table are such forms of wealth as land and houses. The division of the above forms of wealth into quintiles excludes those Japanese who have no forms of wealth-holdings and also does not give much indication of the overall concentration of all forms of wealth. The table reflects the high propensity to save on the part of the Japanese that cuts across all class lines. This is reflected in the fairly close ratio between the holdings of cash, time deposits, and insurance held by the lowest and highest quintiles of wealth-holders. There is a much wider disparity in the holdings of other forms of wealth, particularly bonds and trust funds.

The Effect of Inheritance and Gift Taxes on Wealth

Given the fact that the Japanese economy suffered tremendous dislocations as a result of World War II, inheritance and gift taxes would have had less time to exercise an impact on the accumulation of wealth than they would in the United Kingdom or the United States. Although the Japanese inheritance tax is progressive, with rates reaching a maximum of 70 percent on estates in excess of 150 million yen, the base of the tax is reduced by a number of exemptions. The end result is that only a small fraction of the total property of decedents is subject to the inheritance tax. In 1971, for example, 24,500 decedents out of a total of 716,313 had taxable property. The total number of heirs of all types numbered 67,248, the taxable value of the property amounted to 664 billion yen, and the amount of the inheritance

TABLE 7.10

Distribution of Various Types of Wealth
in Japan by Quintiles for 1971
(100 million yen)

Quintiles	Currency	Time Deposits	Insurance	Stock	Debentures	Trusts	Other	Total
First quintile	22.1	56.4	37.7	7.2	1.6	2.1	9.3	136.5
Second quintile	23.1	74.4	45.7	3.0	3.3	11.7	9.3	170.5
Third quintile	34.0	82.6	54.9	7.0	3.7	20.4	24.5	227.0
Fourth quintile	40.2	147.6	56.3	0.2	12.8	17.2	25.9	299.7
Fifth quintile	68.6	198.5	74.4	36.5	12.2	29.4	38.7	458.3

Source: Bureau of Statistics, Monthly Statistics of Japan (Tokyo: Office of the Prime Minister, March 1973), p. 513.

231

tax was 134 billion yen.[29]   As a source of revenue, the inheritance
tax accounted for 1.3 percent of national taxes in 1971.

The gift tax is used as a complementary tax to the inheritance
tax. Without the gift tax, a decedent could distribute his properties
to his successors prior to his death in order to avoid the inheritance
tax burden. The gift tax is imposed on properties acquired by gift in
a calendar year and is progressive, reaching the highest rate of 70
percent on gifts of 30 million yen and over. The impact of the gift
tax would appear minimal. In 1971, for example, 136,942 persons
were subject to the gift tax, the value of the property subject to the
tax was 189 billion yen, and the amount of the tax was 24 billion yen.[30]
As a source of revenue, the gift tax accounted for less than one-half
of 1 percent of total revenue.

SUMMARY

The growth rate of the Japanese economy has been the highest
for any major industrial country. There has been a rising rate of
productivity in industry as well as in agriculture. Productivity increases until rather recently have been in excess of wage increases,
and the margin has made possible a high rate of capital accumulation
by companies and thus a high rate of capital investment. Labor has
been released from inefficient areas, such as agriculture, and has
been more efficiently used in connection with modern equipment. A
result has been a rapid increase in both national income and personal
income, along with an improvement in living standards. Paradoxically,
this rise in income, with the concomitant demand for more and better
consumer goods, may very well result in a reduction of personal
savings, which has been one of the cornerstones of economic growth.
Income distribution has shown a shift toward greater equality
over time. In 1939 the top 20 percent of all taxpayers received 55
percent of income before taxes. However, by 1955 the share of the
top 20 percent had declined to 44 percent. By 1969 the number of taxpayers had increased 20 times over the 1939 period, and the top 20
percent received 41 percent of before-tax income. However, the point
has been made repeatedly that much of Japanese income is not included in the tax returns. This fact, plus the fact that certain forms
of Japanese income, that is, capital gains and dividends, are subject
to different tax treatment, makes it rather difficult to reach firm
conclusions about the distribution of income in Japan. Given the institutional arrangements of the Japanese economy, it would appear
that there is greater equality in the distribution of income in Japan
than in the United States or West Germany.

NOTES

1. Herman Kahn and Anthony J. Weiner, The Year 2,000 (New York: The Macmillan Company, 1967).

2. National Accounts Statistics, 1960-1970 (Paris: Organization for Economic Cooperation and Development, 1972), pp. 368-386.

3. Ibid., p. 370.

4. Ibid., p. 377.

5. Ibid., p. 386.

6. Bureau of Statistics, Japan Statistical Yearbook, 1972 (Tokyo: Office of the Prime Minister, 1973), p. 353.

7. Ibid., p. 353.

8. Ministry of Finance, An Outline of Japanese Taxes, 1973 (Tokyo, 1973), p. 246.

9. All information on the Japanese tax system was obtained from Eibun-horei-Sha, National Tax Collection Laws, Volume IV (Tokyo, 1973); and Taizo Hayashi, Guide to Japanese Taxes, 1972-73 (Tokyo: Zaikei Shoho Sha, 1973).

10. Mitsubishi Bank, Mitsubishi Bank Review 4 (May 1973): 165.

11. Bureau of Statistics, Japan Statistical Yearbook, 1971, (Tokyo: Office of the Prime Minister, 1972), p. 50.

12. Ministry of Foreign Affairs, Statistical Survey of the Japanese Economy, 1972 (Tokyo: 1972), pp. 72-75; Council of Economic Advisors, Economic Report of the President, 1973 (Washington: U.S. Government Printing Office, 1973), p. 252.

13. Statistical Survey of the Japanese Economy, 1972, p. 71.

14. National Accounts Statistics, 1960-1970, pp. 368-377.

15. Ibid., pp. 368-377.

16. Economic Planning Agency, National Income Statistics, 1971 (Tokyo, 1972), p. 34.

17. Ibid., p. 35.

18. Japan Statistical Yearbook, 1972, p. 500.

19. Statistical Survey of the Japanese Economy, 1972, p. 73.

20. Japan Statistical Yearbook, 1971, p. 501.

21. Ibid., p. 502.

22. Ibid., p. 505.

23. Ibid., p. 506.

24. Ibid., p. 508.

25. Unpublished data provided by the Tax Administrative Agency of the Ministry of Finance at the request of Senator William Brock of Tennessee.

26. Ministry of Finance, Annual Report for 1971 (Tokyo, 1972)

27. National Income Statistics, 1971, p. 7.

28. Ministry of Finance, Annual Report for 1963, Tables 1-4.

29. Bureau of Statistics, Quarterly Bulletin of Financial Statistics (Tokyo: Third Quarter, 1972), p. 42.

30. Quarterly Bulletin of Statistics, Second Quarter, 1972.

MARTIN SCHNITZER is Professor of Finance in the College of Business Administration at the Virginia Polytechnic Institute. He serves as a consultant to the Joint Economic Committee and the House Ways and Means Committee of the United States Congress and has served as a member of a Presidential task force on welfare problems.

Professor Schnitzer is a past editor of the Virginia Social Science Journal and has published a number of articles and books, including three Praeger Special Series titles: Regional Unemployment and the Relocation of Workers, The Economy of Sweden, and East and West Germany.

Dr. Schnitzer earned his Ph.D. in Economics at the University of Florida, has done advanced work in summer institutes at the Harvard Business School and the University of Virginia, and has been the beneficiary of grants for research work abroad.

EAST AND WEST GERMANY: A Comparative
Economic Analysis
                          Martin Schnitzer

EUROPEAN DEVELOPMENT POLICIES:
The United Kingdom, Sweden, France, EEC,
and Multinational Organizations
                          Overseas Development
                          Institute
                          edited by Bruce Dinwiddy

INCOME REDISTRIBUTION THROUGH STATE
AND LOCAL BUDGETS
                          Yung Mo Kim

MONEY AND ECONOMIC DEVELOPMENT
                          Milton Friedman

THE SOVIET ECONOMY IN REGIONAL
PERSPECTIVE
                          edited by V. N. Bandera
                          and Z. L. Melnyk

REVENUE SHARING: Legal and Policy Analysis
                          Otto G. Stolz